Second Edition

MW00977325

Table of Contents

Introduction

The Why Question

1. Family Backpacking Adventures
*Starved Rock Illinois*River-To-River Trail, Southern Illinois* Sawtooth Mountains, Idaho*Lessons*Life Transitions*

2. Pacific Crest Trail
*Trail Overview*The Gods Send a Clue*Hat Creek Rim Water Lessons* "Becky" and the Descent to the Faucet*Scrubby-Less and Getting Water* High Points and Forester Pass*A Bear Is Not A Bear Until You See His Hair*Never Be Tame Again*Dell*Leave No Trace*Vermillion Valley Hiker Barrels* Hawkeye*Things Learned /Happiness Just Is *Trail Guides-The Books*Nine-Eleven*Border Fever*Manning Park*

3. Appalachian Trail
*A Winter of Preparation*Fierce Farts *Temporary Setback* Males*Smokey Mt. Fortress* Fear Factor*A Word on Weird Gear*Stove-Less*Expert Newbies*Games for Soloists*Eight Pound Pack*Ultralighters, Gram Weenies, Minimalists* Night the Hikers Hung*Warning: Ball Alert* The Whites Are For Infants*Phoenlx Goes Fasting*The White Blaze Boat*Doing The 100 Mile Wilderness*The Green Circle*Katahdin*

4. John Muir Trail
*Trail Overview and Logistics*Ice Axes, a Leash, and the Abyss*A Photo Opt, now?*Don't Tell Me That*Loss at Muir Hut*Next Time Take a Compass*Day Hiking to the Valley* Wading Mosquitos*A Serious Chunk of Cheese*

5. Colorado Trail
*Trail Overview*Near Death by Strangulation*Fire and Ice*Of Bikes and Bears*The Poncho Lesson-Take 2*Trail Gods*Sudden Stampede*A Desperate Resupply*A Desperate Camp*

6. Continental Divide Trail
*Trail Overview and Guides*Bear Lure Area* Mule With Issues*Blow-downs From Hell*Love Under the Bridge*Karaoke in Helena*Obsessions*

7. Bartram Trail
*Trail Overview*Writing the Free Trail Guide*Georgia Trail Guide and Notes*North Carolina Trail Guide and Notes*

8. Foothills Trail
*Trail Overview*Never Camp Near A Gravel Road*Who Took the Lake?*Test of the Hobo Stove* When the Horse Dies*Postscript*

9. Vermont Trail
*Rainmaker's Skills*When Reality Sucks* Bailing*

10. My Ultralight Gear List Evolution
*My Ultralight Philosophy*True Cost and Sleeping Bags*Evolution of the Gear List*Keep the Cook Set Handy* Trowels* 9-Ounce Silnylon Backpack * Electronics and Batteries* The List*

11. Other Stuff
How to Fully Utilize a Garcia Bear Canister Food List for 7 Days*My Hiker Resume* Other Books I've Written*Web Links and Blogs*

Introduction

I'm not even going to make any excuses for the stories that follow. Honesty, posterity and survival of the human race demands it be done. Let the chips fall where they may.

In all seriousness, this is sort of a How-To book, maybe even more of a How-Not-To book. Take everything at your own risk. No one cares more about your ability to walk out alive than you do. Seriously, even Mom will get over it.

The Why Question

I share these stories for fun, too. A couple years back a co-worker asked me what I did the previous summer. My eyes filled with an unholy gleam as I got carried away describing months of backpacking while wearing the same shorts and tank top, sleeping on a ¾ inch blue closed cell pad in a tiny ultralight tent, taking water from a beaver pond and making do with one cup of instant coffee for breakfast. I waxed eloquent describing the long trail miles while carrying twenty pounds of food, hauling five quarts of water through blistering desert heat and eating oatmeal for supper seven nights in a row. I paused for breath sure she understood the wondrous journey, smiled and waited while she cocked her head, considering this adventure. At last my co-worker looked at me and asked dubiously, "Why would you **DO** that to yourself?"

I looked at her, flabbergasted and speechless. I didn't have an answer quite then. Opinions vary why the torture keeps calling us back. If you're a long distance hiker, you probably know, but how do we put that into words and still sound sane?

Driven to find an acceptable response to the bewildered friend, I decided my reasons were to stand on mountains that can only be accessed by foot, to gaze into hidden valleys unseen by motorized travelers, to drink from glacier melt while the sunset lingers over distant peaks, to wake each morning with fierce independence and to experience self-determination at the very core of my soul. The saying goes: The worst day on the trail is better than the best day at work. Wanderlust, vision quest, remedial self-therapy and honeymoons are all excellent reasons to pack up, head out and make miles on foot.

Rainmaker, my hiking partner, and I were preparing for an 825 mile segment on the Pacific Crest Trail in 2000. It would be my first real taste of long distance hiking. He told me to write down why I was going. I resisted at first. I just wanted to get out there and hike. But, he warned, "Once you get out there and things start hurting, you'll ask yourself why and you'd better have an answer."

I thought about it. Wasn't it enough to just go for the adventure? After several days I finally wrote:

Wondering
---written by Carol Wellman February 2000

Modern life seems so soft, in a physical sense.
A person could live their whole existence on this earth
Without ever breaking into a sweat,
Without ever needing to use every inch and fiber of their being,
Without ever tasting a physical struggle, defeat, or conquest,
Or ever making a conscious decision to live.

I guess that's the purpose in pursuing these trails,
to use and explore every inch and fiber
of myself, of my world.
Pressing to the outer limits of my abilities
and when I have been there, to press further.
Wondering if what I am will serve.

Hoping to realize that what I am
has served.

There is a line in the movie Ben Hur.
In the hull of the slave galley
there are men chained to their oars.
The captain of the ship warns them,
"You are here to serve this ship. Row well, and live."
That line always runs through my mind when I think of my body.
It is here to serve my purposes.
I feed it and allow it rest
but I chain it to my will.

Some athletes have that attitude.
The record setters
Not content with what has been done,

Always looking to push the limits,
Asking their body for more.

Survival in extreme conditions has always fascinated me.
It takes an indomitable spirit.
Willingness to do whatever it takes, and never say die.
There are stories of men and women eating ants,
bark, cadavers, and sled teams,
Reports of coming back from nowhere
when given up for weeks as dead,
People improvising shelters and clothing
living and surviving,
forcing their bodies on
though in pain and agony.
It's not fun.
It's not a good time.
It's life with the minimum of resources.
But I think it then becomes
the ultimate experience. So I am wondering.

Wondering what every mountain top will feel like.
Wondering what each valley will hold.
Wondering what it will be like to ask my whole being
to surrender to the primitiveness of self-reliance.
I am not going alone this time,
but it is my responsibility to hike the miles, and survive.
I am not afraid.
It takes a measure of misery to make memories.

I think I will love it all.

Until then, I will be wondering.

These concepts have motivated me all through my hiking career. Pushing the limits and when I think I've reached my limit to push farther, to push harder. Rainmaker was right. A person does need to put all of this into words. Those words become personal mantras when things get rough.

Common themes run through every trail journal, things like water, food, logistics, crappy hiking partners, gear choices and bodily functions. This book is written with the adult reader in mind, not that your average teenager couldn't understand the stuff I'm talking about. It's just pretty raw sometimes and rather than edit for the youthful novice, I chose to just put it out there. Often I'll refer to my comrades or hiking buddies as trail bums, maybe even trail trash. I say it with admiration and fondness. I happily count them my peers, thankful I got to hike these trails and meet these great characters.

Many of the stories have never been told. Some have been touched on briefly in online journals. At the time my journals were posted, I couldn't tell it all because it was just too PG-13, or might hurt someone's feelings or worse. As I edit this second edition, I am no longer with Rainmaker. We split in early 2012 and I moved out west. This event allows me the freedom to add a few more details.

So while I've divided the book into trails, all of which I've completed save the Vermont Trail and the first two family adventures, the recurrent themes overlap and reminisce about lessons I should have under my belt at this stage of the game.

In Chapter 10, I talk at length and even detail an ultralighter's gear list. That essay is called: My Ultralight Gear List Evolution. Gear Lists are in constant flux. Just because something works fine and weighs next to nothing doesn't mean we're done messing with it. It's just the nature of the beast: maybe there's a fabulous adaptation right around the corner. Just this summer I met a guy named Josh hiking up in Colorado. He had some innovative down gear from a new company, one that would custom make a down quilt for you to your specs, even adding extra feathers to the place of your choosing.

What I espouse for one trail you wouldn't catch me dead with while hiking another. I wouldn't haul a bear canister on the Appalachian Trail. Heading out on the Continental Divide, I'd better have it in Montana and Idaho unless I'm camping near bear boxes. While I might carry an actual coffee mug on a two day trip, I'd never have one on the PCT, hauling it over tons of miles and packing it up every morning, squeezing it in beside mounds of food for the long sections without resupply.

And, while I don't pretend to be an expert, I do have a few solo miles under my ultralight drawcord. I list my Hiker Resume in Chapter 11 in case anyone wants to vet me.

We ponder not whether to wander, but where. May All Your Trails be lighter.

1. Family Back Packing Adventures: My Start

I started backpacking late in life, although I'd been a girl scout and spent a lot of time in the woods camping and day hiking. The lure of open fragrant meadows, tall snow covered mountains and transparent rock-bedded streams worked on me like the romantic Zane Grey novels of my childhood. I absolutely lived the Betty Zane drama. Holding down forts and waiting for mountain man Wetzel to appear out of the woods, scalps hanging off his war belt, I'd dream about the daring it took to settle in the deep forest, fend off wild creatures and build a homestead.

As the gods would have it, I married and had kids instead. We played Indians and snuck around stealthily at Starved Rock State Park in Illinois, built Wikiups in the back yard and sewed leather medicine pouches and moccasins. We built snow forts and slept out in 7 degree weather, mid-January in hot pursuit of survivalist skills.

We saved milk jugs and studied water displacement as part of our homeschooling Earth Science course. Then I turned my sons loose to build a raft out of these jugs and old barn wood. It sat in the barn unused until a family friend finally came by and saw it. "Let's give 'er a try!" he said with his Arkansas drawl. "Looks fine as frog hair split four ways!" After obtaining the husband's permission, five of us loaded it into the back of his pickup truck and hauled it down the road to the Kishwalkee River. We launched the mighty raft along with a canoe and rowboat escort and floated down the swollen river. It was early April and the rains had done their job. The river was in flood stage. This was one of the best ever home school projects. The raft made that five mile trip fine, careening around wide bends, crashing into the shore. We found the thing floated great but it was a monster to steer with long poles and scanty paddles.

Once, my son picked up a road kill raccoon. I put it in the freezer until I finally got up the nerve to thaw the dude and attempt to glean cool accruements for mountain man projects. That idea was discarded when the raccoon's paw flexed as the pruning shears bore down on his little tendon. My daughter screamed. I jumped back wondering if he had come back to life. We took the raccoon tail for a hat and gave him a decent burial along the fence row.

Sometimes I'd grow restless living in northern Illinois. There were no long trail adventures or trails getting lost, trails going hungry, or trails getting thirsty. Survival at that time was all about getting the kids in bed, one more night then getting up and doing it again. Did I mention we had gardens from hell? We planted rows upon rows of vegetables. The kids weeded and harvested and we canned enough vegetables to last the entire winter. All of this required massive amounts of time and cut into my creative longings for adventure. That was probably a good thing. Who knows what else we might have gotten into?

Every fall our family would go camping in Starved Rock State Park. Legend was an entire tribe held out against their enemies atop the bluff, choosing to starve rather than face torture. They would lower buckets down to the river in an attempt to secure water, but the enemy cut the ropes so the embattled tribe would be thirsty. Weeks passed until one day some French Trappers were traveling through the area and noticed vultures circling overhead, diving down onto the bluff. Wolves were abundant, slinking around the forest, unnaturally reluctant to flee. The trappers hiked up to the top of the limestone bluff and found Indians dead, starved down to the last man.

Starved Rock State Park is loaded with poison ivy. Very quickly our family learned to recognize the variations of this toxic plant. It can be found climbing up a tree as a beautiful vine, growing tall like a lush lilac bush or hugging the ground like huckleberry bushes. The leaves can be huge or tiny or non-existent. They usually have jagged toothed edges, but not always. In the fall they sport incredible color making them favorites for leave pickers. But this is serious stuff, especially when someone throws it into the campfire. A few times we had to return home with at least one child nearly unrecognizable and unable to take class photos.

But the fun stuff didn't really start until I heard about the River to River Trail in southern Illinois. At that time, only 8 people had ever hiked its entire length, just 168 miles. I wondered why. The guide book wasn't difficult to read and supposedly the trail wasn't rugged. There were places to park the car, jump on the blue blazed trail and buy food in little towns along the way.

But what did I know? So far all my knowledge was theoretical and I knew those theories had to be tested before any truth could be known.

My first experience with backpacking came on the River to River Trail. My children were great accomplices. The lure of Snickers bars and no real school way overrode any concerns they had with the homemade gear, day packs and ponchos their mom loaded into the station wagon. I had talked two into coming with me on this wild adventure. The rest decided to hold the fort back home and await results. If their siblings didn't make it back, they had wondered aloud, could they have their stuff?

We had three days to play, a tiny trail guide book and plenty of online friendly advice from internet friends met on a backpacking site. Thus armed, three newbies drove five hours south, found a place to park and drug out our gear. After checking to be sure our food bags were loaded, we headed east from the Post Office parking lot. The lady inside behind the US Postal Desk had assured us our blue station wagon would be fine and waiting for us when we returned three days later.

Joyfully following blue rectangular blazes amidst trees barely budding out, we headed out, one enthusiastic mom and two kids. It was early March in southern Illinois. We were unarmed and unaware of any human danger. What could be wrong with this picture?

After hiking a few damp trail miles we pitched out tents and set up a little camp on a picturesque bluff. Nearby, a few raccoons played in the trees but we were sure none would steal our food. After a cozy little campfire, we opted for an early bedtime. My kids crawled into their dome tent. I crawled into my little homemade pup tent.

Sometime during the night it began to rain. Phooey, I said to myself glancing up at the canopy, just a tiny homemade tarp I was fearlessly testing. My pup tent had some mosquito netting and seemed pretty comfortable though it was a little small. I rolled over and listened to the patter of rain. Packing up was going to be interesting if it was still raining.

I listened for several minutes longer. The kids didn't make a sound. My teenage daughter and preteen son slept on in spite of the rumbling of distant thunder. I remembered the geography of our camp and realized we were the tallest thing around. Phooey. Double Phooey. This was back when I still went to church and didn't swear.

I jumped into action, crawling out of my tunnel configuration and stood up, put on my rain jacket, puzzling how to approach the dome tent laying bottom side up. Two kids were still sleeping soundly on the door, in the rain as dark clouds continued rolling in, thickening in the early morning. How do I get them out of that thing, dressed and ready to hike? I asked myself, what is the most efficient way to get this project done?

The operative word: Calmly.

My daughter, Christine heard my voice calling her name and groggily replied, "Ok, ok." I explained the predicament. She replied she understood the situation. She woke her little brother and said, "Come on, Josh, crawl over there, next to me." As they both crawled over to the same side, the tent began moving, slowly rolling down the hill, slowly revealing the door.

"That's fine, that's good enough, stop!" I called. The door was now exposed enough to reach the zipper and begin excavation. I reached over the tent, got the zipper moving and then Christine took over. Minutes later two kids popped out, disheveled and confused. Now it began raining and thundering pretty loud. "Get your packs," I said, "We need to get below the trees." Each of us quickly located our packs and threw stuff into them. We donned our ponchos, made sure they hung straight and grabbed Snickers Candy Bars for breakfast. They have nuts and milk chocolate so I figured, why not?

Object lesson: stake down dome tents. Stake them even if you only stake just two corners, even if it's not windy. You never know what the night will bring.

I'd love to say that was the worst of it and that things got better. Nope.

We headed east, stepping through puddles, walking in mud, crossing streams, weighed down with dripping ponchos, hand sticking out of wet sleeves grasping hiking poles. No one was talking. That's never a good sign. I watched my kids, noticing how the ponchos managed to drain directly over sleeping bags double bagged and stuff sacked, cinched below their day packs. We hadn't tested all this at home. I hadn't realized the rain would be running directly their most vital protection against the elements.

Object Lesson Number Two: test stuff before committing to it.

Plugging onward, we eventually arrived at The Garden of Gods and marveled at the huge boulder formations, their colorful deep crevices and steep slopes breaking away from naked woodlands, all very beautiful in the right circumstances. My son pointed to a large cathedral type cave with a huge mound of dry firewood piled way in the back. I smiled, relieved. It was exactly what we needed!

Immediately we built an enormous white man fire, ate and dried out our gear. I took off my outer shirt and dried the sleeves that had become wet clear up to the elbow, hanging it over a hiking pole, just above the roaring fire. Drops of water sizzled into the flames. All was good.

Laughing and talking, we regrouped and admitted, really, life wasn't so bad. The rain turned into a drizzle. The drizzle stopped. The sun peaked out and the air warmed remarkably. We began replenishing the stack of firewood at the back of the cave. If you take advantage of someone paying it forward, don't be a jerk. Keep up the momentum. Pay your dues forward as well.

Taking our time, scrounged farther from our oasis and found a bountiful supply of downed wood and hauled several loads into the back of shallow cave knowing it would dry out for the next survivors. When there was a huge stack, we stood back, assessed the situation and decided to pack up and leave the cave.

Now, warmed up after outwitting the gods of hypothermia, we continued east and hiked through wet trail until nearly dark. At last we found a tidy spot, nearly level and just down from the trail and off the bluff. After setting up the tents, we cooked supper over the campfire, feeling like real warriors. The night was cold but uneventful.

Early the next day we started hiking back. There were deer feeding along the ridge. Falcons soared overhead. There were more animals than people. The trip appeared to be a success. At some point my son decided he couldn't go any further. He sat in the trail. I don't know if he figured a new house could be built on that location and the whole family would move down there to join him or if a helicopter might be summoned to rescue him from further foot travel. Perhaps he figured the mounted Canadian Police would arrive to extract the hostage. He simply offered no excuse, sat down and refused to budge.

I analyzed this little power play and figured he would start to worry and reconsider his options if Christine and I just kept on hiking back to the car. I figured he would get up and follow, scared of being alone in the wilderness. Nope. He was too smart for that. The boy knew I'd never leave him. His sister had a great idea. She brought out her stash of little candy bars and enticed him, one fun bar at a time.

Object Lesson Three: carrots on sticks can be replaced with candy bars.

Hours later we finished out section hike and left the trail. Relieved to be done, we approached the Post Office and saw the car. The station wagon never looked so good with its dry, soft seats and adjustable heat. We changed into clean clothes, dry socks, and dry shoes left in the car. With both kids corralled and falling asleep, our troops headed home promising not to tell dad, not too much anyways. Half way home we stopped at McDonald's and got some real food. I thought about the lessons learned all the way back.

The family holding the fort agreed to try it sometime. Who knows, yeah, maybe it would be fun. In retrospect, I noticed neither of the River to River Contingency wanted any part of it. To their credit, they didn't alert their siblings to possible misadventures.

The very next summer the family planned a backpacking trip in the Sawtooth Mountains of Idaho. My husband and I planned to head out first. This adventure would be a sort of 'couple's thing'. Gear divided into two packs, we drove to the trailhead and parked the car. I noticed a black bear warning sign had been posted. We looked at each other, shrugged, shouldered our packs and headed into the mountains, planning to return to this car, essentially yo-yoing this trail.

Silently we hiked up through glorious mountain passes deep in black bear country hauling a very nice double walled dome tent. We also cooked over sterno type stoves. I thought it was great, though a little lonely. My husband wasn't enjoying the strenuous climbs and he knew in a couple days we'd be heading back on this same trail with three family members who were meeting us at Red Fish Resort. This plan gave us a nice shuttle and 52 miles of alpine experience.

We arrived after two days hiking, the night before our family was meeting us. I sorted my pack realizing I had way too much crap. It's hard to imagine, but my pack weighed in at 30 pounds. I pulled everything apart, wondering what I could leave behind. This goes to show any heavy weight backpacker can become an ultralighter. I stuffed extra socks and shirts into a plastic bag. I intended to stash this extra stuff in my family's truck when they pulled in the parking lot.

My daughter and her husband, along with my buff teenage son arrived the next morning. They parked their rig and unloaded the mule. My son-in-law is a backcountry hunter and has taken plenty of game. He could not for the life of him figure out why any sane person wouldn't use a mule. He loaded the mule with 60 pounds of stuff, all of my husband's gear including half of our shared tent. There was tons of food. They were not going to starve. The mule was only for carrying stuff, not people so John put half his tent on it likewise. Otherwise, he carried a full pack determined not to be outdone by his 5'2" mom. He wanted to tell his little brother, Josh, he manned up as well, and did a wilderness hike for two days.

Our backpacking party of five got separated early on. Two trails diverged and the son-in-law took the one less traveled. My husband took the boat across the lake, cutting off 5 miles of trail. It wasn't until 3 miles along the trail that we three hikers realized the group had split up and had no sure sign that we would reunite any time soon. There were no cell phones at that time.

Two miles later, my daughter, son and I sat down and waited for the boat to arrive at the end of the lake. We considered the options, looked at our watches, and figured that John and I could venture forth, heading down the trail together because we had all of our gear, but only after her dad arrived. Together, they could wait for the divergent pack mule.

If the mule and owner discovered they'd veered off onto the wrong trail, backtracked and caught up, they would join us at the designated alpine campsite. If however, the mule and owner did not come back, or come back with enough daylight to proceed, they could backtrail, and bring the rig around and pick us up next day at the trail head. Everything depended on regrouping at the end of Red Lake. John and I wouldn't know if all this happened until they showed up, or didn't show up in camp that night, 7 miles further down the trail.

Right on schedule, their dad arrived, considered the situation and finally gave us permission. It's hard to believe, but my son and I headed out happily, carrying two halves of two different tents. Sleeping arrangements had put the matching halves with those not coming unless the mule was located with all the gear.

However, John and I were not dismayed. We looked at the comical situation as a challenge and headed out before anyone could change their mind and call us back.

The lesson here is to carry your own stuff.

Meanwhile, the mule and owner, my son-in-law, discovered their error, retraced their steps and got back on the right trail, eventually reuniting with those waiting in limbo at the end of Red Lake. Advised of the new situation, all three decided to come on and do it. As they stumbled into camp, John and I were rigging two mismatched dome tents.

We looked up and smiled. The troops were reunited. We found the missing tent parts and pitched both tents properly. An hour later, things back in order, water was collected and we enjoyed a roaring evening fire. The guys wore blue jeans. My daughter and I wore skirts. Need I say chafing? After hiking all day, jeans can be devastating. As an ultralighter, I've weighed jeans and found I can bring two layers which combined weigh less and dry in a fraction of the time.

The second day we five managed a grueling 13 miles, envisioning the car waiting at the trailhead. We had plenty of food in our packs, but the lure of hot water, soft beds and a real stove waiting at home pulled on our bodies. All swore never to do it again, concluding that's why God made horses.

But I wasn't cured.

The bottom line is you either like it or you don't. No amount of luxury or misery can knock it into you or out of you.

Other valuable lessons from the early family experiences are:

When I want to test a crazy idea I make sure I'm the only one to suffer from it.

If your stuff is on the mule, stay with the mule. Don't let the frickin' mule out of your sight.

Always bring plenty of candy bars.

Keep your sense of humor. This too shall pass.

Life Transitions

Soon afterword my husband and I split. The Sawtooth adventure was only the final confirmation that we were incompatible. Among other things, he told me he hated backpacking and no wife of his was going to be traipsing all over the countryside.

Many people have asked me to elaborate after reading the book I wrote in 2003 entitled *My Journey to Freedom and Ultralight Backpacking.* In the interest of family privacy, I'll simply say he issued ultimatums restricting all of my hobbies and interests, my associations and wardrobe. There are a few more details in that book but the bottom line was that without compliance, I would be divorced and penniless. If I submitted to the demands and continued attending and supporting a very fundamentalist church, I would be allowed to stay.

Suffice to say, he maintained his high ranking deaconship while I moved on to become the ultralighter and survivalist I am today.

Then followed a very difficult time in my life in which I rejected all religious associations and built new friendships. It took long trails and much soul searching until at last, I received the most powerful gift from the trail gods: my identity. Days spent alone on the long trails taught me never to backtrail unless someone's life was in jeopardy. Forward movement is the key to all happiness. Eventually I found myself navigating the path of certain decisions.

2. Pacific Crest Trail
Trail Overview

You will never ever understand water, at least not in America, until you've hiked a long trail. Nearly all water can be made potable with the simplest of techniques and basic gear. Be assured the long distance hiker will learn on a very personal level that water means comfort. They will learn how to hear it, smell it, find it and taste it.

The Pacific Crest Trail is a collection of bewildering anomalies. You parch through the desert, grabbing water from cement tanks with dead rats, then splash across in snowpack, nearly drowning in glacier melt and run off. You'll pitch your shelter or roll out a bed among cactus and sand then wander through moss hanging off trees so thick you figure you missed a turn and ended up in the Amazon rainforest.

Brawny in Snow north of Senora Pass. This was my first year of serious long distance backpacking before I was a bona fide Ultralighter. Skin out weight, including shoes: 17 pounds.

You'll hike past icy lakes and decide to have lunch and a quick swim. You'll mark the hot springs on your data sheet and plan a long break. Will they be skinny dipping today? Highly possible. Will I? Probably not.

Two days before you hit town, you'll be making a mental list of all the fattening stuff you'll eat in the first half hour knowing once you head out it'll be near famine regardless of the mad volume of food hanging off in plastic bags, stuffed in pockets and claiming every last inch of available pack space. Ultralighters have learned to leave town stuffed and make miles on that belly of food. That's one day's worth of food, perhaps two pounds, they don't have to carry on their backs or cook.

The Pacific Crest Trail will find you hiking along barbwire fences and steel gates in the middle of nowhere. Often hiking solo, I would arrive at a barbed wire gate tight as a drum, fastened snug, top and bottom, with wire loops around a 6 foot post. A boldly lettered sign would be posted saying **close the gate behind yourself**. Then, I would struggle just to crack it open enough to squeeze through before the high strung wire swings back, whacking me in the butt, catching my gear in the barbs. Sometimes I would swear vigorously, creatively exploring my growing repertoire of profanity I had learned while living with Rainmaker. After several such experiences, I stood wearily before a stubborn gate. I tried hard to budge the wire. Nothing happened. I swore viciously.

Suddenly a man was standing beside me. I hadn't even heard him walking in the deep sand. I was very embarrassed at my frustration and verbal explosion. Nevertheless, I smile because the trail gods have sent another soloist just in time. The hiker had heard me and came to help. I made lame excuses for a temper so early in the morning.

Later, the trail guide will warn you there are 200 miles of no roads. Don't worry. You'll be through there before you know it, but a warning to the wise, just decide how you want to get food. There are options for resupplies but make sure the establishment is still in business before you count on them.

PCT hikers measure each other by the tiny packs overloaded with food and the weird hats decorated with dust, dried blood and sporting maybe a feather or two. I was warned to put a chin cord on my hat. Good thing I did. One friend lost his as he hiked up on a ridge. A sudden updraft from a mountain sent his hat sailing into the abyss. When PCT hikers met in town, we would sit around telling stories on each other. Lessons would be learned and maybe a trail name bestowed from a hilarious escapade.

Everyone wears trail runners on the Pacific Crest Trail. There's not an overkill trail boot among us. Most of us have weighed them on a scale before dropping serious cash on one of the most important pieces of gear. The desert will cook your feet, turn beautiful soles into blistered mush and serve them to you on a plate of misery.

You really don't hear as many trail names out there as you do on the Appalachian Trail. There are fewer people out here, and we recognize and remember each other's idiosyncrasies. The year I hiked there were four Daves hiking in the same section. We named one Early Bird Dave because he couldn't get out of bed in the morning. His partner would tell how long Early Bird took to pack up and get on the trail. Everyone loved Early Bird. One particularly hot day six of us hunkered under a Joshua tree, taking a break from the sun. The cold water I picked up at the last creek crossing was now hot enough to make coffee. Finally, he stretched, shouldered his pack and said, "Well, let's go hurt ourselves some more."

A second Dave we dubbed Long Dave because he was a really tall dude from Illinois and had a very long stride. A third Dave was deemed Crazy Dave when he tried to leave bottled water for himself at the trail angel's house in the middle of the desert. The angle, a grizzled old war veteran, loved living in the Mohave Desert and always invited hikers inside for some "magic." When Crazy Dave tried to pull this stunt asking if he could cache some water at the house, the old man growled, "I'm in charge of the fuckin' water around here!"

The fourth Dave we called DAVE Dave. He was a military dude who hiked in black speedos. It was somewhat shocking when I first saw him because his legs were really pale. I imagine further up the trail, his legs tanned up or he put on long pants.

The Pacific Crest Trail remains my first true love, and like all true love, hate surfaces soon enough which is soon followed by a begging for forgiveness and a vow of faithfulness forever. At times I cursed my love, all 2,658 miles stretching from Mexico to Canada as it took the long way around California, Oregon and Washington State. Other times I blessed the views which a camera could not adequately capture, and the strength the long stretches built into my legs.

Come prepared to suffer or die trying. That's what it takes to hike for months at a time. It wasn't unusual to be running low on food or staring 2,000 feet into an abyss which has the water you thirst for. Its not uncommon to have the long path aimlessly routing 30 miles west from the nearest town while routing you through land where you'll be sharing prime water sources with free range cattle. In those first 500 miles, you'll be trudging through six inches of deep sand, then meet it again up north at the Hat Creek Rim, then later be breaking through bramble 10 feet tall in section O: Overgrown and Overlooked. That's the Pacific Crest Trail and god, I love it.

At some point you'll need an ice ax, debate crampons, learn self-arrest and eat snow. At some point your pack will more than double in weight by sheer food alone. At some point you'll grab a few extra soda bottles for water capacity and then ditch them in town during record rains.

Volume 1, The Trail Guide, is a must have and weighs 1 pound 11 ½ ounces. It's a beautiful book and covers the first 1300 miles in California. There are 525 pages of essential maps and town information artfully inserted in mind baffling paragraphs which may end "but this won't get you to the post office." It's painful to cut such a magnificent book apart, discard the introductory pages and cover, choosing to haul only 400 miles of guide description at any one time. To lighten my load, in the evening I'd burn the pages I no longer needed. It helped to supplement bare fuel supplies. A warning, though, if you're going to do this. Be careful burning anything. Large sections of burnt over landscape remind us it is the desert, after all, and fires get whipped along by hot winds. If you are cooking in pine forests, several feet of duff are below those trees. A tiny spark can smolder for days, even weeks, eventually bursting into flames.

I shipped several boxes of hexamine tablets in my bounce box. When I got the bounce box containing among other things, my ice axe up at Kennedy Meadows, I pulled out a box of 24 fuel tablets. This had to last until I got my box again, up in the Sierras where I could flip the soda can stove over, use one fuel tablet and sneak a pinecone alongside it to gain a little more burn time.

But, I had to be very careful because the duff will burn too. All those dry pine needles create a tinderbox for the least stray spark, burning downward and spreading underground to later erupt in a wildfire of biblical proportions. My solution was to set my stove on a large flat rock or sheet of aluminum foil.

Volume 2 of the Pacific Crest Trail Guide covers Oregon and Washington State. You will need that too, farther up. Slip it in your bounce box and disassemble it as needed.

The Data book is a great supplement, giving mileages and elevations to water and key intersections. Together they provide information essential to a long hike. We used both. Rainmaker preferred the data book. I'd read the guide book aloud and we'd match it up with the data and altimeter readings from the watch he wore then journey forward. After a while, trailing becomes second nature. Whereas in the beginning we'd come upon footprints wandering 100 feet down trails in any given direction, later those same prints left a junction sure.

Rainmaker in Sierra City, taping his bounce box for shipping about 300 miles up the trail. Ship this monster parcel post, insured and pack it with essentials like 100% Deet, solid fuel tablets, a spare bandana, needle and thread, sunscreen and spare socks. I ended up with an aerosol spray can of 20% Deet in this town on my first year, a two month hike through the central portion of the PCT. I thought I could outsmart the mentor and do drop boxes instead. This was a silly concept, as though I could figure out when I would need any given thing. Mosquitos laugh at 20%. No ultralighter is caught dead with an aerosol can. My bad.

Heading out alone through 698 miles of desert, during the second year, in early spring, I got in touch with poison oak, rattle snakes, deep dry sand and temperatures over 117. I carried five quarts of water at a minimum and picked up water beneath unlikely places filled with poison ivy, then later in cow tanks, also from gushing cement holding tanks and a couple times out of tiny trickles that for all practical purposes might have been cow piss. This same water is soon hot enough to solar cook ramen in an empty peanut butter jar, brew tea, or make instant coffee.

The Gods Send a Clue

Five miles north of the Mexican border on a hot spring morning, I took my first break. It was the beginning of an epic solo journey. If all went well, that night I'd be camping with others at Lake Morena: well-wishers, PCT Association members, and some other backpackers undertaking this same life changing journey. All of us were attending The Annual Zero Day Pacific Crest Trail Kick Off Party, held the last weekend in April.

Rainmaker had done this 1,000 mile section before. If I wanted to finish with him in Canada later that year, I would have to get these thousand miles done first. It was an enormous task.

When I planned this section during January, I hoped that maybe I'd find a kindred spirit early on, but if not, I would be soloing. So far, without a partner, I was hiking by the seat of my pants, my trail guide and data sheets tucked into a pocket made out of silnylon and sewn onto the left front of ultralight shorts. You can get rid of a fanny pack with such a pocket. Weight saved: about 4-6 ounces.

Time Line Note: The previous year I had hiked with Rainmaker from Sonora Pass to Crater Lake, 825 miles of continuous life lessons. It was his second year on the PCT. We went home in the fall. He planned to finish at the Canadian Border the next year. I thought about that. He would be celebrating and I would be thinking about the first 1000 miles I had to do yet. Nope. I decided after a winter of preparation, I would fly out in April, hike those

1,000 miles starting at the Mexican border and meet him for the final leg of our journey. Because I completed the PCT over a 14 month period, this is not a thru hike. A thru hike is defined as an entire trail finished in a calendar year. I originally had a hiking partner lined up. She couldn't make it and I decided to go ahead anyways.

On my first day out, I crossed Campo Creek and paused watching it bubble merrily. It looked clean and what the hell, the day was young. I took off my pack in a nice spot near the creek. I walked off a ways, took a pee break, came back and sat down and ate some jelly beans. At some point my bare skin came in contact with poison something. By that evening I was itchy and miserable. It took five days to get over that mistake.

Lesson learned: sit on a silnylon jacket, backpack, or stand. This is also a good way to avoid ticks and Lyme disease.

After my nice break, I came to a road crossing. The guide said *next you undertake a contour north and you can see your trail snaking ahead.* I puzzled this sentence. I didn't see anything. Standing only 5' 2" my view of the world is different than whoever wrote the guide, god bless them.

I considered the challenging text several more minutes while standing at the crossing. A woman on horseback rode up and showed me the way. I thanked her, feeling foolish. The trail was right behind the huge road sign. I'm only five miles into this five month adventure and things aren't looking too good. I ate some jelly beans and crossed, thinking to myself, follow that horse!

Lesson: watch for tracks. Wait for folks. The gods will send a clue.

Frequent sign of border jumpers, like discarded clothing and glass bottles, old shoes and plastic sheeting told me I wasn't out here alone. I had been warned to get 100 miles north as fast as possible.

Later that afternoon I took another break at nasty Hauser Creek, wandering along the stream, shaking my head. Horses had taken several dumps on the bank of an otherwise doable water source. I saw a guy sitting in the shade and gave him a quart of water from my stash because the data sheet showed serious elevation gain then a drop into my target zone. Why carry 2 extra pounds?

One good climb remained. I crossed the road "to begin an earnest, sweaty ascent of the southern slopes of Morena Butte". After I topped that monster, I descended rapidly and arrived at the great Kick-Off Party, Lake Morena, by 6:00 p.m.

I was fat in this picture. I would soon tone up and lean down, dropping about 12 pounds of body fat, a very desirable thing for an ultralighter. I have no idea what is in my hand here at the kick-off party.

On that perfect late April evening I wandered into a large grassy gathering with long folding tables laden with savory food. There were quite a few dogs on leashes and a few dogs running loose. There were huge colorful tents, small tarps and various homemade shelters. Among this interesting assortment of structures milled crazy wild eyed hikers and support crews. A few of them I recognized and smiled. They were new friends I'd met online. It was one huge trail party going on, all crowded into our designated portion of the campground. At one picnic table, a buff and bearded hiker was giving a spontaneous demonstration on how to make an ultralight soda can stove using only a jack knife and three soda cans.

Hikers wandered around the assortment of shelters asking weights and admiring innovative designs. I'd never seen Frog Toggs before and asked a guy if I could touch his pants. He looked at me weird and smiled while I pinched some fabric near his thigh. It looked like paper and I was wondering how it could ever shed rain. Apparently, it does, quite well.

The Pacific Crest Trail Association organized this annual event and it was the perfect way to start this trail. I highly recommend that anyone hiking north on the PCT try to attend it. There were presentations, introductions by trail angels and seminars on water caches. I didn't fully appreciate then that trails were loved and lost over a little bit of water.

George, on the left, came to meet me. I felt very honored. Charlie, the man wearing the white t-shirt, met me last year hiking up in Northern California. He is the one who picked me up at the San Diego Airport that year, let me sleep at his home, woke early to cook us a fine breakfast before daylight and took me to the border the same day. He was prepared to come looking for me if I didn't show up before dark. Charlie will always hold a special place in my heart.

The Kick-Off Party starts on a Friday night. Saturday I met Lightingbolt and we scrutinized each other's ultralight gear. When he pulled out a Styrofoam cup, I frowned. Having worked at a hospital, I knew these cups will harbor germs. You cannot sterilize them. I watched him describe his ultralight tarp but finally had to say, "I'm not sure about the cup." He asked why and explained the germ thing. He stopped, looked at me a minute and told me how sick he'd become on the Colorado Trail. He had used a Styrofoam cup.

I pulled out the plastic peanut butter jar I carried for my cup. I told him it needs a preliminary shrinking. He asked how to do that. I told him first you pour very hot water into an empty jar, then put the cover on so it doesn't warp. You leave that way until it is cool and voila, you've got a perfect cup with lid.

Nearby, a polite young man was listening. He told us he hoped to one day set out on a thru hike. For now, he was all about support. His eyes light up as he says, "Wait here. I'll get my stove." He also brought a gallon of water. Various plastic bottles soon appear from bystanders and jack knives for cutting things to size.

We started experimenting with various sizes, temperatures and waiting periods. The experiments showed that if cut, a plastic bottle should be taped to maintain its shape until the water cools. Now that plastics have come under scrutiny for leaching chemicals into water under hot conditions, I say do this at your own risk. We also proved that it only shrinks the first time. Boiling water poured into a preshrunk container created no additional change.

Some thru hikers headed out on Saturday, eager to get their adventure underway. Others waited until Sunday. I decided to head out early Sunday alone, after breakfast. Partnerships come with baggage, but I would have welcomed it. The desert is vast. My mentor always said that the difficulty of getting any group up the trail multiplies by the same number in that group.

The skies were clear, the weather perfect. By the first night I'd gone 20 miles and camped in a place with pit toilets, a rare find. The cement tank had water and was mostly covered with a lid. I dipped my soda bottles in and filled them completely. Not too bad. Added three drops of chlorine apiece to purify. Checked my trail watch hanging on a cord with the LED light. In half an hour, I'd have potable water. A bearded backpacker came up to me and said, "They said there's a dead rat in there." I shrugged and added two more drops.

Hat Creek Rim

The previous year, when I hiked the section from Sonora Pass to Crater Lake with Rainmaker, we went through the Hat Creek Rim. Located in northern California, this 32 mile waterless stretch is very hot and dry. Fortunately dedicated trail angel leaves water caches, more than 15 gallons of clean water, about midway. There's also a notebook and pen at the cache in case any hikers want to leave pertinent information or offer words of wisdom.

A significant water cache. *Trail etiquette is to take the water but not the jug. Trail angels will return, refill the empties and check on the trail journal. Although one should never rely on a reported water cache, they should definitely be enjoyed when found. May the gods bless every water angel.*

The Hat Creek Rim trail angel had written a note in the front cover of his spiral notebook tied to a tree, along with a pen attached in like manner. "Don't write thanks. We know you're grateful. Please add your thoughts and favorite quotes." Right off hand, I can't remember what or if I wrote anything because all I could think of was, "Wow, Thanks!" I do remember drinking two quarts of water and reading that register with Rainmaker. One of my all-time favorites and a mantra I repeat often is "**In the end you find no one wins and the race was only with yourself.**"

Another gem: **It doesn't matter what anyone says. In the end the only thing you can do with cucumbers is make pickles.**

Rainmaker and Brawny at Sonora Pass, What a Newbie I was!

"Becky" and the Descent to the Faucet

She was from Maine and 20 years old with short dark hair, a ready smile and shoulders built for backpacking. The girl's stride matched that of many a much larger man. She carried a backpacker's guitar and wore all black like me, just a sleeveless tank top, shorts, decent socks and trail runners. But, she didn't have anything to cover her head. No hat. I wore a beige wide brimmed felt cowboy hat and would stick feathers in the band whenever I came across them. I first met Becky on my resupply in Idyllwild, California after going down early in the morning. After breakfast, I washed clothes and stopped in for pizza at a nice joint before heading back to the Devil's Slide Trail, a short steep 2.5 miles trail that headed up from the parking lot and intersected the PCT.

I'd like to tell you her real name was Alexa, but when I e-mailed her telling her I was publishing my first book, **My Journey To Freedom and Ultralight Backpacking,** she requested I send her the file first for inspection before I published. She told me to change her name and e-mailed some weird moniker to use instead. Well, I don't do ultimatums very well. That's not gonna happened. So, I named her "Becky" and pressed forward with my work.

Anyways, when I entered the pizza joint in Idyllwild, she walked over and asked, "You wanna split a pizza?"

"Sure," I replied.

"I got a ride lined up. You going back tonight?"

"Yup, just resupplying and heading back," I said.

We grinned simultaneously. We were two peas in a pod. It was the beginning of a long and strange trail friendship, a summer of random

28

encounters and mother-worry when she'd disappear for days, circle back and rejoin us after hitchhiking and hanging out with strangers. I fondly named her the Trail Animal. She loved it.

Becky and I caught our ride, thanked the man profusely and offered him money for gas. He refused, bid us happy trails and let us off at the parking lot trail head. We grabbed our packs, shouldered them and hiked up the Devil's Slide, pitching camp just beyond the sign that said no camping. Other thru hikers joined us that evening, throwing down shelters and sharing hilarious town stories of getting the gear shop to open early so they could buy some stuff and make it back to the PCT by nightfall. Becky had a bivy sack. I carried an ultralight silnylon prototype tent I had made myself. It seemed perfect, if only 6 foot long. It was bug proof and I could sit up in it.

At daybreak Becky and I packed up and headed out before 6 a.m. It was a gorgeous morning. She quickly outdistanced me. Every once in a while she let me catch up. We'd chat and she'd take off again. After a nice climb up to Deer Springs, we compared notes. It was early, the whole day ahead of us. We could really make some miles today. Off she went, heading north with that long purposeful stride while I spent a lot of time sliding through snow pack and wishing I had my snow baskets now on my hiking poles. One thing for sure, there was water enough and to spare.

Leaving Fuller Ridge Campground after a light lunch break, Becky and I realized it was only 16 miles and mostly downhill to the water faucet at Snow Creek Road. Doable, we were sure. She's a much faster hiker than me, young and fearless and still carrying stuff an Ultralighter wouldn't dream of. It didn't slow her down for a minute. Every once in a while she'd decide to wait for me. We'd sit on some rocks and share some stories, then off she'd go, blazing trail.

Again she would let me catch up to her. We'd take a break and I'd read the guide book aloud. She'd burst out laughing in delight. She loved the descriptions of west facing promontories rising from a north oriented saddle, various knobs mentioned just to spice it up and confuse the literal reader.

The trail seemed easy, all downhill, no worries. The sun began to set and we headed off again. Suddenly I remembered my bandana. I back trailed half a mile to retrieve it off a rock, then spun around, hurrying in the waning light. Becky was gone, way ahead, but that was O.K. I had my gear. As the light left the mountain, the undulation became maddening. You could see the houses way below, but the trail took the scenic route, wandering through the desert. Interspersed were boulders in deep ravines and tall saguaro cactus whose sole planetary purpose was to ensnare the wayward bushwhacker.

Suddenly I spotted a piece of paper laying on the trail. I picked it up, read quickly, "Brawny, there's a rattlesnake on the left, under those rocks. Go across." I couldn't believe it. Not now, not in this waning light. Maybe it was gone. I took a few tentative steps. The rattler shook his warning. The sun began to set in earnest. I glanced across the canyon at the obvious trail winding onward to another gulch. Many enormous boulders would have to be climbed, many obstacles backlit by the setting sun. There could be rattlers waiting for me there. Or, even the dreaded Green Mohave. Singing Steve had warned us about the Green Mohave rattlesnake. They will leap at you, stretching their body full length, an airborne missile of venom. One leapt at him and missed. That's encouraging. They don't always hit their target.

Reluctantly I took a few steps. The rattler under the rock was seriously pissed and rattled furiously. I paused, thinking, if I run across, he might get me. It seemed I had no choice but to brave the canyon.

Carefully I slid down off the trail, scrambled over a bolder, slid onto another one, watched my foot touch base, longing for the far side. I glanced over my shoulder at the setting sun, all the while cursing courageously, bemoaning the time I'd wasted during the day sitting around chatting. I took a deep breath, knew not to rush, still determined not to be marooned in the rocks. Focus, I told myself, just focus. Each bolder was a challenge, each cactus a peril. Slowly but surely I made my way across, keeping my eyes on the goal. Eventually I made it over to the northbound side with just a few scratches.

The light nearly gone, I began sprinting, my pack bobbing up and down, poles raised like spears, desperately scanning the trail for a place to camp. Finding no place to throw down a sleeping bag, I kept going, wondering if I might have to sleep smack dead in the middle of the trail. But that's not happening, I hoped, because that's where critters, night critters like scorpions and rats roamed. That's where snakes hunt in the dead of night when the sleeper is most vulnerable.

As the last orbs of light sunk beneath the horizon, voices called out, "Brawny, over here!" My eyes focused on three black forms up ahead, a small light shown from the edge of the trail. I smiled. It was a thru-hiking couple named Eric and Pam sitting alongside Becky. All three had their sleeping bags spread out on a little overlook adjacent to the trail.

"How far is it to the faucet?" I asked.

"About half a mile," Eric guessed. After a 27 mile day and descending 8,000 vertical feet, we were despondent. I ate fig bars and swigged the last of my water, picked cactus needles from my socks and hid irritation. I had no one to blame but myself. But, I vowed, next time I bite off this kind of day, I won't be sitting around chatting. I'll haul ass.

It was hard to sleep. Lights in the valley winked at us insomniacs wishing we had made it down. The stars came out, lighting the desert sky. It had cooled off to a luscious 60 degrees. Snakes and scorpions were in their element. Around midnight a strange glow appeared above. Another one followed it, and a third. They bobbed in erratic unison. "Look, Brawny," Eric said, pointing to night hikers winding their way down around myriads of switch backs, the same ones I'd run a few hours ago. We watched them for ten minutes. Finally, they stood beside our makeshift camp, paused and greeted us. "Goddamn trail is designed by Satan himself," Colorado Steve said.

"Damn straight," we agreed.

"Well, happy trails," another said and led his troops onward. Silently we watched them head down the trail. It was the first time I saw someone really utilizing head lamps to night hike.

At daybreak, we four packed up at our own pace, silently miserable after a sleepless night. Quickly we made our way to the faucet perched three feet up, attached to a single pipe coming up out of the ground. Each of us filled every water bottle and platypus from the rare treat of potable water. It was strange turning a knob and seeing clean water coming out of a pipe at thigh level. A few feet away, four night hikers were snoring, still asleep. They had camped there unmolested and no one was the worse for wear.

Scrubby-Less

As the sun peeked over the morning horizon the heat began to rise. I threw a poptart in my pocket, packed up the rest of my gear and strapped on my pack. It seemed late. At soon as it's light enough to see I feel compelled to hit the trail in order to get some miles in before the incredible desert thirst takes over and the ground shimmers in scorching sun.

Becky was already gone. She was known to get her miles in before breakfast. Somewhere up the trail she'd be sitting under a Joshua tree, cooking oatmeal. When she finished licking the pot, she would pour a cup of water from her platypus into the pot, scrub it with her finger, swish it around and drink the entire contents. Then, she'd wipe her mouth with the back of her hand and grin.

The first time I witnessed the ritual I pronounced it genius. I loved the fact this cut down smells which draws in rodents and bugs. It eliminates germs breeding in food particles caught in a scrubby. Immediately I chucked my 2x3 inch green scrubby pad into my trash bag and threw it away at the next town stop. I've been scrubby-less ever since.

Object Lesson: Don't waste water or calories on the trail.

Farther up the trail, Becky and I teamed up with a nice middle aged guy who had hiked the Appalachian Trail a few years ago. He was dubbed Cobweb by his peers because like us, he often broke cobwebs as an early morning hiker.

Things had gone so well with us three hiking together that at Kennedy Meadows Cobweb suggested we call our loose confederation the Jamaican Bobsled Team. Sure, I replied, what the hell. I'd never seen the movie and had no idea it referred to a group struggling against all odds to accomplish their dreams. None of us kept the same pace. I just don't hike fast enough and refused to trail run unless absolutely necessary. I hike long and take few breaks. This works for my body and prevents shin splints and trashed knees.

The three of us would leapfrog each other and by evening end up in the same camp together to trade stories and feel a certain safety in numbers.

Early one morning, we gathered by the side of the trail and watched water drip from the overhanging rocks. Intermingled with the seepage were vines. We agreed, it was poison ivy and in beautiful display. This was the day's water. In the desert, intermittent supplies are taken seriously. If you can get it, by god, you better.

I grabbed my plastic margarine tub. It could hold eight ounces. I stood under the seepage and offered, "I'll collect and you pour."

"Are you sure?" Becky asked. Cobweb saw the brilliance. No sense all of us coming down with poison ivy. They filled my four bottles to the top, then theirs. After all the bottles were filled to capacity and the iodine, chlorine or filters of choice utilized for purification, we collected our gear. I washed with the cold seepage, ran rubbing alcohol over my arms and legs and never broke out.

Days later, I approached the water supply with trepidation while analyzing the long burn section. You couldn't stop and set down the pack because it would soon be covered in soot. It was hot and desolate. Fire from the previous year had stripped the canopy. These areas are legendary for dried up streams, but I hoped the data book was still correct. At last, the burn section ended and greenery once more flourished. I was getting down to the last swallow.

Becky and Cobweb sat in the shade chatting. "Is there water?" I called.

"Well, not much," Becky called back. Ben only smiled. I arrived and stood over the tiniest of streams peering at the trickle.

"I guess there's some. Says in the guide book it's supposed to be intermittent." Suddenly the flow ceased before my very eyes. "What?" I asked stupefied. "You got to be kidding me." I waited and the trickle resumed.

"Guess a cow just pissed upstream," Cobweb said.

"Well," I muttered, shrugging, "Guess I don't have any choice!" I pulled out my water bottles and the little 8 ounce plastic bowl I'd scavenged from a margarine container. I could feel Becky and Ben's eyes on me a I stooped and let the bowl fill, then slowly poured it into the bottle. "This is going to take a while. Hope that cow is hydrated."

I met Lightingbolt again while going through a recovering burn section on the PCT. He started using a fanny pack to carry extra food and gear, wearing as a hip belt of sorts. It provided a ledge for his ultralight pack to rest on. As the months passed, food weight increases due to incredible hunger.

High Points: Mount Whitney and Forester Pass

There was a pit toilet on top Whitney the year I hiked. They tell me it's gone now. I used it just for bragging rights. The only wall was about four feet tall and directly behind the can. But, look at the views! Normally, a person sitting on it will be visible above the shoulders. It was a little embarrassing, but you only go around once in life.

Marmots also live on top of Mount Whitney. They actually will join you as you lunch, and steel from your pack if given half a chance. While Mount Whitney is not on the PCT, few hikers will pass up a chance to summit.

Pacific Crest Trail thru hikers can request a "Whitney Stamp" on their permits which allows them to summit when they get there. As the southern Terminus of the John Muir Trail and highest point in the contiguous United States, it's a very popular place. More on this in *Chapter 4: The John Muir Trail*.

After doing Whitney, Cobweb and I descended to Crab Tree Meadows where we camped, then headed towards Forester Pass the next morning. Forester Pass is the highest point on the Pacific Crest Trail. The mountain was covered with snow and we soon found ourselves searching for the actual PCT while hiking through punky snow and snow banks undercut with rushing water. Becky had camped alone at Guitar Lake, then met us on the trail.

We decided to spread out to lessen the chances of breaking through the snow or post holing. Periodically I'd glance up, watching Cobweb and Becky, trying to figure out if they had located a marker. They'd look over, wondering if I had been lucky. "See anything?" one would call. "Nope," would be the answer, so we just headed towards the mountain. If you find yourself standing on or above pink snow or hear a river under your feet or start post holing, you better get moving.

Far ahead, bits of brown trail snaked up a huge snow covered mountain. We approached it confidently, knowing that had to be it and somehow we'd reach it. Finally arriving a little wet and winded, I marveled at the purple violets punching their way through the frozen barrier.

At the foot of the mountain I breathed a sigh of relief. Back on trail, all we had to do was climb the thin trail, hiking poles punching tiny holes in the snow pack, while flowers reminded us it was mid-June. Once at the top of Forrester Pass, we met other hikers. Turns out they were doing the John Muir and had started at the Yosemite Valley Northern Terminus. We pulled out our cameras and asked them to take our photos. They admired our light packs and checked out my pack-less system. We came to the same conclusion. The longer you're on the trail, the less stuff you carry.

We said our good byes to the southbounders, wished them happy trails and began heading down the north-slope. The sun warmed the trail. We were able to slide-ski at a transversal. Most of the slope was covered with mushy pure snow. Half way down we paused, pulled out our empty plastic peanut butter jars and filled them with clean snow. We each dumped a package of hot chocolate powder into it, smiling at the novelty of making ice cream in the middle of the wilderness, in summer. The trail spoon and peanut butter jar is always nearby to enjoy these spontaneous treats.

Trail heading up to Forester Pass. Do not look down into the abyss. I survived this treacherous strip, and then turned to take Becky's photo. I thought of it as a log over a rushing creek: I can do this. The drop off was over 2,000 feet of sheer terror.

After enjoying the trail ice cream, we headed onward to find the sodden trail, fight off multitudes of mosquitos and watch the marmots scurry away. Marmots don't seem to fear people. They will rob your pack just as soon as look at you. We keep an eye out for the "mini bears" of the PCT. When they're aggravated, they'll sit on top a rock and whistle, warning other marmots some enemy is approaching.

A Bear is Not a Bear Until You See His Hair

Becky finally showed up late one evening, appearing out of nowhere from one of her side-trail jaunts. Chatting freely about her wild adventure, she threw her bivy bag down beside a boulder and told us about some food she had yoggied. Cobweb and I were used to this. It was like we were a family, he and I patiently listening to our teenage daughter just home from school.

Cobweb's tent was pitched nearby. We were nearing Yosemite National Park. It was early. The crowds hadn't arrived yet in spite of the lush greenery. It was very good to have company. Three of us camping together were less likely to have bear trouble than just one camping alone. While Cobweb swore by his Ursack, both Becky and I swore by our trail nerve. None of us carried bear canisters. Those things weigh 2 pound 11 ounces empty and you have to figure a way to strap a slick cylinder without any hardware embedded into it, onto an ultralight pack.

Becky grinned; dug into her pack and hauled out several small baggies of food she had been given. We were on the way to Vermillion Valley and it felt like I was starving, but I would never admit it to anyone. I had packed all I could and left Kennedy Meadows with seven real days of food. Stretching it to ten days of trail was an ultralighter's dream but a human's nightmare. My pack weighed 28 pounds on the scale at Kennedy Meadows. Seemed like that should be enough food for 192 miles which included the day spent doing Mt. Whitney.

Every day I picked wild onions to add to my ramen. Whatever food supplies my trail friends carried had no bearing on me. Solo hikers and true ultralighters never ask for a bailout. I wouldn't even think of asking or mentioning it, but when Becky offered me food and repeated she had plenty, I gratefully accepted.

That night I dreamed I was washing clothes and buying food for a lengthy resupply. My grown kids were asking me all kinds of questions while I was trying to pick out a bunch of candy bars at a local convenience store. Paydays, Snickers, a few Three Musketeers and some bags of M&Ms had been carefully chosen. My arms were full as I headed towards the check- out counter, licking my lips, looking forward to devouring several after I paid for them.

But, my kids wouldn't quit harassing me there in the store and I grew very angry. "Shut up and leave me alone," I yelled furiously at the top of my voice. Suddenly I awoke, startled. I glanced around the dark tent and remembered where I was and realized I had shouted that last sentence out loud. Oh my god, I thought covering my mouth with my hand, as if I could retract the words, those trail bums must have heard me. I waited breathlessly, listening intently, but there was no sound from either tent or bivy sack. Suddenly I burst out laughing. Still no one said a thing. I covered my mouth, giggling. What a crazy thing to shout in the middle of the night! Finally, I turned over and fell back to sleep.

In the morning I asked Cobweb if he'd heard anything last night. He said, "Yeah, I heard you yell, *shut up and leave me alone*. I thought it was a bear, but it sounded like you had everything under control so I went back to sleep."

I looked for Becky to get her reaction but she had already packed up and headed out. We didn't see her again until we hit Yosemite National Park where she confided she had taken a notion to head down to Bishop and hang out with people she'd never met before.

Stories abound of close bear encounters while hiking the trail. I think the encounters might be wilder out west. Tamer is not pretty. We'll talk about tamer in the next section. The Appalachian Trail has a whole colony of black bears that travel up and down the length just to intimidate you and teach you how to use those stupid mouse things in the shelter, but ok don't get me started. Back to the PCT.

Long distance backpackers sat around the picnic table at a rare town park sharing favorite black bear stories. One young guy told us he and his girlfriend were sleeping on top a tarp under the stars. During the night he felt sweet licking on his face and figured his gal wanted to get it on. He narrowly opened his eyes, turned to reach for his woman. Instead he found a big black bear standing over him, licking his face. Immediately the guy flung his arm out and yelled, "Go!" The bear took off running, completely astounded by the human voice.

I'm told if you use strawberry shampoo you probably will have a similar experience, even wake to find your head in a bruin's mouth. That frightening vision made me decide to keep all flavors and scents at home.

One evening, during the first year I hiked the PCT, Rainmaker let me chose a campsite. Up until then, he had done all the choosing, carefully making sure the slope was perfect and it had at least one solid tree where he could lean his external frame pack to use as a back support. He would inspect the tree, making sure the brush or roots would not interfere with his evening comfort. It didn't matter to me that he took this time to scrutinize our surroundings. We would be in camp twelve hours and worth the extra minutes. I admit, there were times alone I slept on slopes and tucked beneath scraggly trees, just too tired to care.

So, late this particular afternoon, we hiked one mile past a car accessible campground. There was relatively clean water coming out of a pipe into a nice cement tank. But we knew to never camp in a car campground. All kinds of food smells and bear lures are in campgrounds. And unlike a car camper who can jump into their vehicle, or pull out a shotgun to drive off the bear, we're pretty much just out there. So, in compliance with my mentor's instructions, I hiked further and picked out a campsite back off the trail. We dropped our packs and pitched the tent then took turns going for water, hiking way back to the tank while one of us stayed back to watch the site just in case a bear ambled through.

After the water situation was under control, we sat leisurely against our respective trees and cooked our individual suppers of ramen. Then we each washed our individual pots. Rainmaker had always insisted on keeping our food separated. He said in 1992 when he hiked the Appalachian Trail he had witnessed so many fights over food that he wanted no part of that. This was fine with me. Seems women tend to get corralled into meal preparation and I could see the wisdom of keeping it separate.

After washing my pot, I went down the hill to brush my teeth. Toothpaste does have a smell. I took my time, enjoying the beautiful evening light. Afterward, I came back and leaned against my tree. Rainmaker had a firmly established evening ritual. He carried a wash basin that he set beside his right thigh. He would brush his teeth sitting down, leaning against his tree, spitting into the wash basin. Just before bed, he would walk away from camp and dump it. His wash basin was just a sawed off milk jug.

With clean up over, we both began writing in our journals, getting it done before darkness necessitated using a head lamp. I struggled to write something interesting. I paused, frowned, just couldn't think of anything spectacular and said, "I don't have anything to write about tonight." Suddenly I looked up and here came a bear up the hill, straight for us. "Rain, there's a bear!" He stood up. Sure enough, walking right past where I brushed my teeth, a mid-sized bear is ambling straight for us.

Rainmaker leapt into action, grabbing some nearby rocks, striding quickly right towards the bear, yelling, "Get the fuck outta here!" I jumped up, prepared to back up my partner, all I needed was someone to just tell me what to do. The bear was still coming, boldly walking right up to our camp. Holy cow, I worried, and picked up a large rock too. "Get the fuck outta here!" Rain yells furiously, marching towards the uninvited guest. The bear finally veers to the right, skirting our camp with Rainmaker close behind it, hurrying it along. Now I'm scared. Yeah, I wondered, what if the bear gets angry, turns on my partner and scratches him up?

Rainmaker chased him a few more yards and returned. He casually dropped the rock and resumed his seat against his chosen tree, stuffing extra padding against his external frame backpack. I watched the procedure, knowing his back needed all of this or it would rebel and go into debilitating spasms, trail-ending spasms.

But wasn't not over.

The bear circled around and came back from the left. Rainmaker was seriously pissed now. This bear was cutting into his downtime, the reason for pitching the tent and setting up camp by 5 –ish or 6 at the latest. By god, this bear was cutting into his extra cup of coffee time. So he picked up another rock and I could see all hell was about to break loose, goddamn it! I shuddered. When his face looked like that, anything or anyone better just back away. I always did.

I've never seen this kind of chase and Rainmaker wasn't giving up after a few yards. He would have routed that bear all the way to Canada if that's what it took. So me, I picked up a rock and followed to offer back up, suddenly rethink our camp vulnerability and return. What if the bear got back into our camp and started ravishing the food bags feeling he has earned ownership rights? No, I decided, that can't happen. But I'm still worried about Rainmaker. I run back up the trail, then back to camp, back and forth between the pending confrontation and our camp, not sure where I should station my 5'2" 110 pound mighty force to be reckoned with.

Running back and forth, trying to see where they went, I felt very foolish but couldn't come up with any reasonable line of action. Finally Rainmaker returned unscratched and said, "Pack up, we have to leave. That bear will be back tonight and we won't get any sleep."

In uncharacteristic spontaneity, Rainmaker shoved all his gear into his pack. I dropped the tent and we threw everything together, checking to be sure nothing is left behind.

Instantly we headed north. Rain's long legs covered remarkable ground. I was running to keep up. Just as dusk arrives, we pitched the tent and crawled in, once again arranging our sleeping bags, corralling loose gear.

During the night, a buck snorted near our shelter. We listened, watched closely, slept fitfully, but there are no raiding bears. I never picked out another campsite, not because Rainmaker wouldn't have it but because while we were together I deferred to the master.

Bears are widely hunted out west, which makes them more skittish. In the middle of one night, however, a continual crashing just a few yards down trail from our tent brought things to a head. "Plug your ears," Rainmaker said. "I'm going to blow the whistle."

"Yeah, ok," I replied, turned over and thought whatever, go for it. Rainmaker put his whistle to his lips and gave his all. Simultaneously the bear ran off, crashing in midnight retreat while I jumped two feet straight in the air. Next time I will plug my ears.

From my trail journal, I must include here one of the most intense bear encounters of my life. It was at this juncture I realized how brave Rainmaker was and how seriously fortunate I was to have my trail partner. I've added a few details not shared before.

August 7 - Tuesday. We'd heard there was free camping for PCT hikers at the RV Marine Campground 1/4 miles east of town. Free camping in town works for us. We could get in during the afternoon and eat real food at a restaurant. We would spend the first night in a tent, then take a zero day gloriously relocated in a sweet motel as soon as the proprietors would allow us to check in. Cascade Locks had plenty of nice motels to choose from. It's a cute little town south of Washington State before crossing over the Bridge of the Gods spanning the mighty Columbia River.

Happy with our plan, we packed up and got on the trail by a normal 7:30 a.m. after a breakfast of steaming hot coffee and cream cheese spread thickly on a blueberry bagel. I always start out faster than Rainmaker especially when it's cold. Walking fast warms me up. There were ripe red berries along the trail, delicious thimbleberries. Lots of noisy waterfalls cascaded far below, deep in the canyon. Rainmaker and I amble along, casually picking berries, nibbling at the edge of a steep drop off, getting further and further apart.

I rounded one of many curves and heard some noises down in a small canyon. I figured it was people and wondered what on earth they were doing way down there. The trail became very narrow, dropping off into the canyon while the wall rose straight up on my left. I continued munching berries, rounded another tight bend and suddenly heard something swish the right side of my pack. I wondered what had brushed my pack and figured it was a low tree limb I hadn't noticed before.

I glanced back over my shoulder. There was a black shape next to the tree at the trail's edge. "David, a bear!" I shouted as I turned to face the tree, searching it and seeing her cub so close I could touch it.

I began backing up, knocking my metal hiking poles together. A million thoughts raced through my mind. What on earth? Is that a bear? How on earth did I not see her? Oh my god, I just walked right past a mother bear and cub. Not wanting David to walk past her as I did, I shouted several times, "David, a bear, there's a bear!"

She rose up with an angry bear frown, huffed and woofed at me. I kept backing up. It occurred to me she might have another cub up ahead. I glanced behind me at the trail, making sure I wouldn't back off the edge and fall into the canyon while scanning for a second cub. But I couldn't get too far away from the bears. What if my partner was about to be attacked?

I couldn't scream, all my focus was on the pending confrontation. All I could do was shout loudly as I kept watching her challenging me. I expected a bluff charge. "A bluff charge?" I wondered silently, "Is there any room for a bluff charge?" My body tense and alert to every signal, all my senses preparing for a charging mother bear, I was determined no matter what happened, not to run.

Somewhere around the bend Rainmaker was calling to me, "Carol, don't run! Don't run." Because of the waterfall and landscape, neither could hear the other and neither had any idea what the other was doing.

He told me later he had seen the cub scurry up the tree and knew I had just passed that tree. Bravely he kept advancing on the mother bear, yelling to me, hoping I could hear, hoping she would become confused, perhaps be distracted and even turn her attention to him. Finally, she dropped on all fours and galloped down into the canyon. Her cub soon followed. Then Rainmaker came around the bend.

Rainmaker took me in his arms. Silently we held each other close. Minutes later we began comparing notes, reliving our experiences over and over. I have never had anyone risk their life for me before. I don't think I ever had anyone willing to. It is something I will never forget.

At last, safe and sound we continued on the Eagle Creek Trail, a marvelous section which brings one past Tunnel Falls and unpaintable beauty. There is cable embedded on the canyon walls for hand holds. Rainmaker warned me to stay away from the edge while I stoop to take close ups with my disposable camera. It's slippery he chides patiently and reminds me we've tested fate enough for one day.

Never Be Tame Again

I wrote this poem as we neared the Canadian Border after living out of my pack, on the trail for nearly five months. After many close calls, whether its bears or heights, hunger or thirst, bad weather or bad men, a real life change takes place. It's hard to describe what comes over the long distance hiker but I know for certain I'll Never Be Tame Again.

Up in the heights I walk the ridge,
Look way below and I see the bridge.
I crossed that log this early morning,
In spite of all day hiker warnings.
Wind blowing through my hair, an eagle cries.
I'll soon be there,
Never be tame again .

I hiked ahead of Rainmaker. There remained only 60 miles from the Canadian Border. It had been an incredible trail, increasing my wilderness skills until I'd become alert to small noises. As we neared a rocky outcropping and prepared to turn a blind corner, I heard gruff noises and huffing. Please, not another bear! We'd had so many bear encounters in the last month I knew it was about that time again. I started hitting my hiking poles together, backing up, and calling Hey bear! Just then a surprised long distance hiker rounded the bend, laughing. He admitted he was practicing his belches and apologize, saying "Sorry!" I blushed, replied, no, no problem." I was embarrassed to be so jumpy, but Rainmaker found it hilarious.

This photo was taken near home on one of our many remote trails. When I first started backpacking, I had mixed emotions about possible bear encounters. They both fascinated and terrified me. Now, I carry bear spray on daily hikes and talk out loud when nearing streams.

Dell

The man was a mile maniac. I mean, who takes two weeks off a Pacific Crest Trail thru hike to run a 100 mile ultra-marathon and then return where he left off and continue north, undaunted?

This tall lean guy had many peculiar traits. Unless he was in town, he only ate cold food. He would hike until he got tired. Then, he'd find a flat spot and roll out his bag and ¾ sleeping pad smack dab on the trail. He would sleep about 4 hours then get up and go again. He could maintain this rhythm because he was solo and could listen to his body instead of watching a clock. I met the dude on and off. While the rest of us were making camp, cooking supper and sleeping eight hours, he'd be hiking, day or night and get ahead of us.

One hot day while Becky, Cobweb and I were heading into the Mohave Desert, the winds blew so hard that a person couldn't stand up straight. I leaned forward, fighting for each step. I glanced at Becky. Even she was struggling, though I'm sure she was grinning with pleasure. Cobweb led head down, beating his way against the blinding grit.

We staggered into driving sand, our faces covered up to the eyes with bandanas. Suddenly we glimpsed a tall thin man coming towards us, holding his hand and fighting the wind beating against his back, driving him sideways. We paused as he came abreast, "Dell! What the hell, Dell?"

"I blew over in the canyon, up ahead," he said, holding up his finger inviting our inspection. It looked really nasty, bent sideways, grotesquely skewed and gnarly. "I've got to get to a doctor. I'm sure it's broken," he told us. We nodded, agreed and turned to watch as he bravely back-trailed to the nearest road and hitched into town. A couple weeks later, we crossed paths with him again. His finger was in a splint and he was back on the trail, going night and day, making up for lost time, never missing a mile.

The man was a trail animal, inspirational and eccentric. He taught me the meaning of no boundaries hiking, of finding your style, regardless. Completely brilliant.

Dell was 60 years old.

Solo is fine. It's pretty nice once you get used to the intense solitude. You can actually burp or belch at will. You can fart or sing out loud, take a pee break, snack on candy before supper.

Sometimes I'd hike for days without seeing anyone. One especially hot day I had my program lined out. Trudging uphill in heavy sand, I'd count out 100 steps, then stop, lean against my poles while allowing myself a count to 20 break then continue another 100 steps. I repeated this micromanaging style, knowing if I kept at it, eventually I'd make the summit. Suddenly I glanced over to the left and there was Lone Wolf under a rare shade tree, observing my count to 20. I hid my embarrassed grin, swallowed my pride and asked him how it was going. He nodded thoughtfully and replied, 'good.' I've learned just because you think you're alone, doesn't mean you are.

Leave No Trace

Ultralighters practice Leave No Trace because as ultralighters they don't carry enough stuff to Leave a Trace even if they wanted to.

For instance, I have an oral bridge and I have to use a threader to floss this permanent tooth structure. But, I only bring one threader. If it falls into the dirt, I pick it up and wipe it off. I use one length of floss per week, over and over. I count tent stakes when packing up. If one is gone I don't leave the campsite until it is found. Every inch of cordage is accounted for. Spare change, excess toilet paper, extra clothing? Ain't got none.

Before an ultralighter leaves a campsite or rest spot, they check over every inch of ground, rock or root because anything left behind would be dearly missed. You don't have to worry about an ultralighter feeding the wildlife. We fight 'em for every last scrap.

One sunny afternoon we were taking a break, sitting on the ground eating some lunch. Suddenly I felt some weird tickling against my skin. I checked out the trouble spot and learned reconnaissance ants had crawled into my shorts and bit my butt. I jumped up and dropped a few bits of my poptart into the dirt. Immediately worker ants grabbed those crumbs and began high tailing it, heading straight to the ant larder for the ant babies waiting underground. But, the workers weren't fast enough. I caught up to them and with a smash of my hand, recovered my crumbs.

Admittedly, Rainmaker has a softer heart. He will generally spare a few Fritos for "Camp Robber" Jays. But on a particularly long stretch, hungry and sick of the beggars swarming around, he called out his challenge, "Come on. Make my day, you bastards!" The birds perched on limbs petulantly watching us eat. I started keeping a pile of rocks at my feet. No bird is taking my hard earned supper.

And be assured those wild creatures do know what you're talking about. You just have to let them know what the situation is. There was a particular persistent squirrel running too close to our packs, food bags and personal space. He wasn't even scared of me and I couldn't chase him away. Rainmaker was bathing in a nearby pond. I called to Rainmaker saying that although I was watching his pack, this one squirrel had a lot of guts and what should we do about it.

"Well," he said thoughtfully, "If I kill him and skin him with this knife, do you figure we could cook him?"

"Sure," I answered, "And I'll make some gravy while I'm at it." Suddenly, the furry monster totally disappeared. We did not see nor hear one sound from him the rest of the evening.

Vermillion Valley Hiker Barrels

I'd been warned about this place from a previous PCT hiker but apparently it was really upgraded by the time I arrived to enjoy a great time, starting with a 6-mile boat ride across the lake to the last blueberry pancake breakfast.

After 10 long days on the trail, covering 192 miles through the high Sierras, my supplies were running low. At Kennedy Meadows my bounce box had been shipped to me, with the ice ax, extra layers of clothes and 100% Deet. I bought a lot of food, packed it tight. Heading out from there, we hiked to Crabtree Meadows, did the Mt. Whitney day hike of 15 miles round trip, then headed north without taking any side trails into town. According to the scale at Kennedy Meadows, my food, ice ax and extra bag liner (made from an army blanket I bought of the proprietors for $2), along with my pack, weighed 28 pounds.

The rugged trail's elevation change along with lots of snow and cold nights had taken its toll. By the time I reached the resort I was Starving! I caught the first boat in, after turning down a joint from another hiker patiently waiting nearby. The boat ride was nearly unreal after being on foot for six weeks. Upon reaching the dock, I quickly disembarked, checked in at the store's front desk and chose my free "Welcome" beverage. The clerk smiled and told me where I could spend the night. Immediately I left and threw my pack on a free-first-night-cot in a spacious cabin tent.

Word was there was free food laid out in the guys' nearby cabin tent. I immediately headed over to check it out. White bread, cold hotdogs, cookies and chips were spread abundantly on the bottom bunk. No one was in the tent. I eased in, calling, "Anyone here?" No one answered. The buffet of junk food beckoned. I ate a ton of food and then pulled back, slightly embarrassed. I've been told I could eat like a trucker.

Next I went to find out if there was a hiker box. I should use more restraint but that's the reality of staying on budget while hiking a long trail. Within minutes I walked past two enormous barrels, both made of cardboard. I'm not sure what was shipped in them but they had been commandeered for hiker boxes. They were wonderful, standing over 3 feet tall with a diameter of 30 inches, nearly half full. I wondered, "Where did all these hiker donations come from?" Then I found out that Vermillion Valley is a good place for hikers to ship themselves a drop box. If the box is not claimed within a month, the contents are shared or dumped in the hiker barrel. I figured I could totally resupply out of those barrels, then buy some real meals, cooked over the grill with my cash.

I dove in, head first, arms reaching the goods and sorting through packages of noodles, gourmet coffee, dried tomato leather, feminine products and shampoo. Hanging by my stomach, feet off the ground, I nearly fell in head first. When all was said and done, I hauled out some Irish cream coffee, shampoo for the $5 shower, sunscreen, oatmeal and Alfredo noodles. My next stop was Red Meadows, just two days away. This was going to be a sweet low pack weight resupply.

A young dude approached and introduced himself as Carrot Top. He said he recognized my stuff from online and asked me to set up my gram weenie tent. I told him sure, I'd be happy to.

My tent on the Pacific Crest Trail was a tunnel type configuration which I designed and made myself. It weighed 18 ounces. I named it the Cherokee. The front was supported by my two hiking poles, spread wide and held in place by an elbow fitting for PVC pipe, which had a hole drilled in and was tied to the apex. The back end was held up with a café curtain rod. Eventually that rod bent during high winds while camped just 10 miles from Echo Lake. I kept bending it back, as straight as possible. That crease in the metal started to rust. I hoped and prayed it wouldn't break. Once Rainmaker joined me, I could throw it away. We would be sharing a two person tent.

Some things I have learned so far:

· A hiking boot makes a great cup holder.

· Don't hike with your shorts on crooked.

· Thistles are edible when boiled, but they may be hallucinogenic.

· Becoming chemically dependent on pain reliever while hiking long distances is highly probable. Don't worry, you can wean yourself later.

· Have everything firmly secured to your pack, or it may become history. A friend lost his sleeping bag near Muir Hut this way.

· Leave no trace, Protect and Enjoy signs do not apply to Loggers or horseman.

· We only have here and now. Plans for tomorrow often change.

Hawkeye

Rainmaker and I had just finished a rough waterless climb. Down below in the valley, a sweet crystal clean stream flowed abundantly, sending reflected river glimmers our way. Always seeking the crest, the Pacific Crest Trail skimmed the mountains high above. But the trail is marked and those so enthralled by this border to border trail purposely chose the harder path away from life giving water.

Gratefully, Rainmaker and I paused to pick up water at the edge of the narrow trail as it trickled off the embankment, wiping our faces with wet bandanas, continuing onward hoping to find a level place to camp. It was the five o'clock hour, time to wrap up the day according to Rainmaker's Rhythm. Anything more was in overtime, and what was the rush?

Finally topping the ridge, Rainmaker noticed a place flat enough, if we felt like moving some brush and scraping some rocks away. "Sure, why not?" I asked, exhausted and not wanting to march any further. Rainmaker found a suitable tree to sit against. He slid his pack to the ground, leaned it against the chosen tree.

I slid my pack to the ground and waited as he eyed the camp, walking in a tight circle, at last saying, "Put the head here, my door here." I nodded. I understood. Within half an hour, the tent stood proud and taunt. Rainmaker was settled in against his tree rest. Nearby I was washing up, coffee was brewing on my little stove, ready to jerk off my shirt and put on my sleep fleece. Suddenly, a man's rough voice was heard swearing up a storm. He was voicing his displeasure valiantly, unseen, oblivious to us camped a hundred yards up trail.

Just as he topped the hill, he halted mid-step, peered into our tiny camp and swallowed hard. "Sorry, didn't know you were up here," he apologized. This was my first year on the PCT. I grinned, glad I was still dressed. He was the epidomy of the rugged outdoorsman.

While Hawkeye and Rainmaker introduced themselves, I listened silently. Both are long distance veterans of the Appalachian Trail. I feel admiration as they compared experiences from their thru hikes. Hiker lingo flows easily. I am mesmerized.

Hawkeye asked permission to camp with us. Rainmaker replied, sure, help yourself. Briskly, he unrolled a tarp, spread it on the ground and laid out a sleeping pad, topping it with his sleeping bag. Within minutes he had his supper cooking.

Hawkeyes is a gifted story teller and soon began telling us about the Deer from Hell. He precludes the story by revealing it's not bears that scare him, it is deer. I hold back my smile and wondered how a brown eyed bambi could scare a man like this. "A deer?" I ask.

"Well," he said, "A bunch of backpackers were camped in a clearing. As usual, my friend was camped nearby. He would always keep his cooking set next to his head while he slept under the stars, rolled up in a tarp tortilla style. In the morning, he'd just roll over, smooth out the tarp and cook breakfast in bed." Rainmaker and I nodded. We could imagine this being done.

"But late one night, a sudden rattling was heard," Hawkeye continued. "I didn't think anything of it until my friend screamed in pain. Everyone grabbed a flashlight and aimed them at the wailing man. His head streamed blood. The whole camp jumped up and flew into action."

"That's terrible," I said. "What did you do?"

"I hiked out 6 miles for help, while the others monitored the dude, staunching the blood and keeping him calm until help showed up. Rescuers arrived by helicopter and air lifted him out to safety." We nodded, imagining the midnight drama. "They figured it was a deer that had approached him sleeping during the night and stumbled on the metal cook set. It startled the animal so bad that it lashed out with hooves, landing one square in my friend's noggin."

As Hawkeye finished his story, I made a mental note to not let that happen to me. "Maybe we should wear helmets to bed!"

Hawkeye was a lightweight backpacker who carried a blue sit pad strapped to the outside of his pack. The pad was small and handy enough to pull out at a moment's notice. This is how I learned that sky blue is very visible along the trail. We'd see this blue thing first way up the trail and wondered what gear had been lost or left. As we neared the item we finally noticed Hawkeye picking up water.

Hawkeye is also an artist. He took this self-portrait year ago and e-mailed it to me. I thought it was pretty cool. I have no idea what the man's real name is, neither his first name nor the last.

A few truisms I've discovered:

Happiness is an empty bladder. Pee before climbing hills. Who needs the extra weight?

Happiness is a trail marker that has useful information. Happiness is any trail marker at all. Or even a water bar that indicates someone has been out here before, a rock duck or even some fresh boot prints.

Happiness is clean water. While I will drink water out of anything once it's purified, I do draw the line when something is swimming inside my bottle, wild eyes staring back at me.

Happiness is a bug-less Ramen Delight. A delight has known ingredients, all edible food. Ramen Delight should not to be confused with a Hiker Surprise which could contain any number of inedible grains, seeds, peas or dehydrated stuff.

Happiness is hiking with your best friend.

Gear Up for the Climate

The PCT has at least five different zones with distinct climates. This determines how much gear the savvy ultralighter is going to haul with them. In the desert you can get by with a tarp, a 30 degree bag and a rain jacket which can double as a vapor barrier, but be prepared to carry serious water, at least five quarts. Be prepared to punch out the inline filter that gets clogged with sand, a good reason to carry a cotton bandana for filtering and chemicals such as chlorine or iodine for purification. Bring serious sunscreen and a wide brimmed hat with cinch cord so you don't lose it in the gale force winds. Even though the first 600 miles are desert, there is still rain and snow crossing passes above 8,000 feet.

Head into the High Sierras and the liquid fuel for an ultralight stove needs to stay warm or else it won't even light. Denatured is the best for that altitude, but it's hard to find. Use Heet successfully by first warming that little stove with a cigarette lighter before filling it. You'll be cooking above 10,000 feet. Take lots of food, lots. There's plenty of water. Smart wool socks are sweet. They keep your feet relatively warm in spite of being soaking wet. A bag liner can supplement the 30 degree sleeping bag. A good fleece pullover with a hood, gloves and a hat make those cold nights tolerable. Reclaim those snow baskets from the bounce box for your hiking poles and carry decent bug dope.

I'm told the natural bug repellant doesn't work a bit out here. The mosquitos have about one month to eat, reproduce and get on with life before they freeze and die off. One dude hiked with his mouth wide open, saying, "They bite me, I bite 'em back." Another tied grasses to the brim of his hat so that when he walked the movement of the swaying stems swatted the critters. Some wear a bug net over their faces. Once, a trail friend of mine took some newbie advice and sprayed Deet on his ball cap. When the drizzle began, the Deet dripped steadily onto his nose, eventually getting into his mouth and eyes.

The Pacific Crest Trail is beautiful beyond description, even while you are glissading down rugged snowfields, steering your controlled slide, using the ice axe as a rudder. Happily you can ship the ice ax home from Tuolomne Meadows.

Once you reach northern California, you'll be back in desert conditions and deep in cow country. *Shoot More Cows* was written on a cardboard sign, posted near a muddied water hole. We had to agree. Cows have a way of trashing out even the best water holes. I picked up two more soda bottles for this section after ditching two in Vermillion Valley, back in the High Sierras. There are big cats out there. Don't let the human-sized prints freak you out. The first ones I saw were the length of both of my hands held together lengthwise.   My friend Patch routed the same mountain lion twice because he wanted to camp by the creek. Patch says he yelled at the cat, threw a few rocks and told the cat to go find his own spot.

We neared a long green building midway through the Hat Creek Rim. There had to be water there, we figured. Crossing the parking lot, we noticed a couple doors, went over and knocked on one. A man in uniform answered and offered us water. Soon, the guys working at the power station north of Hat Creek Rim told us about watching a cougar taking down a deer right outside their chain link fence. They invited us to sit a spell, enjoy some cold sodas from their personal frig and tell them about our adventures.

Heading into Oregon we crossed jagged lava rocks, miles and miles of sharp edges and careful footing. If you don't have good shoes now and more rain gear, things could get ugly. It rains a lot. No longer can a hiker just throw down the bag and sleep like a cowboy under the stars. If the campsite is sloping and you decide it's not going to rain that night, you could find a river in the morning, right under the sleeping bag. But, if you're pressed for a camping spot, lay down some logs parallel to your shelter and build a temporary water bar funneling the water down the slope. Whoops! Leave no trace! In the morning, kick out that water bar, smooth down the dirt and cover it with leaves if there are some. But, I'm sorry, I don't feel guilty at all for my little camp reconstruction. Having walked through trenches created by pack horses and strained water from bovine ponds; I sometimes get a little feisty and dig a tiny trench to protect our 4x 8 sleeping area. Rangers want us to forget about all the horses and cows tearing up the trail. We backpackers do our best and leave no trace.

A picture of me after 6 weeks with the Packless System, south of Muir Pass.

Once you get up into Washington State, you'll be stronger, feeling that border fever and an expert in what works for you. Probably some parts of your body are hurting. My feet were complaining, mainly because my boots were so heavy because they seldom had a chance to dry out. Rainmaker's instep was hurting so much he couldn't wear trail shoes. He wore sandals all the way to Skycomish, drying them each night in camp. In the morning he had dry socks and dry footwear. As I watched him cross snowpack with dry feet, I wondered about the sandal concept. It made sense at the time.

It was damp and cold nearly every night. Now my ultralight pack has an extra fleece and Johnnies stuffed in it. There are plenty of hunters in the fall and the berries are ripening. I tied my blue closed cell pad to the outside of my new Nike Pack. No longer do we desire to be unseen, or hiking stealth. Please see me, I pray. Hunters with high powered rifles and scopes are waiting on the ridges for their game. I worried about being visible because I've been mistaken for a bear before while sitting in the shade. Wearing all black is not so good anymore.

One night we camped near Rainy Pass in northern Washington. Early the next morning a huge buck wandered through our camp, not 10 yards from out tent. He merely glanced at me while I tossed my stuff out the tent door and crawled out behind it. Meanwhile, Rainmaker slowly emerged from his side of the tent after placing each stuff sack methodically out of his vestibule.

The 6 point buck watched us out of one eye while wandering downhill a little and continues grazing. Rainmaker arranged his breakfast nook and soon had coffee brewing. Up past the trail two men were scoping us with high powered rifles. I watched the men sitting in the morning sunlight as they watch the buck taking his sweet time to munch the choicest grasses. The men continued monitoring our camp. They knew at some point we would be packing up and leaving and that damn conniving buck belongs to them.

Half an hour later, I finished eating and drinking my coffee. I dropped the tent, shook out the condensation. We were packing up as usual, going through the typical procedure. Rainmaker has his stuff in order, his pack fully loaded. He stood tall and began warming up his back, using full range exercises, rotating his arms in wide circles, lifting his legs one by one as though climbing a hill. The buck wanders a pinch more downhill, loath to leave the tranquility. I glanced up the hill. The hunters were still there, long rifles perched across their laps. I strapped the blue pad on the outside of my pack. I wanted them to see me. In all black, I've been mistaken for a wild creature before.

Months back a horse named Murphy would not pass me while I sat under a pine bough, waiting for Rainmaker to join me. The owner had laughed and explained that she named him Murphy because anything that could possibly scare him would. Horse people usually asked us to talk to their horses because we freaked the animals out when we were standing just off the trail, silently waiting for them to pass. The owners said, to the horses, we look like giant scary turtles, our houses on our backs.

When Rainmaker finished his 15 minute routine, he lifted his pack and slid it on. I shouldered my pack and watched him loosen his black back brace. We slipped our gloved hands into hiking pole straps and glanced around, looking for any piece of gear we might have missed, noting the buck had eased off downhill. I watched the sleek brown creature enter the forest and immediately blend into the foliage. As we left the camp and hiked up the hill past the hunters, we waved and hit the trail.

If you've made it this far on the Pacific Crest Trail, you might be the walking wounded, but you definitely got your act together, or should have. But the Ultralight disease is never cured. At this point I decided to bounce my pot support ahead, thereby saving an ounce, along with some solid fuel tablets. I planned to pick these items up again in Skycomish where Rainmaker had a package coming. I figured to use little rocks or tent stakes for the one meal I cooked each night. Rainmaker frowned but he wasn't going to say anything. He had already declared ultralight extremists as nuts but as long as it didn't negatively affect him, he would not protest.

But I was visualizing the next section. Heading over the passes in the Northern Cascades feels like doing tines on a fork. Way way UP then way way down. Way Way UP then way Way down. Every ounce I could get rid of would be so worth it.

Two days later we camped on solid-rock embedded turf. It began to rain. We set up the double walled Coleman tent. Each of us had our own small vestibules and we reached out to cook from the comfort of our sleeping bags stretched alongside the door. My pot-support tent stakes would not go in the ground no matter how hard I pounded. I searched the vestibule, leaned outside getting soaked. I frowned. There were no little rocks available. I considered the situation silently, at last coming up with something that would not burn.

Carefully I laid my hiking poles down inside the vestibule a close parallel position. Gently I placed my pint sized pot filled with water on top, slid the soda can stove underneath and lit it. The thin ultralight foil lid and aluminum foil windscreen were eased into position. I sighed as my water came to a near boil. Rainmaker sniffed suspiciously from his side of the tent and asked, "What's that I smell? It's like rubber burning."

"Humm," I said, lifting my pot with a gloved hand, "Just the snow baskets." Sometimes a person needs to carry another ounce.

Trail Guides-The Books

A couple years back I walked into an outfitters shop and approached the front desk. My kids and I wanted to do some day hiking up in the Sawtooths of Idaho. The sign outside said they had trail guides. Perfect. "I'd like to see a trail guide," I told the clerk. Frugal as sin, I wanted to be sure it had what we needed before parting with cash.

The young lady looked at me and tilted her head, "What kind of guide are you looking for?" she asked.

"A good one," I replied, eyes darting to the shelves lined with books on Idaho backcountry. "I want to be sure it's what we need before I get one."

"Oh, they're all good," she said, "And cute too. You want me to call one for you? He's in the back."

My teenaged daughters blushed and I hurriedly explained, "No thanks. We meant a Book."

I've since learned a perfectly fine trail description may baffle you completely. Once you get out there, it starts making more sense. Here's an excerpt from the absolutely necessary Official Pacific Crest Trail guide:

"North across the road, the PCT soon veers east, recrossing the road to climb easily under the Lagunas steep eastern scarp to a saddle with the end of a jeep road (5540-0.5). From it the route undulates northwest on scrub-bound slopes while keeping just above the rough jeep track. Your path crosses jeep spurs to the summits of Peak 5663 and Garnet Peak and then strikes another spur at a saddle (5495-1.6) west of Garnet Peak. The PCT next traverses around Peak 5661, passing through hoary-leaved ceanothus brush..."

Just for pure entertainment value, I'd often read the upcoming portion to Becky, trying out various inflections at key phrases. We'd laugh and check out the Data Book, a very straightforward itemized list of water sources and main road crossings. They complement each other. The data book will not tell you how to get across the state park and find the correct underpass nor will it tell you to exit the road to the left. Unhappily you won't find any trail markers to assist, either.

In keeping with the beauty of this guide and our experience, I wrote this little parody:

A PCT GUIDE BOOK version of Directions to our Room:

From the dining area cross a table and chaired saddle (.002m) turn west until you see a ladies room. There you'll find a refreshing faucet, although late comers may find it seeping (.00012m) Descend north on an east facing staircase. Pass a room. Pass another good room. Pass an old abandoned room (.0035m). On an east facing west rising door you'll note the number 24 which has been posted since the new easier route was established in 1983. Head north. Open door. Close door. However, this won't get you to the Post Office. So, if you need to go to the Laundry Room, head east from your saddle. Those who complete this section may want to celebrate at the licorice bowl, (4,290-.003m) a seven way junction where intense PCT Register Logging is going on.

I've already confessed my absolute love and fascination with the Pacific Crest Trail. Other trail guides may be confusing too. I find once I get out there they make a lot more sense. I usually buy an updated guide because after 10 years some of the "jeep" roads have disappeared. Of course, the new version may still have the original text and a person just has to rely on dead reckoning and a sense of adventure.

Nine-Eleven

As if this trail wasn't mind blowing enough, my last week on the trail proved to be historical. I count myself very fortunate to have experienced this event while secluded and not in front of a television.

Every American knows what Nine Eleven means. It was the day we woke to an unbelievable terrorist attack. It was caught on tape and broadcast live. Those of you who watched it unfold must have felt as though it were a Hollywood Movie, only why on earth are you watching a horror flick at 8 in the morning?

On September 10th Rainmaker and I briskly hiked 12 miles, hurrying down the trail so we could catch a bus that the trail guide said would take us into Stehekin. For $6, we could ride into the last town on the PCT, only 89 miles from the Canadian Border. I'd been on the trail for nearly five months. Rainmaker had been out nearly two months. It was bitter sweet but it was time to wrap this up and go home.

Stehekin is a sweet little burg with only 11 miles of road. Most people get there by ferry across the lake. With so few cars, it was a difficult hitch. For sure we would take the bus. The Wolf-Pack was waiting for the bus, too. This man and his grown sons looked nearly as trail trashed as we were.

The bus driver was friendly. He knew long distance hikers were incredibly hungry and part of his routine was to stop for an hour at the Pie Shop. Hikers would scramble out, crowd the counters, laying down serious cash for delicacies made with berries, sugar and cream. Rainmaker and I devoured a fantastic homemade pie and bought a couple loaves of real bread. Just the tender squeezable-ness made my mouth water.

Hikers reboarded the bus, laden with sacks of goodies. Because of the delay, we nearly missed the critical post office stop along the way. We needed our drop boxes shipped there from Skycomish for the last few miles into Canada. Just as we neared the Post Office, Rainmaker leaned over and asked the driver to let us off. The driver nodded happily and stopped the bus, opening the door. Immediately Rainmaker jumped off the bus, raced into the post office and jerked open the front door just before closing time. I was right behind him as he implored the postmaster to let us pick up our box. He grinned, said, sure, he understood our need and went to find our cardboard boxes. We nodded our thanks, smiled and left, heading into the little quaint town just up the road.

Seeing lots of hikers and bikers walking around town, Rainmaker told me the first priority was locating a camping spot. They were free but they were limited. We headed to the campground, quickly grabbed the last spot then registered at the visitor center returning to the grassy spot to set up our home for the night.

With camp pitched, I set off to locate the coin Laundry housed in the same building as the free showers. Without hesitation, I took advantage of both, throwing in a load of clothes, adding a bit of detergent from the vending machine, using my rain pants and tank top to maneuver between the two rooms. Rainmaker put off his shower until later. He likes to relax after all this commotion. I like to check it all out. After being together 24-7, we go off in different directions to enjoy some personal space.

I found many hikers hanging out on the deck in front of the main restaurant but I discovered that if you want to eat supper there, you must register early in the day so the cooks know how much to prep. I also learned the store and restaurant both close at 8:00 pm. I guess no one eats after that. After gleaning all this information, I walked back to our campsite and told my partner.

Unfortunately, the hot water had run out in the free showers. Rainmaker had taken a cold shower and changed into his sleep ware. We hurried to the store and bought food before they closed, creating a supper out of hiker type snacks. We would have loved eating a fine restaurant meal but failed in the requirements necessary because the sign- up sheet for supper wasn't available for the late bus people. Bummer. The good news was we learned there was a serious breakfast buffet in the morning and vowed to make it in time, really hungry, really focused and do some serious damage to whatever they offered. With that plan made, we crawled into our sleeping bags and slept peacefully.

Early the next morning Rainmaker and I dressed silently and started walking down the road to breakfast. We sure didn't want to be late. Maybe they quit cooking after the place fills up. Who knew?

This is the kind of day forever imprinted on the minds of every American. Like the day President Kennedy was shot or our team landed on the moon for the first time, we shall always remember where we were, what we were doing, who we were with and what we were thinking.

The lush green valley was still smoky. There were wild fires raging in the back country, up in the mountains, fires which could only be fought during the daylight. At night the firefighters paused their efforts and the fires got an upper hand. In the morning the battle resumed.

Stomachs growling, we thought about all the great things we'd eat. There'd be perked coffee and orange juice. We'd get lots of scrambled eggs, toast and hash browns. We'd check out the fruit salad if they had any. We would take our time filling the hunger void building over the last week.

Many of my trail friends were in town and leaving right after breakfast, heading back to the trail on the morning bus. I wanted Rainmaker to meet them, especially Dell. After Rainmaker flew in to meet me to finish the trail north of Crater Lake, I had lost track of my thru hiker friends.

John was walking towards us. His big white dog was by his side. We stopped and he asked, "Did you hear? A ranger told me he heard that 3 planes crashed, one into the Pentagon and both World Trade Center towers are gone."

It was 7:30 on the west coast, 10:30 a.m. in New York. "No, it can't be true," I said. "It can't be true." Rainmaker didn't believe it either and we kept walking. But, I started thinking, what if John was right? No, no, it couldn't be. All three of us continued walking down the road, stepped up on the wooden porch and entered the restaurant. Eleven hikers were seated at two long tables. The waiter came over and told us what he knew. The information was sketchy, but verified John's initial report. In 2001, Stehekin had no outside contact except for radio. There were no t-vs, no cell phones and no internet.

The food smelled wonderful. The waiter poured coffee all around. Somehow I wasn't very hungry anymore. We hadn't talked politics, jobs or families for over four months. Suddenly heated political discussion broke out and an aged hiker angrily left the table. We watched him stalk out of the restaurant.

The buffet was laid out in deep silver steam tables and included scrambled eggs, sausage, bacon, pancakes, fruit, milk, oatmeal and coffee. At last I found my appetite. We ate ravenously and quickly demolished the buffet. The cooks brought out more. We talked trail, conjectured about world events and surmised that sitting isolated 89 miles from the border, we really didn't know for sure what was happening out there, way back home.

Photos were taken with disposable cameras. We kissed each other good-bye, shook hands and smiled fondly into faces we would probably never see again. One guy said he was taking the boat out, his country needed him now. I couldn't see that. Not with just 89 miles left to go, just days from the border.

Finally stuffed, Rainmaker and I headed next door to the store where ten or so people stood around listening intently to the radio. One New Yorker is describing the people she sees jumping from the windows. She fearfully describes people fleeing up the street in total confusion while incredible suffocating smoke keeps pouring out into the streets everywhere. My god, I thought, this is real. This is America. The reporters say the country is in readiness. Yet still no name has been given to who is responsible. Who are these terrorists? We are told the borders are closed. No planes are flying. All have been grounded. A fourth plane has crashed. What is wrong with the people who would do such a thing?

Nothing makes sense. I feel sick and nauseated. I must get some air. I must do something that makes sense. I go to work on my resupply. Other than one guy at breakfast not a single hiker considers not crossing that border. We have come too far, suffered too much, been out here too long. Not me nor Rainmaker will turn back now. Some of us discuss the possibility of hitting Manning Park in Canada, resupplying and re-crossing the border, even illegally and back trailing south into the United States.

Back in camp, I searched diligently but couldn't find my magic trail spoon. It had been with me ever since the Lassen Park stream crossing last year, when I found it by river's edge. I looked high and low, through every sack and every corner of the tent. I combed the campground five times asking myself how can one little spoon just go missing? Then, I stopped looking and chided myself. Get real. People have lost their lives today and you are mourning the loss of a spoon.

Hikers continued to come into town for a resupply and were met with the news. We shared the utter amazement and shock which soon turned to anger that some crazy terrorists would do this. We thrilled at the story of 4 brave men on the last flight who heard via cell phone of their pending doom. They banned together and rushed the terrorists, took over and crashed the plane into a field. I hear this story proudly; clench my jaw and think, "Never Again". Never again will a hijacker be allowed to take over a plane or take us anywhere. We are not sheep. Never again will we allow it. There won't be sit down and shut up mentalities ever again.

But Rainmaker and I must focus on the last leg of our journey and get resupplied for the trail. I take a deep breath and buy five days of food, ship home any extra ounces of gear and plan for an early ride out in the morning.

That afternoon I met Zion. He's a really cool 23- year old who hopes he will not get drafted. Bob Walker from Canada pulls into town. He's hiking for Parkinson's disease and tells Zion to come hang out in Canada with him. Bob finds a shop selling mouse traps and buys two, hoping to eliminate some constant pests beneath his tarp. Jack came in. I haven't seen him since Echo Lake. He's looking hungry and really tired. I hope I can get a newspaper tomorrow when the ferry comes in. I'm told there are no newspapers in town, anywhere. Our only information filters over the radio waves in the convenience store.

The next morning, Rainmaker and I again eat breakfast at the buffet. He agreed to wait for the ferry before catching the bus back to the trail junction where we caught it. I'll buy a newspaper, regardless of the cost or weight. I have to know what is happening.

I saw many other people were waiting for the ferry. They had the same idea. As the boat swung to the dock, several of us jumped on, heading to the newspaper rack.

The man ahead of me scooped up the last newspaper. He was vacationing there at the resort. We left the boat, following him closely. Total strangers crowded around the tourist as he stood on shore slowly opening and paging through the newspaper. Eight of us read over his shoulder, standing closer than family, seeing for the first time horrifying photos of people leaping to their death and burning towers, of the dust enveloping all of upper Manhattan. No one was in any hurry to turn the pages.

Finally, Rainmaker and I grabbed our packs off the porch and caught the 11:00 a.m. bus. When we got off at the trail head, Pam and Eric were there waiting to get on. They hadn't heard the news yet. We hugged and gave each other some quick updates. I knew they would hear more in town. It was just too overwhelming to talk about now. I wished them happy trails and waved as they got on the bus.

Rainmaker and I hiked 5 miles and camped at Bridge Creek Campground with Paw Bunion. Back in the forest, things got back to what we considered normal. Paul saw a huge abandoned cooler suspended from a tree. He wondered if we ought to check it out. Rainmaker cautioned us against such a raid. Just because there were no cars didn't mean the owners wouldn't return soon for their cache. Nevertheless, Paw lowered it, looked over the various contents. Whether he took anything or not, I can't recall.

Rainmaker and I fell back into our comfortable routine, each of us silently pondering our own deep thoughts. A couple days fled by without much comment. We met some weekend backpackers and asked them what they knew. So far, nothing had changed. Days later the planes started flying again. We saw one overhead and knew that if we could get into Canada and were allowed to cross back into the United States, we would soon be flying home to Georgia.

Border Fever

With Canada just a few days away the fever grows. Suddenly Rainmaker and I didn't feel like stopping for breaks or early suppers. We hiked on. The fall colors were outstanding, little blueberries ripe on red bushes, golden mountain sides contrasting with dark evergreens. One of my favorite places on earth is Fire Creek Pass. I don't think it was so much the place as the time and tranquility about to be lost as we neared the end of a life changing journey. The photo for the cover of this book was taken there.

There were many kinds of berries and we ate those. Grouse startled from beside the trail and flew loudly into the air. Then one day, we were accosted by a determined male grouse.

Cobweb sent me the next photo. Apparently he had the same type of encounter we did. I was hiking along minding my own business when out of the blue this little bird comes roaring down the trail. I jumped into the weeds calling out, "Help!" Rainmaker turned around and laughed. This little male grouse had me cornered.

Amused, Rainmaker walked back and told me to go ahead while he kept the bird at bay. I watched them go around a few times, the bird hanging onto Rainmaker's sock while Rainmaker attempted to shake him off. The grouse would finally have to turn loose, only to try again. Finally the bird retreated. Rainmaker walked past me, and once again led us northward.

Within seconds I heard a *swoosh* and turned just in time to catch the creature in a flanking move. We broke out laughing. Didn't he know he could be lunch?

I wrote this poem in commemoration:

'Twas the Night before Manning:
A PCT Version of: 'Twas the Night before Christmas
---"Account of a Visit from St. Nicholas"
by Major Henry Livingston, Jr. (1748-1828)
(previously believed to be by Clement Clarke Moore)
--corrupted by Brawny on December 24, 2001

'Twas the night before Manning, And all through the park
Not a creature was sleeping, Though 'twas plenty dark.
Rocks were all piled Near the tent door with care,
In hopes that they wouldn't be needed against bear.

Hikers were nestled ,Just barely been fed,
While visions of real food danced in each head.
I on my short pad , Rain on his thermarest,
Had just settled down for a review of the quest.

When out in the camp there arose such a clatter,
I unzipped the screen to see what was the matter.
Away in the dark and just under a tree
Were two camp counselors holding one flashlight, to see

And swinging some food bags by the end of a rope
To fool all the bears and sleep tight, was their hope.
The moon on the breast of the new-fallen leaves
The day's heat now spent, I tucked my hands in my sleeves.

Then, what to my remembering eyes should appear,
But a grouse with an attitude showing no fear.
With a little red comb, and so lively and quick,
I knew in a moment he was up to some trick.

More determined than mice, more ferocious than bear
He pecked and rerouted, as Rain tried to move him from there
At last we hiked by, then I heard on the trail,
Such a swoosh, so I jumped to avoid getting nailed.

As I drew in my feet, Rainmaker was turning around,
He shouted with surprise, and came with a bound.

That bird was all attitude, from his head to his toe,
What had pissed him off so we may just never know.

Rain pushed him aside, I got back on the trail
Safely hiked on ahead, turned to see those two males.
He was feisty and angry, kept attacking Rain's shoe

I laughed when I saw them, this bird with no clue;
That grouse was fresh meat, and had a little round belly,
That wouldn't taste bad with some cranberry jelly.
If a hiker so chose, and gave a twist to his head,
He could be lunch meat sliced thin between bread;

Rain marveled and laughed, as he out flanked this bird
Who tried to get to me with a passion absurd.
But the sun started setting, the border 3 miles away;
The grouse stood his own ground and his stance seemed to say,

"Don't you dare come back, or I'll give you some more
I'm lord of this trail and I've done this before"
But I heard Rain exclaim, 'ere we hiked out of sight,
"You'd better be glad we're bound for Canada tonight!"

   An online trail angel met us at the trail head and took us to her home,
helping us do laundry, feeding us, lavishing us with care.
   Then, she took us shopping. I bought a fleece turtle neck and swapped out
my pack. I was sure the Nike was big enough. I strapped the blue pad to the
outside to be more visible during hunting season.   All along the trail I spent

nightly sessions refining the pack by sewing a hip belt out of a cannibalized stuff sack and a portion of the blue pad.

Manning Park

At last it was late enough to get up from the restless sleep. I checked my watch. It was 4 a.m. Rainmaker and I made peanut butter sandwiches and drank coffee by red photon light. Both of us were eager for daylight. Neither one of us wanted to miss the 10:00 a.m. bus that would take us to Vancouver where we would get on the Am-Track train bound for Seattle.

Although we were ahead of schedule and still had a few days to kill before catching our flight for home, we wanted to get the border crossed before anything else happened to make things worse. Neither of us had our passports with us. Back in those days, passports weren't needed to cross the Canadian border.

Rainmaker and I were happy to just hang out in Seattle a few extra days instead of risking complications in an attempt to change the dates on our tickets. Nine eleven was just one week old.

Sitting in camp was one of those bittersweet moments. With snow predicted any day and a cozy Georgia home awaiting us, there was no reason to delay. But the trail, the memories, the freedom was intoxicating.

Wordlessly Rainmaker and I packed up in the dark and headed out just as enough light revealed the treadway. There remained three miles to the terminus. An hour later we faced a wooden message board at the road to the Manning Park Resort. We tagged that. Is this the official terminus, we wondered aloud? We walked up the road, looked for a sign saying something like Northern Terminus, Congratulations. We tagged several other possibilities. Who would want to go home unsure they actually hit the terminus?

Satisfied the requirements were met, we followed the road and wound up at the Manning Park resort. We took photos, headed inside and bought a delicious hot breakfast. We shopped a bit in the store, figuring out the exchange rate, then headed outside to wait in line, catching the bus with others bound for the States. It seemed really weird, like I was out of place, a spectator in civilization. Really weird feelings surfaced as I struggled to weave my way through crowds, hearing traffic, reentering civilization fixated on material goods. Skeptically I stood around watching all the people shopping, bustling through stacked aisles of goods made in China, souvenirs for relatives. I bought a tiny Canadian Flag, pulled out some bills, exchanging cash.

We caught the bus and headed for Vancouver. The border patrol scrutinized Rainmaker's driver's license carefully. This white bearded, thin, darkly tanned man standing before them did not look like the blue eyed, nearly blonde man on the license. I waited silently, wondering what would happen if they chose not to let him enter the U.S.A.

Minutes passed. Finally, Rainmaker said, "Sir, it was a long trail."

The agent looked at me, back at Rainmaker, handed him his license, and said, "Alright."

That was it!

We spent our Canadian money at the Vancouver train station, carefully calculating out food purchases until only a few coins remained.

The trail had been very good to me. I grew emotionally after spending 25 years in a male dominated fundamentalist church. I found that God is in his people, his earth and his wild creatures. The wind brought His gentle touch, and yes, a frequent testing of wills.

I send a shout out to the nicest people I've ever met, Brenda and Ralph from Ashland, Oregon. We met Brenda and Diane the first year in California as they horse packed near Sierra City. Their understanding husbands would keep the women supplied, bringing hay for the horses, meeting them at trailheads and taking them out for a night in town. The women would ride over a hundred miles of trail, keeping notes. We met them later on, at Colahan's and enjoyed trail story telling. They told us, when you are ready, call us, we'll come get you.

Brenda and Ralph picked us up at Crater Lake when we completed the middle section that first year then took us out to eat and gave us a place to sleep at their fine home. The next day they drove us 6 hours south to my sister's to get my Geo Metro. They never would accept any money to help cover these expenses. These are God's real people. They never criticized or tried to shove religion at us. All I felt was non-judging love from these trail angels.

The next year, they got us back on the trail after hosting us again at their house. May God bless them in every imaginable way.

Re- entering society is strange, almost like an out of body experience after that kind of adventure, for me anyways. I went back to cooking at the hospital. I was just on some other level. Earning money for retirement or having health insurance seemed unimportant. I felt no urge to buy a house or settle down. My friends said I was on some "wild woman thing." They had analyzed my summer tan, my toned body.. They claimed to notice a wild look in my eyes.

They were right. The Appalachian Trail called to my soul. In February I put in my two week notice. Human Resources told me I needed to rethink my life. I told them they could rethink this job.

In 2003 I wrote *My Journey to Freedom and Ultralight Backpacking*. It has a complete chronological narrative of my Pacific Crest Trail hike and Appalachian Trail Thru Hike. It is also available in digital format at Amazon.com or Barnes and Noble.

You can find my contact information at the end of Chapter Eleven.

3. Appalachian Trail
A Winter of Preparation
There are so many ways to approach this trail which meanders from Springer Mountain in Georgia to Baxter State Park in Maine.

The trail has been run in 47 days as a totally supported, slack-packing effort. It has been yo-yoed, which means hiking the entirety, tagging the terminus atop Katahdin or Springer, then retracing your steps back to where you started. It's been hiked as a third of the Triple Crown One Calendar Year Hike by Brian Robinson in 2001.

In 1948, a war veteran became the first person to prove it could be done at all. The first thru-hiker was a young Earl Shaffer. He did it again 50 years later. Amazingly, thru hiking the AT was believed impossible before this man did it. Back then gear was very heavy and there were no hostels or trail angels leaving stuff to help a body along the way. Maybe that was a better time. Few women hiked this trail unless accompanied by men. The equipment necessary for a thru hike was just too heavy for a woman alone and the trail was considered too rugged and dangerous.

Things have really changed.

My point is to hike your own hike regardless of all the hype of power hiking or of spending a night in each and every shelter. Keeping in mind that I might never have another chance to be a Thru Hiker and desiring to do the Appalachian Trail as a purist, that's exactly what I set out to accomplish.

At first, I was sort of a reactive hiker. Someone would encourage me to keep up, someone would piss me off or someone would arrange to meet me up the trail at a given time. I would listen and change my plans accordingly.

But a person can't blame *"someone"* else for reactive hiking. I had to learn to maintain my own style, regardless of others on the trail. It would be my experience of a lifetime. In the end we are our own masters, so hike your own hike. Search deep and find your style and hike that way. That's what I kept reminding myself, repeating the mantra adopted on the Pacific Crest: In the end you find no one wins, and the race is only with yourself.

Some backpackers told me I was already a thru hiker because I completed the entire PCT, a feat so rare statistics show that more people have summited Mount Everest. I replied that while I hiked the entire PCT over a 14 month period, it was not the 12 month calendar year required to define a thru hike. I don't feel any need to lie about what I have done or play with terms.

After returning from the Pacific Crest Trail in September 2001, I got my old job back, knowing full well I'd be on the trail come spring. I made my living behind a stove, feeding old people and hospital staff. I would get up at 4:00

a.m., throw clothes on, grab an instant coffee and head out the front door. I'd jump in the car, back it out and head down a steep driveway, throw it in first, set the brake, open the gate, move the car, run back to relock the gate.

Half an hour later, after driving the little Geo in the dark 14 miles over winding northeast Georgia Mountain roads, I'd be fully awake. I would pull into the hospital staff parking lot, lock the doors and enter by the emergency doors, nodding to the nurse on duty.

I would head downstairs, pull out the keys and unlock the heavy kitchen doors, hang up my coat, done an apron and immediately fire up the stoves and steamers, turning on a score of lights in the process, pushing the Brew button to start a huge pot of perked coffee. I'd grab Danish from the cooler, unwrap it and take a huge bit, while heading over to the cook's station. There I would flip open the notebook maintained by the manager to see what's on the menu today.

My coworkers soon arrived, washed their hands and threw on aprons. We'd go through the day automatically as though the same things had to be said over and over. I would mark my Styrofoam coffee cup with my name. Later, I'd sketch in a tent and some mountains. After lunch, I would clean up my station, glance at the clock and sigh. Only 2 more hours and I'm outta there. I would pick up my cup and sketch in a trail, then glance out the enormous floor to ceiling windows the kitchen has by accident. This was supposed to be a dining room but the board of directors changed their minds at the last minute and turned it into the new kitchen. Excellent idea, I thought. The place was huge and well equipped. The windows faced the woods and there was a trail heading out behind the pavement. The trail, so enticing, I can't wait for spring.

That year the hospital was getting rid of their entire Y2K inventory. The world-wide digital changing of the century-disaster didn't happen and now cases upon cases of dehydrated food packed in #10 cans, expensive stuff that purportedly had a shelf life of 25 years, needed to be disposed to gain space in the storeroom.

Immediately I sensed the opportunity of a lifetime. This would be perfect trail food for my upcoming AT thru hike. The kitchen manager said she'd give me a deal, seeing how I was such a loyal cook. I suspect she was tired of working around this mass of food product every time the Sysco delivery guy hauled in our real food.

Eagerly I bought dehydrated eggs, onions, mixed vegetables and a stew blend, figuring this would really make my hike nutritious and cost effective. It would make for a seriously ultralight food bag. I tried a few ideas at home and every food seemed viable. I never tested any of the products out on a trail though.

Mistake. Sometimes your stomach just doesn't want to go with the plan. I subsequently learned that survival food has lower moisture content than normal dehydrated food. This is why it will last 25 years. It requires more water for reconstitution and often a lot more cooking time. If you don't take the precautions you could end up like I did with fierce farts . I didn't learn all this until much later.

If I knew then what I know now, I don't know if I would play. -- from My Story, by Michael Jordon, NBA legend

Michael also said "I can't accept not trying." I figured that's what this was all about. There are no guarantees and nearly everything is worth a try, at least once.

Fierce Farts
This next story is seriously embarrassing and I haven't told anyone before writing this book. Maybe I can save you some misery.

While I hike away from Springer Mountain on a rainy dreary March 12, Rainmaker takes my photo. Underneath the custom packcover is the 9-ounce prototype silnylon backpack I designed and sewed for this journey. I'm wearing my silnylon gram weenie rain suit and Nike sandals.

Rainmaker hiked over 200 miles in Oregon on the PCT last year wearing sandals over smart wool socks because of a foot injury. Every night he took off his wet sandals, and hung his socks to dry. Our feet would get soaked from going through snow. Every night he wiped his sandals down with his bandana and they were dry come morning. I know, because I watched him pulling on dry crusty socks and strapping on dry sandals. Meanwhile I would pull on dry crusty socks then yank on high-top trail runners soaking wet, weighing nearly ten pounds apiece, I swear they did. This is hard on the foot. The instep will suffer excruciating pain from all that weight. Wet shoes turn socks wet and blisters can form extraordinarily fast. Even though I remove my wet shoes every lunch break and allow my feet to dry, the constant moisture starts to break down tender skin. I study Rainmaker's sandals and vow, next spring on the Wet AT, I will have sandals, too.

So, wearing brand new Nike sandals I pitched my custom tent on the first night at Hawk Mt. Shelter. I cooked my fancy dehydrated stew in my pint pot, adding a nice dash of dehydrated onions to boot. After simple hygiene, I settled down into my cat's meow sleeping bag, expecting to get a good night's sleep.

Or so I thought. A light drizzle began, changing into a steady patter. Then it really started raining. My stomach began churning, rumbling noises that foretold of misery to come. I laid my hand over my stomach and pressed down, trying to relieve the pain. Things were not looking good. Quickly I threw on some clothes, left the tent and dug a cat hole back in the brush. I could hear laughing in the shelter. It was packed full of spring breakers and they still partied on. Other tents were pitched near the shelter, but they were dark.

Unobserved, I eased back to my tent and smelled onions. This was not good, not in black bear country. The onion odor lingered in the tent until morning and I knew what I had to do. I chucked all my dehydrated stuff at Neel's Gap and went back to ramen and oatmeal. These are simple foods my stomach likes and can digest without complaint.

I was really glad I learned this before I started using the trail shelters. If you get the farts from hell, please choose a place near the wall and stay in your sleeping bag. Keep your back next to the wall, away from your neighbor and pray no one kills you in your sleep.

Temporary Setback

It wasn't long before I knew the sandals wouldn't work for me. All the mud and rain caused foot slippage, which tweaked my ligaments in debilitating pain. I finally figured out that there was too much play in the footing or grip. I tightened the straps, adjusted my socks, but nothing helped. By Woody Gap my knees were calling it quits. I wasn't sure I'd even be able to climb Blood

Mountain. A wild thought occurred and I glanced into the blue sky. Maybe some helicopters could air lift me out or maybe they'd send men with stretchers. Slowly I inched my way over Blood Mountain and descended to the road, feeling like a complete failure. I hobbled into Neel's Gap, climbed the steps one at a time and called home.

Rainmaker and I chatted a few minutes, then he told me to sit tight, he was coming to pick me up. A young man watched me making coffee beside the parking lot using the soda can stove. He told me he was taking a week off, his knees were trashed. I bid him good luck, held back my self-pity. Others were facing the same thing.

When Rainmaker arrived, I got in the car. I cried pitifully and sobbed my heart out, broken while he drove home consoling me, telling me it wasn't over. He reminded me that he had suffered a setback when he thru-hiked, too.

The next day we went shopping. I bought trail runners and two knee braces and faithfully spent 13 days doing rehabilitation exercises. Those braces weighed 1 pound but wearing them allowed me to get back on the trail right where I left it. I tagged my touch point at Neel's Gap and continued a purist.

A few hikers scoffed at my knee braces and pitifully slow pace asking me how did I expect to get to Katahdin like that? The saying is: if you put enough 10 mile days together, you'll have a thru hike. Ten miles a day, I replied philosophically. If it took me from dawn until dark, I would do whatever it takes.

I learned last year on the PCT it's not so much how fast you hike, but how long. By rising with the dawn and staying focused, a two mile an hour pace will produce a 20 mile day by nightfall. Thirty nine miles after Neel's Gap, we were crossing into North Carolina. I'd be arriving late and thru hiker friends would greet me, "Hey, Brawny! You finally made it in." I'd grin, find a spot and pitch my new prototype: the **Tacoma Solo.**

Males

After returning to the trail wearing two knee braces, I began relying on my hiking poles even more, taking tiny steps when climbing hills, stepping sideways off steep logs. Rainmaker taught me to treat the knees like a hinge, not a muscle. Slow hiking isn't so bad. You see more, you hear more, you interact more with nature and human beings.

One day as I rounded Rocky Mountain, Georgia, I came upon several groups of fire fighters, each wearing a thick helmet and bright yellow jacket. The burly men were sitting on logs, taking a break on a perfect spring morning. One man stood off to the side talking on his cell phone. I could hear him saying, "Yeah, I'm on some mountain in Georgia." They watched me casually hiking past, trying to hide the fact I get a little self-conscious going around a group of men, alone.

I kept going, eventually meeting another group of six. One stopped me and asked politely, "Where are you heading?"

"To Maine," I replied, thinking, don't they know this is the Appalachian Trail?

Mouths fell open. "Hunh?" one asked, surprised. "Can I take your picture?"

"Sure," I said. A camera went off, then we stood chatting for a while. Finally I decided to share the fact that they were sitting on the Appalachian Trail. "Yeah, I heard about that on Dateline," one nodded to his friend.

At last I bld good bye, waved and walked north while they continued with the controlled burn that would protect one of America's greatest treasures.

Sunrise found me nearing Dick's Creek Gap. It was a brisk morning; I was cold so started out wearing tights on under my shorts. As the sun rose, the day began heating. I found a nice log, leaned my poles against the tree and glanced up and down the trail, waiting a minute, making sure no one was in sight. It was still early, way early.

Quickly I removed my shoes, slid off my shorts and quickly stripped off my tights, rushing to grab my shorts and pull them back on. Need I whisper: no underwear? Suddenly, here come two men in total camouflage, carrying big long guns. They approached silently, ominously. "Are you men out on maneuvers?" I asked.

The darkest man whispered some response. "Pardon me?" I replied. Another whispered answer from a bearded face. "Excuse me?" I asked, still uncertain what he said.

"We are turkey hunting!" he says loudly, clearly irritated. He exhaled roughly and led his teenage son past me, paused a moment, reconsidering

76

the shoeless woman standing beside the trail. "Ya hear any gobbling?" the man asked.

"No Sir," I respectfully replied. He nodded, touched his hat and continued onward. I turned to watch them walk away, then put on my shoes, tied the laces and headed north. From then on, I wore shorts with my rain pants over them. I could slip the rain pants off without removing my shoes or shorts.

Unlike the PCT, the AT offers very little privacy within the official corridor because of the easy access and scouts that frequent the shelters.

Smokey Mountain Fortress

After enjoying a zero day with Rainmaker, I rejoined my trail friends at Hwy 28, near Fontana Dam.

Briskly I crossed the parking lot at the marina and picked up my Smokey National Park permit. The shuttle van from Fontana Village had just pulled in and was depositing several backpackers. I smiled. My comrades were disembarking from a zero day, too.

I, the spoiled rotten hiker had spent a zero day at home thanks to a life partner who had thru hiked the Appalachian Trail in 1992 and knew this luxury wouldn't last. I have to hand it to the man. He supported my hike, my freedom and my need to test crazy ultralight techniques in the field. Such men are rare. Men who can let go and trust their woman to hike their own hike, knowing there would be long periods of separation yet trusting them to stay true.

Back on the trail, we thru hikers headed up the hill, past the "Hilton" AT shelter and onto the road leading up to Fontana Dam.
I spent some time hiking with Corncob, Wonder and Charlie Foxtrot. The early spring heat and sunshine was draining. I got hot and complained about my pack weight. Something just didn't feel right. This pack should feel much better. It had a hip belt with padding and weighed in at 15 pounds fully loaded.

Charlie, an ex- Navy dude from Kansas with calve muscles the size of basket balls threatened to trade packs with me. I laughed heartily. Oh sure, I sassed. I don't think I could have budged his from the ground.
Every day, Charlie Fox trot would hike twenty miles, set up his Wanderlust for Two and do push-ups. He said it kept his upper body toned.

But his pack wasn't quite as massive as Badger's backpack. Badger held the record for heaviest pack weighed at Neel's Gap in 2002. He started at Amicola Falls, which is the approach trail to Springer Mountain, with over 100 pounds and arrived at Neel's Gap, 30 miles later, with 87 pounds. He lightened his pack there by shipping 40 pounds of gear home. Some call this process "tuckerizing". That is progress. One evening I watched Badger cook a three course supper with gravy, mashed potatoes, and much more. The rest of us sat around eating out of our one pot, marveling at the work load for a single meal. Badger had plenty of cookware and spices. No wonder his pack was so heavy.

A close up of the 9 ounce silnylon pack. Note the water bottles bungeed to the front straps. This pack made it the entire thru hike.

One hiker tells us the outfitter sold him a mallet to pound the stakes in for his tent. We grin. A friend shouts out, "Just use a rock!" You don't need a clean pair of socks seven days in a row, either. Just wash them out. The more stuff you carry, the longer it takes to pack each morning. Ok, back to the trail.

AT thru hikers continued on at our own pace, leap-frogging along until we hit Birch Spring Gap. The shelter there had been totally dismantled but tent sites remained. There was a good place to pick up water beside the stream. "Better get some," Charlie warns, "It's the last for five miles." Five miles doesn't sound like much if you've hiked the desert. But on the AT with its frustrating PUDs and high heat humidity, it takes longer than you'd think and you get way thirstier than you'd imagine.

As Charlie takes off his pack, digs out the water filter and sits down to pump a couple quarts, I remove the soda bottle from my front sling, bend my knees and scoop a quart. I reach into my pocket and bring out the tiny eye dropper bottle of Chlorine and give the water two drops and stand waiting. Charlie watches me skeptically. "What?" I ask. He studies me a moment longer and I explain, "This is all I've ever used, on the whole PCT, in the Sawtooths. I don't carry a water filter, ever. It's too heavy. I've never gotten sick, either." He smiles, shakes his head, and continues pumping.

We passed Mollies Ridge Shelter and looked in. It was shocking. It was my first glimpse of a Smokey Mountain Trail Shelter and it reminded me of the **forts** from Last of the Mohicans.

Made of rugged stone work, all were three-sided shelters closed off on the fourth side with a chain link fence reaching the roof. It was fully enclosed on four sides, thus creating a fortified home for all who stopped to rest there that night. Inside was an aging, double decker shelving situation with thin slats nailed to the boards to section off individual spaces. I was instantly reminded of the Amistad slave ship. But this o.k. with me. The Smokies are Bad Bear territory and I definitely wanted a slot in the shelving unit.

Inside the shelter the dirt floor was solidly packed. There was an enormous fireplace at one end. Outside were blackened fire rings and huge logs for sitting. Farther on was a grassy area big enough for several tents. A wooden sign pointed the path to water and another indicated the path in the opposite direction to the toilet area.

Wow. We hiked farther and I thought about which slot would afford the least mouse traffic. Two and a half miles later, Charlie and I arrived at Russell Field Shelter. I had decided I could not tolerate sleeping next to the stone wall whose multiple crevices housed infinite generations of rodents. I always imagined a mouse caught in my long hair.

I dropped my pack, pulled out my pad and unrolled it along with my sleeping bag in the center of the top bunk. Poptart and Geek were already set up. Mice scampered in broad daylight. Smurf threw a snicker's wrapper into the corner figuring that would keep the critters busy. It is forbidden to harm any living creature in National Parks. I think that means spiders as well. I operate on a don't ask, don't tell basis.

We hiker claims a space and begins cooking supper, selecting odd packages from individual food bags. Someone smears peanut butter over crackers.

Another boils water to pour into a plastic pouch. Garbage and food wrappers are stuffed into Ziploc baggies, added to the ultralight food stuff sacks then hung on cables 30 feet off the ground.

Everything was brought inside the shelter except for the food bags. Packs were hung on the inside of the fence or from the rafters, long straps and belts intermingling, creating a forest of black webbing. Water bottles were set around inside the fortress, clustered in groups to prevent being stepped on or spilled. Everyone goes out and pees before dark. We're warned by Radio Flyer, if you go out during the night, BE SURE to latch the gate behind you.

It's almost 9 o'clock, bedtime and nearly dark. A south bounder finishes his supper and hangs his 6-liter platypus full of water outside on the fence 5 feet from the ground. He comes into the gated community and prepares for bed.

Smurf waited for us all to climb into our sacks, settle down and be quiet. His British accent was very entertaining especially as he hikes along, making observations on the bloody green scenery. No one set an alarm but most will be up before the sun. At last Smurf launched into our bedtime story of monsters and ghosts. One by one we drift off for a visit to dream land. Long miles and plenty of pain relievers worked wonders, making wooden bunks seem soft, filling the air with the sound of snoring

About 11 p.m. it started raining; a steady drenching rain. A couple hours later it lulled to a steady drizzle. I jerked awake at the sound of a big Whoosh. I wondered, "Who is tenting out there and now dumping the water off his fly?" There was some banging and then all was quiet. I felt sorry for the poor souls out in that bad weather, then fell back to sleep.

As a female soloist, I learned how to get dressed inside my narrow sleeping bag early on. Basically you keep your clothes in a stuff sack for the pillow. In the morning, open the stuff sack and pull out your trail clothes. Then sliding deeper into the bag, pull your sleep shirt off and slide your trail shirt on. Then you can sit up and change your pants. Unlike the miles of solitude on the PCT, the AT could have people all along the trail dawn until dusk. You might run into turkey hunters, kids on break, day hikers, kids at risk and Boy Scouts. To maintain modesty, one has to develop some strategies.

I'm a daybreak hiker. I dress in my sleeping bag, slide out and shove all my gear into my pack before cautiously easing to the edge of the shelf where I let my foot seek the floor. Sliding off the shelf, trying not to step on the head shelved beneath me, I land nearly soundlessly, then pause to be sure I have all my gear before tip-toeing out of the fortress to eat breakfast. After clearing the gate, I turn and carefully latch the lock behind me.

Once on soft grass, I walked behind the shelter just to see the sodden tents. But, there were no tents or tarps. Moments later, Charlie joined me and I asked him if he heard anything last night. He said no. I told him I had heard water splashing.

Gradually hikers awaken and start stumbling out of the fortress, making their way along the dewy grass to claim food bags hanging from the cable. Sleepily they wander down paths to water or potty as needed. I sat back watching all this as I eat hot oatmeal, seated comfortably on a log. A person can learn a lot just watching others begin their day. Minimalism: the less stuff you got, the less you have to find each morning. In a wall to wall crowded shelter, your stuff may end up on the other side of several bodies.

Finally, the south bounder sat up, yawned and stretched, and slid out of his sleeping bag. He needed water and his was outside, hanging on the fence. He dressed quickly and walked out the gate.

"What in the Hell?" he suddenly yells. He unhooks his platypus from the fence and holds it up frowning, inspecting the damage. He passes it around, stunned and incredibly mad. It is completely empty with a huge piece of plastic bitten from it. All that remains are teeth marks. "I paid $18 for this fucking thing! A bear bit a hole in my bag!" he screams.

The south bounder hung the ruined platy back on the fence, borrowed a water bottle and stalked off down the trail to get more water. Curious about the teeth marks, I walked over to the fence, bent over and picked up a chunk of ragged plastic off the ground.

"That must have been a bear you heard last night, Brawny," Charlie said. "When you heard the water being dumped off a fly."

Fear Factor

When hikers arrive at a shelter, immediately they find the trail register and begin searching its recent pages, learning who's up ahead, who is heading to town and what did they think of the rain. Sometimes there will be crazy scribblings and we'll pass around the crayon sketch of a last hiker standing at the outhouse. There will be stories of things that went bump in the night, mice and snakes, a bear sighting, a hiker with a nightmare.

Today there were several pages devoted to the Rant **"Fear and the Ultralighter"**. This dude wrote that he had been disrespected for carrying so much weight by an ultralighter who said that if he weren't such a pussy, he could dump some extra crap and go lightweight.

The dude wrote more, going on to charge that it's the ultralighter who is the pussy because he's afraid if he doesn't lighten up he'll never make it all the way to Katahdin. It sparked a great debate.

The entire argument ignores the fact that it's not the gear that gets you to the terminus, you get the gear there. Whether I've got a Gregory pack or a Go-Lite, or one I've made myself, my feet have to carry it all those 2,172 miles. If the gear is not working for you, whether it's heavy or light, you switch it out. I opened a fortune cookie at a nice restaurant once and it summed it up: Nothing of value is accomplished without passion. It takes heart to live on the trail, passion and a clear vision of the goal: Katahdin!

A note: I never heard this debate on the PCT. No one cared what we were carrying. Your weight is your problem. Most PCT hikers are very lightweight because of the distances between supply points. Plus, long waterless stretches necessitate carrying many quarts of water and pounds of food. Long distance hikers soon learn what they need and what they don't. It's the **can do or die** attitude that gets the gear to the terminus.

Ultralighters have been disparaged by outdoor writers who claim we are parasites and always needing to borrow stuff. This is wrong. I've lent my G2-can opener to a group of guys on a weekend vacation up in Pennsylvania. They had brought canned food but totally forgot the can opener.

I always carry this tiny can opener. Once on the PCT, while hungrily anticipating a feast near Beldon, Rainmaker and I were crossing a state park campground and saw a can of Vegetarian Meat Loaf lying abandoned. We picked it up, found a picnic table and opened it. Rainmaker and I each grabbed a spoon and dug in. I've never eaten canned dog food but the flavor made me pause. We checked the label. Nothing said dog on it so we figured it couldn't be dog food. Looks like it, smells like it, but whatever. Rainmaker and I finished it completely, wiped our mouths on grimy bandanas and went to find real food at the Grill.

Little can openers come in handy when you hit town and lust for that can of black olives, canned peaches or tuna fish. Thread it on the tool cord along with the photon light and mini razor knife and you'll never notice the weight.

I've also hiked with a guy who needed to cut off his long shoe lace. The laces were making him crazy because they kept coming untied. It wasn't the weight of the extra length of lace, not at all.

As he prepared to drop his pack and search for his knife, I pulled out my ultralight tool kit from my shorts pocket and offered him the 6 gram razor knife. He was happy for the easy solution and told me where to cut. It worked.

I'm also a very firm believer that a person should only lose the non-essentials as they develop skills. Not everyone is able to creatively come up with solutions to emergencies. Not everyone is able or mentally disposed to hike out when they are too cold to sleep.

A Word on Weird Gear

Being an ultralight gear-head, I could not bring myself to pack verifiable sandals if I was using trail runners. While assembling my gear for the AT, measuring and weighing everything in February, I was positive my flip flops from the PCT weighed only an ounce. But everything on the shelves at local stores registered two and a half or three ounces, so I decided I was going to go without.

I bought my Nike Sandals and used them for 30 miles on the AT, expecting them to be my all-purpose footwear. I'd met plenty of people hiking in sandals. I'd even heard of the barefoot sisters, hiking barefoot all along the AT. But I'd like to ask them someday how that worked in Pennsylvania.

When I switched out to trail runners, I figured the shoes could be worn in town or in camp or I'd just go barefoot.

Rainmaker couldn't see it. During my 13 days of recuperation at home, he asked me for a pair of shoe inserts, a nice pair that I didn't need anymore. I scrounged around and came up with a set and handed them over. Using his knife and some camo paracord, he rigged sandals for me which registered in at an insane half ounce. I called them my gram weenie sandals and posted the photo online.

All down the trail I'd meet people who would hear my trail name and say, "Aren't you the one with the crazy sandals?"

I'd have to smile and say, "Yup, that's me."

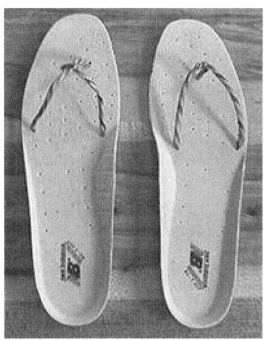

Lesson: You're known by the gear you carry. I think the PCT has more tolerance for home- made-gear weenies. They hold contests at the Kick Off Party and award prizes. I won the "best innovation on the trail this year" contest In 2001 for my silnylon rain suit.

Anyone making gear has to be willing to run the gamut of criticism too. I used to sew tarps for ultralighters. The spacing on the perimeter of the tarps raised the question: is it better to space the staking loops every two feet when possible (an even number length, like 8, 10 or 12) or half then quarter the length. As one adamant client said, "Any IDIOT knows you place staking loops by halving, then quartering the tarp."

Well! I figure, whatever makes you happy. I personally liked the 2 foot staking option.

Then there will be ultralighters cutting off staking loops. I would write them back, "Two loops weigh 4 grams. What happens when it gets windy and you cut off the two loops to stake that shelter down?"

This 3.5 ounce cook set was used for the last 500 miles of my thru hike. It all nested into this cut off lemonade container. The soda can stove fit inside the aluminum pot which is just a Vienna sausage can. This pot fit inside the pot support which was made from a tin can. Aluminum foil serves as the windscreen and lid. The pen is there just for size reference. I didn't carry the pen on the trail.

To use this ultralight cook set I basically heated water and poured it into either plastic container. I used the smaller one for soup or coffee. The larger one was for rehydrating mashed potatoes, ramen or instant cereals. I found my tummy felt better eating simple carbohydrates. When I got to town, I ate anything I wanted. Sometimes that meant a whole pizza!

Stove-Less

After we passed the halfway point, several of my thru hiking friends were growing tired of standard backpacking foods. Some went stove-less, hauling summer sausage, bread, peanut butter and cheese. I met a hiker just eating cold instant mashed potatoes. She poured water into a pot, the stirred in instant potatoes until the consistency was thick enough to hold up a spoon.

GORP, which stands for Good Old Raisins and Peanuts, was always a reasonable choice for the bored palette and takes on a really creative nature. Use the standard Four Food Groups to divide the shopping into categories. Recipe: All sorts of finger foods are dumped into a gallon-sized Ziploc bag. If you get sick of the sweets, just pick out the pretzels and snack on them for a while.

First: are the starches, things like: pretzels, taco chips, crackers, sesame sticks and bite size cookies.

Second: Dump in your fruits and vegetables: dried apples, apricots, raisins, cranberries, freeze dried peas and corn.

Third: Mix in your proteins: peanuts, walnuts, pecans, sunflower seeds, cashews or almonds.

Fourth: Top it off with dessert: candy corn, m&ms, skittles, jelly beans, gummy bears. Don't add chocolate or butterscotch chips unless you want chunks of melted chocolate running through everything. Been there, done that. When it gets hot, the chocolate remelts and it's a mess.

I feel that in the long run going stove-less is heavier because the moisture is carried in the food instead of being obtained from the water source. Water makes up the greatest percentage of food weight. By cooking over a tiny stove, you bring the water as you need it, instead of carrying it from town.

A person has to like their food, though, and if it takes a crazy week of peanut butter and jelly sandwiches to get you back on track, no one's the worse for wear.

I hauled vitamins for a while, thinking to save my hair from the devastation it experienced on the PCT. All the dirt and grime coupled with no conditioners and unbalanced meals added up until finally my hair was dry and lackluster. I found those vitamins absorbed the moisture from the air and turned into a crumbly mess. For a while I tried eating a spoonful a day. They tasted so horrible; no amount of water could wash the chemical aftertaste away. I threw them out next time I passed a garbage can. One guy chucked his four pounds of vitamins and minerals into the trash when they took on the appearance and texture of gray cornmeal.

I learned on the PCT to keep my cook set in an outside pocket. When I hit a good water source, I'd pull out the set and cook a meal right there. The saying is a white man looks at the clock to tell if he's hungry. But we soon learn that meal times on a long hike are discretionary. I try to cook when there's water nearby.

On the AT there is usually water near each shelter which makes it quite handy if you want hot food in the middle of the day during one of many storms. Sometimes I'd stop at a shelter, start making coffee and find some trail goodies left by trail angels: brownies and a fresh jar of peanut butter.

Greyhound and I had just finished hiking 30 miles. It was almost dark but the shelter was up ahead. I checked the data book to be sure. One tenth of a mile before arriving at the shelter, the AT northbound hiker crosses the water source. Having hiked through the Mojave Desert, I learned to keep a close eye on my data book's water information. Pulling out my soda bottles, I stooped to fill them. He followed suit and we pulled in late and finished for the day.

A young man was at the shelter telling jokes and having fun. His parents were footing the bill for this adventure of his and he was only 17. He turned serious and began asking where the water was. We'd just arrived and I said, "Back that way, a tenth of a mile."

"Shit," the youngster replied. "I'll pay anyone $5 to go get me some." An older gentleman took him up on that offer in spite of his injured knees and wearing a knee brace.

Heading north, I'd meet this high school student on and off. He planned to write a paper for his senior year on this adventure and get high school credit. I thanked him for my decision to purchase a down sleeping bag. He carried a beautiful down bag, never got it wet and always slept warm. We discussed the pros and cons at length and he was right. Down is doable on the wet AT.

Farther up the trail the young man lost his gear. Word was someone stole it during Trail Days in Damascus while he partied. That was a serious shame. His parents sent him money and he was able to buy what he needed at the outfitters and continue his journey.

A typical hiker supper shift on the Appalachian Trail.

The Expert Newbies

You've never met so many backpacking experts until you've hiked the southern portion of the Appalachian Trail. Amazingly, accountants, basketball players, tool and die dudes and receptionists have all answers we seek. Of course, I'm kidding. Most long distance hikers learn to keep opinions to themselves on all trail issues, offering information as requested. Styles of hiking and daily rhythms vary greatly and we've learned there's no single right way to do anything.

Gear, miles and timing are all subjective. My mentor says we get the gear to Katahdin, not the other way around. You have to want it and if you can stand the pain, you can keep going.

Three Ultralight tents: all loved by their soloist owners. Note the differences in styles. This proves that the gear is secondary to the drive in each soul. But bad gear will break down even the bravest hiker. A leaking tent, a worn out sleeping bag, insufficient clothing can end an otherwise successful journey.

One particular dreary day it was pouring rain. Greyhound and I hunkered down and trudged silently in a total deluge. I was leading the tall dude from Knoxville. I would have let him pass. His long legs could have carried him to the next shelter way before me. He enjoyed the company and so did I, so he stayed close behind while we navigated across Tinker Ridge near Troutville. Being up high on open ledges was not good in this lightning storm. The white blazes marked our way pretty well if one could see past the dripping visor on the rain jacket.

Suddenly the trail split. I hesitated a moment seeing it went above and below the boulders. He followed close behind while I skirted the base and continued on, not knowing he had retraced his steps. Above the storm, I heard him call, "Hey Brawny, there's a blaze on this boulder."

"Yeah?" I asked but kept walking. He ran back and climbed on top the boulder, just to be sure he could remain a purist.

Being a purist on the AT means following every last white blaze, staying exactly on the trail. The blue blazed trail you take to get to the shelter is the same one you take leaving it. If you left for a resupply from the south side of the road, you return to the south side, tag the sign, cross the road and continue. That also defines continue-ists. There are no missing steps between the northern and southern terminuses. You would never dream of yellow blazing which means taking a ride and skipping actual trail.

Purism is good in theory, but sometimes while crossing a cow pasture, the bull doesn't want to move. Yell all you want. He's standing his ground. That's when I decide to go around.

Sometimes a rattlesnake has claimed the trail. He is hunting his dinner in broad daylight and dares you to just make his day. This is another time I decide to go around. By going around these obstacles, I am still within feet of the treadway. I think that counts.

Sometimes the 10 water crossings of Laurel Creek are flooded and you can't see any blazes as you make your way across. Do the best you can. No other trail is so anal. But as an AT purist, I do hike past every white blaze possible, rejecting the shorter blue blazed trails leading back from towns or AT shelters. I tag sign posts, retrace the exact blue blaze trails to and from shelters, walk the maze around Pennsylvanian Outcroppings.

It's all about Hike Your Own Hike, as it should be. Several nights later, to my complete embarrassment, this same guy called me out as a bunch of hikers sat around camp. He said I could no longer be a purist since I didn't go back and step on top of the boulder. Our companions glanced around, puzzled. Why did it matter to him what I did? And what was his point?

What is the point of me telling this story? The longer a person hikes, the more chill they become. Newbies are known for anal tendencies. They just can't help it. My thru hiking friend, Hoosier immediately changed the subject by asking to see my crazy gram weenie sandals.

Other newbie markers: talking about your real job back home, bragging about your income, refusing to drink out of a hose or asking how many miles someone did just to brag about yours. That dog eat dog competitive nature belongs in the real world, if at all.

Check out the blazes on the stile below. The top offset one shows the hiker that once you climb over, the trail veers right.

Games For Soloists

At some point a person gets over the stigma of talking to themselves. After days of hiking alone over steep hills, racking up long miles, I came up with several games that would keep my mind and challenged.

Break Classifications:

I decided to classify the types of breaks I needed and would give myself pep talks when things got tough.

Type 1= a pee break, I probably won't remove my pack

Type 2= pee break, drink water and eat a snack, I still might not remove my pack

Type 3= definitely drop the pack and sit down, remove shoes, eat, drink and pee. This break will take about 15-20 minutes.

Type 4= all of type 3 spread out over the course of an hour. This serious break gives me time to air dry the tent, sleeping bag and socks. Once on this type of break, I lost my tent stakes. They were in a gray stake bag. When I packed up, I didn't even notice them off to the side, stealthily hiding in the fallen leaves. When I got to town, I bought gutter nails. From now on, I keep my tent stakes in a royal blue stake bag.

Type 5=involves sleep and all of the above

As I hiked alone and neared Albert's Mountain, the bladder began demanding a Type 1 break. The knees chimed in "Excuse me! We could use a 3, at the Very Least!" All this body chatter is draining. I'm listening, thinking of all the miles until the next shelter where I'll camp.

"Hello? Who do you think have pounded the dirt for 3 hours straight? We demand a Type 4!" the feet complain.

I sighed. It was true, my whole body ached. "Ok, ok, everyone shut up," I grumbled aloud, "When we hit that mountaintop, there's a privy and Serious Type 4 coming! Work with me on this!!"

I've learned it's all about negotiation and respect. After a while, everyone got stronger or went home. Once past Damascus, my body learned the more ones and twos we did while holding off on the threes and fours, the sooner we could get to the shelter and have a decent twenty done for the day.

An easier game was **Gorp According To Blazes –** Place the daily allotment of GORP in sandwich baggie in shorts pocket or small ditty bag cinched to shoulder strap. Eat a small bite. Chew slowly. Swallow. Pass 3 blazes before you get to take another hand full.

This game involves others. It doesn't count if you're already hiking with someone else. I call it the **Hiker Factor** - Time how long between human sightings. It doesn't count if you're waiting at a road crossing, debating hitching into town for a burger and fries. Played right, some days, it's about every 3 hours. Sometimes it's only once a day. Vary this game by only counting those with packs.

This is probably the most challenging of games. I call it the **No Thought Game –** Time how long you can go between thoughts. No thinking. Each soloist must set their own parameters here. "When is the last time I saw a blaze?" counts as a thought for me. Your brain is just supposed to register blazes without thinking. If you are wondering if you thought a thought, you probably did. Look at your watch, see how long you went between thoughts, then start over.

This isn't any fun unless you like numbers and can do math in your head. After a while I get a headache, so this is a last resort. Start it with the notion you are rich and   **Plan Next Resupply –** Plan both for ounces and calories. Obtain these figures, then divide by days and multiply by miles. Subtract from your age. Add to your IQ. Start over.

Every once in a while I would sing songs I made up, right out loud. It wouldn't be so awful if I could also think of a tune to match the phrases.

While playing my new game **How Long Does It Take To Pass 100 Blazes?** I was counting 34, we have 34. 34 and going on 35, we have thirty- fi . . . . and suddenly along the narrow, bramble-bordered trail, here comes a southbound, cinnamon colored, Black bear. We both stopped. We eyed each other. I went into scare-the-bear mode, clanking my hiking poles together. He was not impressed one bit. I frowned, bewildered. This has always worked before. Now I'm a little worried, but it's early in the morning and other hikers should be coming this way. Surely this bear is going to run off.

I yelled again, "Go, go bear!" He kept standing there, his heavy shoulders, his huge head above the tall grasses. I scowled. I had miles to go. I couldn't wait forever!

It was time for a new tactic. I called out, "I need to come this way". He turned his head, took a huge chomp of grass and brambles. I firmly believe he was actually smiling and probably thinking, "Is that it, girl? Is that all you got?" I'm getting aggravated. I shout, "Hey, bear, I need to use this trail." I took a breath and added, "But I know you do, too." I figured he would appreciate my willingness to share. The bear looked at me, amused, then shook his big head, back and forth. I wondered, How does he know I don't have a gun or bear spray?

Then I saw the shiny metal tag in his right ear and swallow, fighting back the realization I had a Bad-Ass Bear blocking my way.

Ok, Ok, I thought, this is different. I took several steps back, talking to the bear, calmly, soothingly. Still he's not moving, just eating grass. I started banging my poles while backing away, ten feet this time. The bear starts trotting towards me. My eyes go wide and I wondered frantically, do I jump in the weeds quickly, hoping he passes by like a day hiker? The gut rebelled at this horrid thought and I started yelling, angrily, "Alright! No more Mr. Nice Guy! Do you want me to rock you? Get out of here!!" I stooped to pick up a rock. I'm searching the ground as the bear gains on me but all I can find is one that weighs about 5 pound. Where are all the throw-able rocks in Pennsylvania when you really need one??

I stood tall, rock in hand. At last I see the bear jump off the trail and into the weeds to the left. I watched the weeds. They were so tall he disappeared behind them, easing into the trees. I stood a minute longer and I decide that was good enough. "Attaboy!" I yelled. "I believe in peaceful co-existence, just like you!" I kept talking as I passed the place he left the trail. As I ease by, I glance over my shoulder, then turn around, walking backwards. Eventually the bear got back on the trail and I sighed, nodding my head, satisfied. The passage of two beings was done without bloodshed.

Some of my favorite hiker buddies from the AT:

Smurf loved to tell us bedtime stories. Radio Flyer was from Tennessee. Someone asked him how we do twenty mile days, day after day. He thought hard for about three seconds and said, "We get up early and haul ass all day until we get there."

When we arrived in Harper's Ferry, we headed to the Appalachian Trail Conference Headquarters. They took our individual photos and stuck them in an album for 2002 alumni. I was number 148.

Then Smurf, Radio Flyer and I headed to book a motel. The three of us checked in and I asked the receptionist about doing some laundry. "Well," she replied, "If you'll put it all together, we'll do it for $5 and have it back to you in about an hour." We agreed. That was do-able.

There motel was very clean and were two double beds. The guys said they'd share one and I could have the other. "Sounds great," I replied. "I was figuring on taking the floor, rolling out my sleeping pad."

I stripped a pillowcase from a pillow and everyone pitched in their laundry. The guys wrapped in sheets. I donned my rain pants and a tank top, then took the pillowcase to the front desk and paid the receptionist

Like Romans in togas, the men watched t-v and waited patiently. Eventually they began to pace. I felt restless too and checked at the front desk. Not yet. I checked back 15 minutes later and finally our laundry was done. I returned, poured the sweet smelling bundle on the bed. We sorted the mass, folded our clothes, redressed in shorts and shirts. The guys said, "We're going to rent a car and run around Washington DC awhile. You want to come?"

I'd seen Washington before. "Nope," I said, "but thanks. You all have a great time, be safe." I had gone into Mom mode.

I spent the evening writing my journal, watching t-v, napping. It was nearly 11 p.m. when they returned from some shopping. Smurf reaches in his pack and removes a black roll. He hands it to me and asked, "Do you want these silk shorts? I got new ones."

I lifted the shorts, testing the weight. Yup, they were lighter than my other shorts. "Sure, thanks," I said, adding them to my pack.

Early next morning I headed out alone, declining the offer to join them and play tourist. They decided to stay another day roaming around Washington D.C.

An Eight Pound Pack, for Real

Port Clinton is a cute little town in Pennsylvania, midway to Delaware Water Gap. I had heard there might be food in that little place. But the reports were too uncertain for my liking so I didn't count on it, and packed three extra days of food. Hiking with Main Frame over these notorious rocks was sort of fun. He quipped, "I'd fire the trail commissioner, was it me."

Main Frame was lean and muscular, a computer specialist. He hoped to get into town before the post office closed, otherwise he'd be holed up until Monday. I've learned that post offices are a love-hate situation. You can pay the post office to haul your heavies up the trail or you can shop in towns along the way, hoping they have enough supplies. I choose towns whenever possible. However, when I needed gear for the Whites, I shipped myself a drop box and included some treats. Otherwise I'm basically a stop and shop kind of hiker. I think with postage rates going up like they have and small post offices closing, the habit of shipping drop boxes for long distance hikers will gradually peter out.

Main Frame and I pulled into Port Clinton late in the afternoon. It was nearly closing time for the one outfitter in town. He also had the only phone available for hikers to borrow, a cell phone. Things have sure changed. Satellite towers have sprung up and cell service along the trail has probably increased dramatically.

I imagine lots of hikers carry smart phones now. That's another love- hate situation. Folks back home think you have service and battery power all along the trail. When you don't call home, they worry day and night. Or, if you're sleeping in a shelter and the thing rings, you'll get a lot of nasty stares and comments. Trail etiquette dictates that if the thing makes noise, use head phones or ask permission.

Back in 2002, though, with one lone cell phone available, I quickly accepted the outfitter's offer and called home to leave a message on our answering machine. Main Frame asked where the nearest ATM machine was. According to the outfitter, the town has no ATMs and no one will take a check or credit card. Cash only.

Since we were the only people in the store, this really amicable store owner volunteers to run Main Frame to the next town over where they do have ATM machines. He asked me if I would watch the store and wait for them. I've never seen this guy before in my life. He's never seen me.

"Sure," I said, "As long as I don't have to do anything."

"Nope, not a thing, just stay here, in case anyone comes in."

"O K,"I nod, "Sure." Twenty minutes after they leave they're back. During my wait, I walked around the store looking at stuff, glad I didn't need anything. I studied the large map under the glass display, killing time. There were shelves with Power Bars and candy bars, racks of brand name paraphilia and clothes. I never touched a thing. I know that hikers are ambassadors for the trail. If you mess up, the people behind you will suffer.

As soon as they get back, the owner walks over to the cash register, opens it and counts the money. He puts money back, closes the register and causally walks over, acting overly friendly. He glances down at my homemade pack. "You're pretty light there," he said.

"Yup, I'm an ultralighter. I make most of my own gear," I replied.   Main Frame told me he was getting a motel room. I told him I decided to head down to the pavilion to crash and resume the trail in the morning. He says he has to wait on the post office. He'll be stuck in Port Clinton for two days, at least until Monday morning.

"Would you like to see what your pack weighs?" the owner asked nicely.

"Sure," I replied. "That would be interesting. I have four days of food and 12 ounces of water."

He picked up my pack, set it on his scale and declared, "Fourteen pounds!"

I grinned proudly. If he had asked me to dump out my pack so he could be sure I didn't steal anything, I would have been pissed. I'm no thief.

I said goodbye to the guys and walked down the street to the pavillon. Several thru hikers had their gear spread around. As I looked for a place to lay my pad, one handsome young man said, "There are river rats , be careful, they come in along that wall."

My eyes went wide. I looked around the huge brick shelter. The guys watched me. "Well, you guys seem ok." A twinkle in one man's eyes alerted me. I have always been naive and pretty gullible. "Ok, you guys are just messing with me." I spread my pad, pulled out my bag and fluffed it, resigned to an eventful night. Thankfully, nothing woke me.

The white blaze is at the end of this tunnel formation.
These rocks were cool and shady, an excellent place to take a lunch break.

The AT is a very historical trail. People have lived all along these mountains since Daniel Boone. Some mountains have seen Civil War Battles. Graves and head stones mark the path.

May they rest in peace.

Ultralighters, Gram Weenies, Minimalists

There are ultralighters, gram weenies and minimalists. I fit in all three categories and believe there are many others like me. These are my conclusions:

An **Ultralighter** will weigh gear, spend money and carry things that are insanely light. The amount of items it takes to create a workable system doesn't matter. It's the end weight that counts.

A **gram weenie** will suffer untold hardship to shave a gram of weight. A lowly gram, of which there are 28.5 in each ounce, could make the difference in your tarp being staked down securely in a storm or your wrists hanging out your sleeves. A gram weenie will pick the N off his New Balance Shoes, cut the label off his t shirt, trim the corner off his map and brush his teeth with a finger.

Now, a **minimalist** will make do. It's not that the item weighs too much to carry, like the plastic straw for picking up water off a dripping overhang; it's the mere fact you have to keep track of it. If the tent can be pitched with five stakes, seven being ideal, rather than keep track of seven, they will hunt twigs to make do. Trail journals are kept on spare data sheets and shipped home pronto. Garbage is minimalized and food is streamlined. This week is all about oatmeal. Next week it's ramen. Too many items make packing up take longer. The minimalist will have two pairs of socks. One for sleeping and one for hiking. Numbers count.

Now, I'm not sure what you call the person with tendencies in all three categories. My hiking partner Rainmaker used to call it "fucking crazy".

I decided that mittens are always worn with sweaters. Why not just make a fleece pullover with the mittens attached? When not needed, this special design allows said mittens to be folded back, like little mittens found on newborn baby sleepers.

This concept proved very useful on my AT thru hike. I never had to hunt down my mittens. My wrists were always warm; the sleeves were not too short. Insane, yes, because if you drop a tent with frost on it while wearing your mittens, the mittens get wet. Then, you want different mittens. Solution? Drop the wet tent bare handed, dry hands on bandana then put on mittens.

This same fleece pullover had a hood, which kept my neck warm and eliminated the need for a separate skull cap.

Night the Hikers Hung

Arriving at William Brien Memorial Shelter in New York, I found the shelter buzzing with activity. I love this energy and quickly claimed a bunk in the corner. Some young men, both over-nighters, were pleasantly greeting us as we pulled in and spread out our gear for the night. A roaring campfire was built and we settled in for trail stories, enjoying the creative words from New Yorkers with noticeable accents.

These experiences are great incentives for staying and sleeping on the trail as much as possible. The year I hiked there was an older guy would do 20 mile days, meet his wife and go to a motel. Every morning she would bring him right back and he would continue his thru hike. We called this duo the slack-mobile. Again, to each their own, but I do believe he missed some of the AT culture.

The air cools off, supper is finished, the pot washed, clothes changed. I've taken some pain reliever and eventually, the ibuprofen does its job. Cheerfully I head to bed, slipped off my gram weenie sandals, climbed in my bunk and snuggled deep in my goose down bag. Events soon took an interesting turn and I found a poem writing itself the next day as I hiked out at sunrise.

The Night the Hikers Hung
---on that fateful night, June 17, 2002

One by one we stopped there on a sultry afternoon
An assortment of AT hikers that day in early June
Thru hiker, sectioners and overnighters had a bonfire and evening chatter
Some cooked, some drank, some horsed around, it really did not matter.

I'm early to bed, early to rise, asleep before the others
As smoke from the fire filled the shelter, I prayed we would not smother.
Drifting in and out of consciousness, I slept on that wooden bunk
Benumbed from too much Advil, wasted like some street drunk.

Then, This scraping, crawling and scratching upon the roof was heard
Too organized to be the wind, too loud to be a bird
Exhaustion and darkness claimed me, I could but lay and hope
Whatever had taken up residence was within the human scope.

The sun sought the horizon, I awoke to meet the beast
As I stuffed my gear together,I saw this ungodly feast
Cookies, Chips and Salsa, Tuna Surprise left in a pot
All lay spread on the shelter floor, overnighters sure hauled in a lot!

Then down from the roof they clamored, and their heroics must be sung
Instead of hanging their leftovers, they themselves were hung.

While I packed up beside my bunk, I realized what had happened last night. Both guys were awake, standing at the edge of the shelter. They offered me some food as I prepared to head out. I grabbed a handful of chips as I passed a mound of food in assorted containers, whispering a thank you both for the food and an interesting night.

I paused at the campfire, looking back inside as the sun crested the horizon. On the floor of the shelter, next to bunk beds were the remains of their supper: an open bag of taco chips, a partial box of chocolate chip cookies and a half pot of noodle supreme. I smiled, thinking there sure can't be any bears in this area! Instead of hanging their food, they simply elected to "hang" themselves up on the roof. I laughed when one came over and told me after sliding down the slanted roof all night, he finally discovered if he hung his head off the edge that he would stay in place.

Warning: Ball Alert

I sat on the floor, leaning comfortable against a huge bale of straw. The owner of this new hostel had offered us the use of his pickup truck for a quick run to the local deli. If we had cash-money, we could buy some real food for supper. Across the double car garage, a group of trail bums and AT thru hikers discussed what they wanted for supper. Some were pulling cash from their wallet and ordering up sub sandwiches, some were ordering up pizza.

"Hey Brawny, what do you want?" a young man called. I turned to look at the group and saw a hairy ball sack split by enormous penis. I quickly averted my eyes and turned back around. "I'll get a sub," I said, and dug some cash from my ultralight silnylon ditty bag wallet. I stood up, walked over and handed the cash to the grinning young man. I don't think he knew what I saw.

Please guys, if you're gonna wear a kilt with no underwear (of course no underwear, I don't wear underwear either) keep your knees together. I'm damaged for life. That view comes back to haunt me still.

Kilts keep chafing at bay. Many rugged dudes wore them while I was on the trail. One tall bearded guy wore a flowered skirt his girlfriend made him. His trail name was Flying Kitty. I give the guy credit for his bold statement: Hike Your Own Hike!

I met a beautiful blonde woman hiking solo on the Pacific Crest Trail. She had this gorgeous shawl she wrapped around herself, using it for a trail skirt. Her boyfriend had given her the shawl. I always keep my eyes open for these new ideas and usually learn something. A couple times she had to tighten the shawl, but it never fell off, not that I noticed and it sure didn't slow her down. The gal could travel thirty miles a day, camp, then get up and do it again.

After a while, nudity becomes a non-issue. During one particular rainy spell on the AT, we hiked all day in the rain, stomping through mud, sloshing through puddles. At last arriving at the shelter, we loaded the small building to capacity. A 20 inch width was the maximum floor space any one had. The length that evening was determined by whoever decided to sleep at your feet.

Waldo arrived, stepped up into the shelter and threw his gear just under the eaves. Every one watched this sodden gray bearded hiker making himself a spot. We scooted our bags and sleeping bags closer to the far wall, creating some space at the open side. I scrunched closer to the wall, finished stuffing my trail clothes to create a pillow, then turned to glance out the open side. There Waldo stood completely naked in front of the entire group of hikers. Methodically he stripped off his wet hiking clothes and dried off with a bandana before donning his dry sleep ware. I didn't blame him at all for his blatant disregard of the mixed company of men and women. I averted my eyes to give him some privacy.

I couldn't understand why one of my friends still wore panties in the Whites. I knew she did because in the midst of our windblown traverse, she mentioned how hard it was to get everything up and decent in the gale. I had no clue how she managed.

The Whites are for Infants

Don't get me wrong. This rugged section of New Hampshire spends some time above tree line. The weather can change quickly and gale force winds will make you hunker down just to catch your breath.

On the other hand, there are closely spaced sturdy huts to sleep and eat at. The trails are well marked and well-traveled. Hikers can make reservations and hike hut to hut. I'm told it's much like the hut system in Europe. I've never been there, so I don't know.

As thru-hikers on a budget we stealth camped a few times, forgoing the fees at designated camp sites.

Early the next morning the three of us packed up in the fog and arrived at Galehead Hut. There we ate a bountiful breakfast for $2. The coffee was hot, and the blueberry coffee cake, scrambled eggs and oatmeal was satisfying.

For lunch we hit Zealand Hut and scored the last 3 bowls of soup with pie and cake for dessert. I had heard rumors of this food situation from several southbounders and the rumors proved true. Phoenix and I were on Food Prowl Patrol, enjoying light packs while our friend, Greenbean elected to carry 6 days of food. While she enjoyed the fresh food at the huts, her pack weight didn't diminish much. One word of caution, though. If you're late in the season, all this bounty is gone. The huts close operations in the winter.

Next, we made it to Ethan Pond Campsite after a 17.5-mile day. It was late, but Phoenix, Greenbean and I found out we had caught up to Papa Geezer. After paying our $8 each to camp, we shared an old shelter we several others. The caretaker there composts the pit toilets. The fee system helps provide for that service.

Next morning Phoenix and I left before 6 a.m. and found trail magic doughnuts, soda and peanut brittle in a cooler alongside the trail. I'm was gaining weight, I'm sure of it, in spite of hiking lots of miles.

Near noon, Phoenix and I sat down for pancakes and coffee at Mizpah Hut, surprised the bounty only cost $1 each. The crew there was mopping and cleaning but said, "If you're willing to eat outside, have at it."

"Sure!" we replied happily. They gave us a pan of pancakes, a gallon of syrup and an entire pitcher of hot coffee to enjoy in the fresh air. Then the crew donned aprons over their naked bodies, turned up the music and had a great time, even allowing me to snap their photo.

Phoenix and I wanted to work-for-stay at the Lake of the Clouds Hut, so we headed out immediately with full bellies full. We knew there were limited positions available. Papa and Greenbean had paid reservations, so they were taking it easy.

Phoenix led the way at a steady clip, helping us complete our 14-mile day by 12:30. We were just in time to be approved for work-stay. The cook gave us our duties, and said those duties would begin around three.

The huts had rich people pulling in. I stand back and watch as the bright colors, perfumes and fancy gear crowds the walls. Hikers of every destination and description pull in, chatting about the changing weather and what a marvelous day they had, taking photos and eating up on top of Mount Washington.

Around three Phoenix and I are put to work. We didn't want to pay $8 to sleep in The Dungeon, the name given to the basement bunkhouse. I had looked in the Dungeon while waiting for my shift to begin. It was very crowded and damp. Also, Phoenix and I wanted a good hot supper, which was promised after all the paying guests were finished eating. Dutifully, we filled the condiment dispensers, helped set the table and washed some pots and pans. The aroma of spicy food filled the kitchen. It seemed my appetite was increasing exponentially.

Finally all the paying guests were fed. Phoenix and I stood side by side, waiting our turn to grab a bowl and eat with the crew, managing to get a taste of the stuffed pasta. The veggies were gone but there were still two pots of bean soup. There weren't any crackers or bread, but there was a fantastic poppy seed cake with a buttery frosting. The cook sliced it and passed it around.

At 9:30 the final guests are ushered out of our "bedroom" which is the dining room. Each of us workers claim a wooden table and spread out our sleeping pads and sleeping bags. We brush our teeth in the main bathrooms; take off dirty socks and crash. We are exhausted and glad for lights out.

Early the next morning, Phoenix and I secretly hatched a plan to eat at the table with our friends, like rich paying folks. We began our tasks early, setting the long wooden tables with silverware and salt and pepper shakers, washing pots and pans. Quickly we packed all our gear, stashed it in the corner near the door and filed in to take our seats at Guest Meal Call. We ate with Papa Geezer and Greenbean and decided we had earned our keep with all the prep work we had accomplished that morning. Other thru hikers had arrived asking for work for stay. We politely got out of their way, almost afraid the cook would call us back.

Our foursome prepared to leave the hut. We went outside and gazed thoughtfully up at the mountain. The weather report warned of winds at 50 mph and gusting, complicated by visibility of only 30 feet. There was a light drizzle already. Because of the strong wind it felt like sleet. The thermometer showed temperatures in the 50s. We all looked to Papa Geezer. He had been up here many times and felt an ominous presentiment about this weather. Patiently he described the bad weather route, the Golf Slide Trail that goes to Madison Hut, as we stood around, contemplating the situation. The official white blazes go up to Washington Summit. I am determined to do the white blazes. I have hiked alone, I say, in worse. My friends fall silent. There is no use arguing now. It's time to hit the trail.

Papa Geezer leads with his wooden staff. I follow. Greenbean is next, then Phoenix. At first I am perplexed by the seriousness on Papa's face and the fact he waits for every one of us three to catch up. The treadway is all boulders and there are very few blazes. Some of them are yellow. In the wind and driving rain, it's hard to stop and puzzle the intersecting routes.

As we gain elevation, it gets worse. I am knocked sideways and struggle to stay on my feet. Our packcovers threaten to fly away and we stop to tie them on, hooking them to the pack, anchoring them in multiple places.

"Everyone ok?" Papa Geezer asks. An affirmative nod of our heads and we call out a yes. We continue while the visibility worsens. Papa stops to analyze each cairn. It's a maddeningly slow pace but it's the best we can do. Phoenix is afflicted with several bouts of diarrhea, and we patiently wait for him. The higher we go the more concerned I become about doing this alone. There are so many intersecting trails and the AT is poorly marked if at all. After 45 minutes, we reach the trail junction with the AT and the Golf Slide Trail.

"Its decision time" Papa Geezer tells us. We huddle close to hear him above the wind. We are all purists and strong hikers. We look up the mountain. "It will get worse. There'll be stronger winds and less visibility." We check each other's eyes. There is a sense of pending doom, of vulnerability unfelt before.

This is where the purist must step back and decide: if we take the bad weather trail, the legitimate route to avoid death, will we regret it later? How will this decision affect us going forward? Someone suggested we could come back and do it later as though we hadn't done the entire trail. Does taking the legitimate by-pass trail actually affect thru hiker status?

All these questions seem anal in the face of our own mortality. A CDT hiker would laugh at such banality. It causes us to reflect. Then I say, "If there ever was a need for a bad weather route, it is today, here and now." Greenbean, Phoenix and Papa Geezer offer to come with me if I want to try hiking to the summit. I shake my head no. I'm not having that hanging on my conscious.

Later that evening we would find out that we were the only AT thru hikers to make it on foot to Pinkham Notch. Others who had made it up Mount Washington, grabbed rides with tourists heading down to wait out the storm. They told us the tourists were happy for extra bodies and weight in their cars thereby keeping the vehicles on the road. One woman broke her foot while attempting to hike up and had to be rescued and carried out.

Inch by inch we made our way across the rocky trail, pausing often, wondering if we would make it by dark. Just when it seemed hopeless, we'd cross paths with a few weekend backpackers heading the other way. We'd pause, wish each other luck, and continue on.

Finally we saw the sign indicating Madison Hut and took the side trail. Moments later we were sitting in a small rustic dining room, eating lunch. The soup was fantastic, the bread and cake just like mom used to make. The cook on duty told us the winds were being clocked at 70 mph. That's what a fly feels while sitting on the windshield of a car traveling on the interstate. While we could have stayed there, our goal was the next shelter, just eight miles away. Battening down our gear, pushing open the door into the storm, we headed out half an hour later, hiking hard, over rocks, crawling along, at last reaching Pinkham Notch. It was as if we had entered another world.

All four of us claimed seats at the long table, glancing all along the filled room at satisfied diners. Technically dinner was over, but even though we arrived a little late, the sympathetic cook sent out a fantastic supper which we demolished. Warm dry rooms were available and every one of us rented rooms for the night.

Phoenix Goes Fasting

--Phoenix passed away in an AT shelter in the Smokey Mountains while attempting a second Thu hike the following year. A trail friend alerted me to this tragedy and gave me a link to his hiking partner's journal describing the event. Apparently he died in his sleep after a grueling day. May he rest in peace. I add this note in the second edition out of respect for a great hiker.

The guy was so used to finding trail goodies and trail magic that he simply quit carrying enough food. I don't get it.
I rounded the corner and found Phoenix stopped cold, nearly toppling over. "What's up, man?" I asked.

"Just faint," he replied. He noticed I was eating a candy bar and asked, "Where'd you get that?"

"Out of my food bag. I bought it in town," I replied. It was like he thought I was holding out on him.

For me, the food situation is a psychological thing. Even if I only eat just a tablespoon of instant mashed potatoes stirred into a cup of hot water, I have to know there's something for dinner. I think it's very important that every backpacker believes they have had supper, no matter how meager. But now my temporary companion stood there, dizzy and falling over. He was a rugged guy, but right now, he was weak as a kitten. I reached in my sack I found a candy bar for him.

We arrived at our evening destination, the AT shelter, and he confessed to not having any food at all left in his pack. We still had twenty miles to our next resupply. I'd carried enough to get me to town but this would not work. I sort of felt sorry for him, and besides hiking with a guy who had no calories was mean. I told him I could spare a little but when we got to town, he was going to buy me a really decent lunch. He replied, if that was the case, then did he get to choose out of my food bag.

"Hell no!" I exclaimed, and scrounged some stuff.

I don't get it. How can a full grown man run out of food on the trail, in decent weather without ever getting lost? When things look sketchy, the savvy hiker rations it out. I don't haul food into town, but every day I have a least a nibble until I get there.

The last couple weeks, Phoenix and I had been eating bountifully while carrying light food bags. After chatting with a southbounder who told me he ate at the huts for a buck a meal, after all the high class people were finished, I realized I could get by in the Whites with just a pound of food per day. I learned the reason we were allowed to eat so cheap was because leftovers had to be dealt. The staff found it was easier and more cost effective to sell it cheap to thru-hikers than pay someone to haul it back down the mountain.

This same south bounder told me that so many people gave him food that he ended up with more food when he finished the Whites than when he started. I chuckled at that thought and said, "Dude, that is a sin." He only grinned.

After consistently hearing stories that a savvy hiker could get plenty of food in the Whites, I decided I could go really lightweight and carry a lean four days of food for that rugged section. It was really sweet. One of our companions hadn't talked to any south bounders. She had a heavy six days of food and often begged us to help her eat it.

After that plentiful food experience, I guess my temporary hiking partner began to take it all for granted and let his guard down.

It is true that the Appalachian Trail is loaded with trail angels. I don't know if that's good or bad. Opinions vary. On the one hand, the journey becomes a conglomeration of parties, human encounters, junk food, trail head picnics and distractions. In the old days people headed out to the trail for peace and quiet, to get in touch with their inner being, to get in touch with the higher powers or deal with heavy issues.

It seems the real world has seeped in. Nowhere is it more obvious that a trail shelter loaded with coolers of candy bars just 10 miles into a section. The bad thing is long distance-hikers start using this commonality as a basis for planning. When you have finished hiking your trail, is it days of hunger and self-sufficiency that will be your pride and joy? Or will you be proud of how much crap you scored all along the way? And I am guilty too of using all the trail magic I find.

I lament the influx of trail "magic." Sometimes it no longer feels like magic. It feels like interference and subsidy. True, a person can take a vow of purity and not partake but then how would they know if it was a gift from gods or demons?

And in the end, I philosophize; it all comes down to hike your own hike.

White Blaze Boat

The Kennebec River is part of the Appalachian Trail. Its crossing is done via this red canoe. A white blaze is painted on the bottom so that purists don't have an issue with taking a ride. Upstream water is released on occasion and hikers have died from the unexpected rushing surge. Hence, the boat has been mandated as the way to cross the river and the boatman happily hauls hikers either direction, giving you a paddle to help. I was pleasantly surprised that it was free.

Doing the 100 Mile Wilderness

The sign warned us to bring 10 days of food. This wooden monument posted at the trailhead reminded us it was a rugged trail with many miles to any kind of help or supplies. I had 4 days of food. I'd heard there was food at 50 miles if a person was willing to hike a half mile to White's Boat Landing.

My first clue the "wilderness" wasn't real was crossing a gravel road the first day and seeing cars going down it. While many friends were planning a food stop half way at White's Landing for a hot meal, I really I didn't need anything. Being so close to the end of the trail, I figured I would hike hard and hike hungry.

Twice I passed shelters in the wilderness with candy bars hanging from the rafter. Trail Magic.

The third night I camped at a nice shelter with section hikers arriving frequently. Some were north bound, like us. Some were southbound and only a few days out. It was a fun group. We told stories and crowded into the shelter. Some decided to camp in tents and brought their food bags to hang in the shelter. You could smell the bacon. That was weird. I had never seen a backpacker carrying raw bacon before.

Eventually we crawled into our sleeping bags. All night I wondered what would happen if some critter decided to snatch such a delectable food bag. The owners were sleeping somewhere out there in the dark. I knew that no way were we shelter dwellers going to maintain the perimeter. I scooted closer to the far wall and hoped for the best. In the morning all was well and nothing went missing.

The Green Circle

There was a time I got pretty bewildered while in the "wilderness." The trail wound through the same green tunnel, over and over. It all started to look familiar. Hadn't I crossed that gravel road half an hour ago? Hadn't I hiked near that crystal bubbling stream and gazed at that exact mountain? I kept going, looking for a landmark and wondered if somehow I had turned myself south and was hiking the wrong direction. How could this have happened without taking a pee break or sitting down at any time? These tricks of the mind can become unnerving for the soloist. I began asking the trail gods for any little clue that indeed I was covering new ground. At last I came to the next shelter. It looked different, had a different name and a different register. I sighed with relief. Indeed, I was still on track, heading north.

Later that day I reached my destination. It was only 2:30. Three thru hikers were sitting in the shelter, eating. "Hey, Brawny!" one called.

"Hey, nice to see you, Red and Bruiser," I replied, calling them by name.

One frowned and said, "I'm Packrat." My eyes went wide. Oopsey, I had gotten one of the names wrong.

You know, after a while guys pretty much look the same: brown bushy beards below gleaming eyes. Scraggly brown hair, topped off with a dirty hat, usually a baseball cap or outlander's wide brimmed with chin strap. And then, below the neck, not much looks different: bronzed arms and legs sticking out of ragged trail clothes, lean and muscular, hairy and rugged. Pretty much the same if you're all sitting down, but stand up and let me see your packs and it's another story. I probably will recognize the gear

"Sorry" I said, "Guess I'm pretty tired." As soon as they pulled out I grabbed my sleeping bag and took a rare nap, not waking until 5. I woke refreshed enough to enjoy other hikers pulling in to share the shelter and chatter late into the night.

The next day I hiked to Abol Bridge where Rainmaker met me. He was driving my car, looking stronger after his rough hike on the Vermont Trail. We drove to Millinocket, got a motel and hot meal. He confided he was really worried about me because a hiker dude said he met me the day before but I was all disoriented and called him by the wrong name. My reply: you guys all start looking the same!

Early the next morning, just after 4 a.m., Rainmaker got up, grabbed coffee and drove me back to Abol Bridge. I tagged my sign to maintain a continuous journey, no step left behind, and headed to Katahdin.

My hair is trashed, I'm lean, my shorts and top are the worse for wear. It was an incredible journey. Even if I re-hike it in later years, it can never be duplicated.

The Appalachian Trail is a social experience. I met so many fantastic people and although I may never see them again, they have had an impact on my life. It's funny how long distance backpackers will cross paths later on while hiking various trails. I met Lightingbolt twice on the PCT and once on the AT. I consider these gifts from the gods, random trail-god meaningful experiences.

Damascus Trail Days are held on the second Sunday in May, luring trail friends to rendezvous for a weekend of reunions and parades. We sit around, comparing notes, checking out gear, catching up on trails. Our real jobs are a necessary evil.

My Journey to Freedom and Ultralight Backpacking has a complete chronological narrative of my Pacific Crest Trail hikes, and Appalachian Trail Thru Hike. It is also available in digital format at Amazon.com or Barnes and Noble.

4. John Muir Trail

Trail Overview and Logistics

With two hundred and twelve miles of surreal beauty, this trail by itself tops many backpackers' bucket list. As a PCT thru hiker, you can automatically buy your Whitney Stamp and attach it to your permit. You'll meet many others who are doing the Whitney Portal Trail, summiting Mt. Whitney, elevation 14,500 feet and returning to the trail head as a day hike. That's pretty strenuous, 11 miles each way.

The JMT's southern Terminus is Mt. Whitney. The northern is in Yosemite National Park. Hiking it in either direction is the experience of a lifetime. You will definitely want current information on which ranch, resort or resupply point is accepting drop boxes and how much they will charge for the service. South bounding you'll need a few days of food to Tuolomne Meadows, then to Vermillion Valley, where you'd need a good ten days unless you want to hike out a side trail and hitch into a distant town.

North bounding, I took enough from Kennedy Meadows to get me to Vermillion Valley where I used the hiker barrel and resort store to resupply. Logistically, I would plan to go north for that reason. This has the added benefit that if your pick up ride is late, its way easier to hang out in Yosemite Valley with all the stores and food than sitting in a parking lot at Whiney Portal Trailhead.

Fither way it's a steep ascent. North bounders would be carrying a lot of food. Therefore if you're heading north, you need to be in good shape already for this strenuous beginning. South bounders could shave off about 10 pounds of food weight at the beginning, expecting to spend extra cash on a resupply at a resort and finish with that same food. Either way, just because it's only 212 miles, don't underestimate the difficulty of the journey or elevation gain. PCT hikers are already conditioned. If you stay well hydrated during the entire hike, you will definitely feel better. Altitude sickness is real.

Ice Axes and the Abyss

Arriving at Crabtree Meadows after an 18 mile day, Cobweb and I set up our tents and agreed to a daylight start next morning. We would strip our packs, put everything we didn't need into the huge metal bear boxes, make these 15 miles and be back in time for supper. There's a lot of thru hikers doing the same thing although Becky hiked straight thru Crabtree Meadows on to camp at Guitar Lake, three miles closer.

On June 10, Cobweb and I ate a quick breakfast, stashed our gear in the bear box, preparing to cross the creek and head up the trail. It was quite overcast with a thin line of blue to the west. A few dudes were packing up and noticed we had our light packs and ice axes, obviously preparing to summit Whitney. The warned that they had been up there yesterday and said it wouldn't be a good idea to go today with the weather so sketchy. Also, they cautioned, because it was so early in the season, there was a lot of snow pack, admitting they had post holed for hours and with the heavy cloud cover, there was a good chance of getting snowed in.

Fanny Pack, from Georgia, pulls me aside, lowers his voice and says he didn't make it to the top. He explained that he was a southern boy and didn't know how to use his ice ax. I listened carefully, glad I'd had a little instruction at Kennedy Meadows from a rock climber. Ice ax in tow, I decided that if I went up that steep trail, by god I would summit. Mt. Whitney is the southern terminus of the John Muir Trail. Without a summit of Whitney, there's no point in finishing the JMT in Yosemite Valley.

Cobweb and I are from the east coast. We don't know when we'll have another opportunity to do this. We studied the ominous sky, focused on the strip of blue and decided to go for it. "Worse case scenario," Cob web summarizes, "We turn around and come back to camp, try it the next day."

I nodded, "Good plan." The men look at us, shake their heads. We are older and shorter, but like two pit bulls, determined to have our way.

My external frame pack was stripped and reduced to one stuff sack with clothes, snacks and one full water bottle. I also had my ice ax and rain gear. The entire pack now weighed about 5 pounds total and felt like nothing. We planned to hike fast, make good time and head back before dark.

Cobweb and I bid good bye to the neigh sayers. Both committed to the attempt, we crossed the creek over an icy log. Cobweb and I knew it was time get moving. He led silently. I stayed within sight of his New Balance shoes eating up the trail. An hour later, we came to Guitar Lake. Marmots watched us as we crossed another rushing creek. The clouds drifted eastward, the blue strip widened. Cobweb and I sighed in relief. Maybe the weather would clear.

Heavy snowfields began to appear. Cobweb and I were glad to be ahead of the others who would follow later. Ice covered most of the trail and rocks which were used for handholds. While making our way up the steep mountain, I was thrilled that the snow was still holding my weight and I wasn't post-holing yet.

"Just follow the footsteps, don't worry about the trail," my partner called as I approached a set of 3 switchbacks. He waited for me at the top of that section, cautioning not to grab onto the icy rocks. Inching along on hands and knees, at last I pulled myself up and over. We had gained 4,500 ft. of elevation in just 7.5 miles. It's mentally exhausting watching for ice, snow and loose tread with every footstep. There was plenty of water on the trail and no need to carry extra. To prevent dehydration and altitude sickness, a person has to drink regularly no matter how cold it is.

When we reached 13,000 feet, we sat down for a snack. "How are you feeling," Cobweb asked me. "Any altitude sickness?"

"I don't think so," I replied. "Maybe a slight headache."

"Drink," he commanded. I did as I was told. I had been drinking a bit every now and then, but I upended the bottle and chugged some more.

We began to see other hikers on a switchback above us, then several large packs at the junction. The owners of those packs had planned well and were now switching out to light daypacks stuffed inside the larger packs to make the final ascent easier.

I was surprised to see so many people on the trail. Then I realized it was Sunday and some were day hikers coming up from the Whitney Portal Trail after hiking 9 steep miles. Their trail joined ours just 1.8 miles from the summit. Some also carried crampons, ice axes and heavy packs.

Nearing the snow covered summit, I collapsed one hiking pole, stuck it in my pack and grabbed my ax. Rainmaker had given me this beauty for Christmas the year before. It had a wrist leash on a heavy strap. You slide that leash on over your hand and tighten it securely around your wrist. In case you need to do a self-arrest, the leash prevents the ax from being ripped away. I was surprised others carrying axes don't have leashes.

Cobweb and I joined the Whitney Train, heading ever upward, shoving the pointed end of our axes into ice crusted snow banks at the edge of a 2,000 foot drop off. We make good progress until we confront, right in the middle of the extremely narrow trail, a 6 foot mound of rock hard ice. I stood back, watching as others navigated this. Most of them were much taller than me. Finally I had to bite the bullet. I thrust my ax into the mound and pulled myself over and onto a narrow ledge. I never looked down into the abyss. A slip and a fall and it would all be over. There is no slope to attempt a self-arrest. It's simply straight down.

Gradually we picked our way to the top, winding our way over trail obscured with snow and boulders. An ice ax is about 2 feet shorter than a hiking pole. It was strange holding onto the head, while jamming the pick end into snow banks. Sunspots from the day before weakened areas in the snowpack. Suddenly I'd find myself breaking through up to my waist. After busting through once, I avoided the discolored areas. Once again, Cobweb and I were glad for an early start. By afternoon the snow pack would be softer and less walkable. At least for now I'm staying on top.

Eventually the trail is lost, hikers spread out. Cobweb and I aim for the highest spot. Nearing the top, we see others congregating near a small building and head to that. We reached the top at 12:15 and walk over to the stone hut. I remembered reading Cindy Ross's account of her PCT hike, saying she spent the night there.

Everyone takes turns signing the registry. Then we find a space on a cluster of boulders and stay until 2:00 p.m. snacking and chatting with our comrades. The highest outhouse in the contiguous U.S was up there and several of us took advantage of the facility, gazing out at the great wildness as our wallpaper. How interesting to think of a helicopter coming to empty this facility. I was told the outhouse has now been removed.

Becky met us up there. She was playing her guitar and talking to some young guys. Interestingly, she had taken on a vow of silence from Kennedy Meadows to Tuolumne. She decided the gods wanted her to talk to these guys offering summer employment on their yacht. Cobweb and I just shake our heads. Young people are so interesting.

Two bold marmots attempted to raid a hiker's pack. I'm surprised to see them at this elevation. Some rock climbers appear out of nowhere. They actually summited behind us, coming up a treacherous route.

Left to right on top of Mt. Whitney: Cobweb, Brawny, Alexa, Citrus, Brent and Amy. I'm wearing my award winning gray silnylon rain jacket.

Finally, Cobweb and I decided it was time to head back to Crabtree Meadows. Amazingly we found going down was easier because the snow was soft and mushy. He soon outdistanced me while I stopped to console a frightened day hiker and pointed the way to the top.   Then I met a middle aged woman who was on her way up. She was crying and asking, "Did you make it? I'm scared." She was hiking alone, yet with many others on the trail for support. I told her, "Keep going, you're almost there. The hard part is behind you."

I stopped and faced that mound of ice. From the back side it was smooth. There was no way to crawl over so I chopped some steps into it. A group of day hikers stood marveling. "So that's how it's done. Can we take your picture?" a man asked.

"Sure," I replied while concentrating on not falling over the edge into the abyss. I did my best to look confident, silently realizing at least there would be witnesses and a photo of my last adventure.

I'm a slower hiker than Cobweb. He forged ahead when we left the summit. I made my way down alone across icy boulders and didn't see him again until Crabtree Meadows in camp. As soloists, this is not rude. He's under no obligation to keep me company.

Near Guitar Lake the trail had become inundated with streams flooding the melting landscape. With so much water, I lost the trail and bushwhacked straight down to the dry portion I could see.

Even though my high top trail runner shoes were soaked and heavy, I loved them then. There were fewer stones sneaking inside my boots than if I wore low tops. I also wore a pair of Smart Wool socks and loved them. My feet stayed warm and comfortable, even though they were sopping wet by day's end. You might wonder where my gaiters were. I tried using a pair the year before and found out they made me feel hot and sweaty. After that I got rid of gaiters and never tried them again.

With the evening drawing near, I finally crossed the log and roaring creek, successfully returning to Crabtree Meadows. I got all my gear out of the bear box, set up my tent, made supper and planned an early out in the morning.

Forrester Pass: **Cobweb, "Becky" and Brawny**

Hiking the second week of June at these elevations can be a sobering event if a person isn't used to snow. On June 12th we hiked 17 tough miles up to Sawmill Pass Trail.

A breath holding traverse on the north side required the use of my ice ax. Post-holing caused problems as I tried to extract my leg buried up to the hip. The surface is so slick, I worried about crawling out of the hole, then losing balance and going on a downhill slide.

Reunited with Cobweb, we resumed the habit of getting an early start before the crust thaws on the steep south facing slopes. Often by afternoon the snow is soft even on the north facing slope. Sometimes we elect to get down on our butts and slide.

The days are beautiful, and the scenery spectacular. Waterfalls appear all along the canyon. But we were on a mission to resupply within 10 days. Late that evening we climbed 2,000 ft. in preparation for Glen Pass tomorrow morning. Often I'd pause and grab a bite of pristine snow after becoming so overheated from the exertion of a steep climb.

A Photo Opt Now?

Glen Pass was memorable. Becky was ahead of me. I could see her guitar bobbing along as she edged out onto the north slope. Usually she maintains a quick pace, ski-sliding down these steep snow covered traverses. But today I frowned while watching her inching her way along, slowly edging down the slope today. It must be truly slippery out there. Even she is being cautious. I took a deep breath and started across, deciding to take it just as slowly, every once in a while, pausing to glance over my left shoulder. Seeing the near impossible descent, I realize my self-arrest skills may be tested today.

Suddenly this handsome blonde thru hiker runs up behind me, hands me his camera and asks, "Brawny will you take my photo?" I am astounded. He shows no fear.

"Sure," I reply, "But then how are you getting your camera back?" I stand there, feeling silly, frozen to the spot.

"Oh, don't worry, I'll come get it." He showed me the buttons, then jogged a few yards ahead and posed. I am petrified to let go of my poles, use both hands, aim and shoot while perched sideways on a steep snow covered mountain. After a second shot, I wait while he jogged back, grinning. "Where are you from?" I asked, handing back the camera.

"Canada," he replied. "Thanks." And off he went.

It was still very cold up here, in spite of the calendar saying it was mid-June. There was ice on the lakes. The trail and rock were covered with ice each morning. We all knew it could snow any day of the year. Warm gear was a must, and always is at 10,000 feet. Hikers are prepared to shed layers as the day warms.

This photo shows an easy traverse with rocks to stop a slide and a very discernible path.

Don't Tell Me That!

-*"It's all down-hill from here."* - Somehow those words always precede the worst of sections, but draw one into an insanely huge mile day.

-*"The prices there are pretty reasonable for California."* - Means outrageous to normal folks.

"Those aren't wild onions."- right after you just put a handful of some greenery into your last ramen noodles.

-*"Don't worry honey, he's waiting up ahead for you"*-this is truly disturbing to hear, especially if you are a female soloist. When a day hiker stopped me to reassure me I was being waited on, I could only hope it was someone I knew, but just in case, I prepared to defend myself if necessary. Would I use a hiking pole? My razor knife? Maybe a slap and run?

-*"So are you having fun?"* – Hunh? You mean I'm supposed to have fun? The saying is the more difficult the journey, the more thorough the cleansing. I'm getting seriously clean.

-*"There's a horse camp upstream."* - This just after you drank a quart of untreated water from this lovely creek. Oopsey!

Loss at Muir Hut

On June 14, Cobweb and I planned a big day. Because we seldom stopped to chat, we usually met our goals, however seemingly impossible. The two objectives: Muir Pass, reportedly a heavy climb, and Evolution Creek, cold and deep and 12 miles beyond the pass.

Hoping to ford Evolution Creek it in the evening rather than in the cold of the next morning, we pressed up Muir Pass. I found myself frustrated by lack of calories while slogging through miles of snow. The last miles were more like searching for footprints, avoiding sun spots and under-washed snowfields.

We both knew that The PCT / JMT doesn't always summit the low spot at the pass. At times we were guessing and checking maps to find our way. Two sets of eyes are good at times like this. Footprints of varying snow degradation indicating how long ago someone actually passed this way head in 3 different directions.

Eventually we reached the hut at 1:00 p.m. I cooked a pot of hot oatmeal and coffee and enjoyed this lunch in the cute, stone Muir Hut. Even though it was cold in the hut, it was nice to have a bench to sit on.

Later we heard that Early Bird Dave, upon arriving at Muir Hut, took off his external frame pack for a break and discovered his sleeping bag had fallen off somewhere. This is bad news, anyway you look at it. He waited with his buddy "The Hike Master", so named because he used only one pole while keeping the other hand always on his hip, like a master. Hike Master had hiked this trail 25 years ago and persuaded our Early Bird to accompany him on an anniversary hike. The Master's real name was Jerry something.

Fortunately for Early Bird, backpackers soon came up the slope, hauling the lost sleeping bag, asking if anyone knew who it belonged to. Thankfully, Early Bird cinched the sleeping bag back on the pack. He and the Master continued north. As a note, if you have anything strapped on the outside of your pack, collect all those drawcord strings and clip them together, then secure the bundled cords to the pack. If something falls, it will drag and you'll know it.

We headed north, down from Muir Hut around 1:45, bushwhacking and slogging through snow, often fording snowmelt streams. Every so often we'd come across a 100 yard section of actual trail. Dry feet and dry shoes became moot points as we just waded through stream covered "trail". Surprisingly, once we arrived at Safire Lake and Evolution Valley, it opened up to us. Hiking quickly, we saw a group of four or five backpackers heading for us.

When they came abreast, they grinned and asked to take our photos. We joked that of course, we must be celebrities, here in the boonies. Cobweb and I paused for photos. These new friends returned home and posted them online: This is how they look after 6 weeks on the trail.

Turns out these awesome people had met us at the Kick Off Party at the end of April. We didn't remember them but they remembered us. They were taking photos of every long distance hiker they met in that section with the intention of going home and posting our photos online so our friends and family could see we were still alive and kicking.

After leaving this friendly exchange, we headed north and were able to make Evolution Creek crossing. Quickly but carefully we crossed it around 7:40 p.m. and found it was only thigh-deep on me.

Cobweb reading the trail guide on a snowless section of trail.

Next Time Take a Compass
Finally the end of the long stretch from Kennedy Meadow to Vermillion Valley Resort was only 27 miles away. I had been carefully rationing my food and tonight was almost a celebration. I would enjoy the last bites ramen

noodles and set aside a little oatmeal for breakfast. Cobweb and I had been on the trail for 9 ½ days. No matter what was left in the food bag, anything edible was going to taste delicious. Both of us had been eating young wild onions on the trail, often picking a bunch, washing them and adding them to our suppers at night thereby stretching the food supplies.

At this point, money seemed unimportant, just a means to an end. I couldn't wait to wash my clothes and hair. I thought about how interesting it would be to see how tan I really was or how much of the deep bronze was simply dirt sunk into my pores. I planned to empty my pack and wipe it clean. I grinned. Probably several ounces of grime would be lost in the process, and my pack would weigh even less. I looked forward to the ferry ride, gladly spending the money instead of hiking in around the lake. I planned to call or e-mail home. Oh, the plans and fantasizing while hiking 22 miles! Weary muscles complained that never complained before. Seemed that every inch of my body was ready for a night off, in town and up off the ground.

On the way to the last campsite before the switchbacks heading down to the lake, we meet some new backpackers we'd never seen before. One young man was filled with fear and worried about the dangers so far from civilization. He rambled on as we stood listening, constantly mentioning the vast array of bad things that could happen to people way out here. He admitted to skipping a section due to fear of tainted water. I held in my personal feelings, not wanting a confrontation or argument. I firmly believe fear is a very negative force. It is deadly to dreams and contagious. I have been very afraid many times but usually went ahead with my plans because I hate to let fear beat me without a fight.

Parting with the group and bidding good luck, we hiked on ahead and camped at the top of Bear Ridge. There wasn't any water even though the data sheet indicated there would be some at the top. But it was ok. With only 5 miles and all downhill to Vermillion Valley Resort, we could survive fine.

Dawn found me up before Cobweb had stirred. I was hungry and needed to dig a cat hole. When you're alone, you just go behind a sheltered area, no worries. With a man in camp, I headed down hill, looked back and realized if he woke he could probably still see my head. Modestly, I headed further down the slope and stepped over a big downed tree. Perfect. Maybe I wasn't totally awake but somehow after finishing, I forgot my landmarks and could not see his tent. I started to get worried, where was it? I studied every direction. I headed up hill but still I couldn't see the tent.

At last I called out loudly, "Cobweb?" Totally embarrassed, I waited and called again.

Cobweb responded, "Over here." I could tell he was mildly irritated. He was nearly ready to head out and in a few moments he would have been gone. I realized how dangerous that would have been, me completely disoriented, with no one to voice guide me back. "Next time take a compass," he said angrily and headed out. And he was right. Next time, pay attention. Near misses are good for the soul.

I didn't see Cobweb again until I met him by the lake, but that was ok with me. I hike alone, enjoying the crisp morning. By 5:30 a.m. I was headed down the fifty-four switchbacks leading to food, phone and fun. Half way there, I saw a dark shape moving, two switchbacks below. At first I figured it was Cobweb. I kept hiking, getting close enough to see the creature was too hunched over to be a man. I slowed down, peered through the trees and realized it was a large bear grazing. I stopped, whistled and waited. Immediately the bear ran into the forest and I continued on.

I arrived at the lake and looked around for the dock. I looked for a sign, some indication where to wait. The ferry holds only 5 – 6 people and sometimes it docks at different places depending on the water level of the lake. At last I found a likely spot, soon joined by others wondering if we were in the right place. "I don't know," I replied.   Fourteen hikers waited with me. One section hiker offered me a toke. I smiled at the compliment. Seems I get lots of offers for a taste, which means I look wild enough to take it. "Yes, thanks man, good stuff," I said, and took a hit.

At last the white ferry pulled up. The boatman yelled, "Hurry, I can only take five." I grabbed my pack, ran full out, eager to catch it, laughing as the boat man called again, "I can only take 5 at a time." I jumped on board, the first one, thrilled to be on the first shuttle.

Vermillion Valley Resort runs a tab for hikers. You check in and put your name on a card. Everyone was friendly in this clean and hiker oriented place. The first night in a tent "cabin" is free. I select a lower bunk in a tent with 3 other young 20ish women. The first beverage was also free. I chose a diet Mountain Dew and popped it open, taking a long slurp, closing my eyes in ecstasy as the sweet nectar of gods caresses my tongue. It was really good!

I hear there was free food in a nearby cabin and check that out. A couple guys are chatting outside, saying, "Girls make the best hiking partners 'cause they always look out for you." I listened from inside the tent to them comparing notes. "Yeah," the other hiker said, "She gave me her biscuit, even though she was still hungry."

After a couple cold sandwiches, I left, went to the office and paid for a long hot shower. $5 seemed cheap for the luxury of using the peppermint shampoo from the hiker barrel, surrounded by clean white porcelain while clean water ran over me, head to toe. Afterward, Cobweb and I shared a load of laundry for $2.50 each. Things are looking good.

The resort could be accessed by road from that side of the lake. Several families were there with their boats. Some men are playing horseshoes. Patch walks up to me, claiming he hitched a ride with one of these fishermen. It was hilarious, thinking of my good buddy standing along the shore with his thumb out, and more hilarious the fact he was successful.

I took a nap on my designated bunk bed. Then got up and walked around barefooted, enjoying the wooden floor. My pack was stashed beside the bed for easy access. It was sweet not having to worry about bears raiding the camp. Surely enough loaded weapons were stashed in all the pick- up trucks nearby.

Bret and Amy arrived, then Just Eric. That night we hung around the bar, eating grill steak dinner with baked potatoes and fresh salad. A big bonfire burned in the center of the yard. It felt like heaven.

There was no reason to tarry there at the resort. After a restful day and good night's rest, we decided to leave on the late ferry the next day. We hiked a little while and camped 4 miles up trail. The next day we hiked 23 miles, bringing us within 4 miles of Red Meadow's Resort. I was surprised to find such a small assortment of food. They were just opening for the season, but Cobweb and I were able to buy enough food to get us to Tuolumne Meadows.

My resupply consisted of a 24 oz. loaf of wheat bread, an 18 oz. plastic jar of peanut butter, 13 oz. bag of Doritos Nacho Cheese Doritos, 8 oz. cheese salsa (which I finished and threw away the jar before heading out), 4 king size candy bars and 11 black liquorish sticks. If you starve on one section you tend to over compensate on the next.

After calling Georgia and checking in with Rainmaker, I headed out with Cobweb. We arrived at a nearby campground that offered free hot showers because of the neary by hot springs. Each shower was inside a cement building. I went inside with my pack, stripped and placed the cheese salsa on the ledge of this enormous cement tank that caught the shower water. Then I opened the bag of chips and basically ate while showering and washing trail clothes. Now, if that ain't living, I don't know what is! All the free hot water you could want in a private room while eating junk food and not worrying about the calories!

Day Hiking to the Valley

Singing Steve, who also carried a backpacking guitar, Mark, and Cobweb at Tuolumne Meadows.

We had hiked in to Tuolumne Meadows and found a campsite in the backpacker's campground. There was a huge bear box nearby, but because it was also car accessible, we knew we'd have to come up with a different place to stash our gear. In the morning we planned to pack up and day hike 27 miles into the Valley, thus completing the JMT, then return by nightfall. By not carrying full packs, Cobweb and I knew we could do the distance.

After that day hike, Cobweb planned to head out alone, heading north, resuming the PCT as a thru hiker. I needed to take my time trailing alone, killing time. I was ahead of schedule. Rainmaker wouldn't be flying in to Reno to join me for the final section of the PCT for two weeks.

We asked the lady at the post office if we could stash a few items to lighten our packs for the hike to the valley, explaining that in this very crowded car-backpacker's campground, I was nervous about leaving my gear in the bear boxes. She totally understood and gladly allowed me to leave about 6 pounds of gear.

That afternoon we sat at picnic tables munching food, trimming tags and lightening packs. Already our gear was minimal yet we scrutinized it suspiciously, asking ourselves what else could be removed? The N label from

New Balance shoes was picked off, draw cords were shortened and heat sealed. If any stray label or tag had been carried all the way from the border, we cut it off, disgraced it hadn't been removed 1,000 miles ago. A lot of folks mailed their ice axes home. I kept mine. One thru hiker received a 40 pound box of goodies through the mail. She opened the box, took out what she wanted and passed around the bounty. No way was she hauling all of that north in her pack.

We went to bed early, then on June 22, we got up at daybreak and silently made our way through the campground. After circling some campers, we found the John Muir Trail and began an ascent. Everyone had told us it was all downhill but the first 5 miles were a decent climb. Dawn Breaker joined us. He was from New England and had rented a storage unit back east for all his belongings. He didn't even have a true residence at the time, yet he was far from being homeless. Like us, the trail was his home.

The day went quickly. We passed designated campsites that backpackers registered for in advance. We hiked on, chatting, strong, in beautiful weather. After 24 miles, we passed beautiful Unicorn Peak and the side trail to Half Dome. As we pondered doing that short climb up the famous mountain, Dawn Breaker gave me his nearly empty sack of GORP to finish off. It was really salty but I didn't care.

Another mile on and we met our trail angel, Goslowgofar, hiking south to meet us. She had started in Yosemite Valley a couple hours ago to join us. I first met her online in a backpacker's chat room. I learned she thru hiked the AT in the '80's. We met in person at the Kick Off Party this year. She offered to help us do this shuttle. Yosemite Valley is her home.

The four of us crossed the bridge near gigantic water falls. Many tourists were there, marveling at the enormity of the cliffs. We walked on by, looking dirty and rugged. There seemed to be no exact southern terminus to the JMT in Yosemite Valley. We wandered around, looking for a sign to tag, used the bathrooms then shrugged, it must be unmarked. The four of us went for pizza, then swung by a store to resupply. It was expensive. I bought a lot of food knowing I'd be going slow, killing time while waiting for my partner to arrive. That evening, Goslowgofar drove us back to Tuolumne Meadows. We pitched our tents by LED light, crawled into sleeping bags and instantly fell asleep. At daybreak Cobweb passed my tent, called "goodbye, Brawny," and walked away.

Cobweb was a great hiking partner. I loved the fact he never bailed me, babied me or offered to. He treated me as an equal. Farther up the trail, I met him again hiking to Canada.

The following year, he thru hiked the CDT, met his life love, and married. They now split their time between her home in Switzerland and his in Vermont.

Wading Mosquitos

I learned my lesson. Never ever just wade through the river in your high tops. It may seem like they've been soaked through and through and dried just fine before, but that's an illusion. The mere fact we had been walking through snow melt ever since leaving Kennedy Meadows does not mean one can wade willy-nilly through a full blown stream. It took my shoes one week to dry out after that brain storm.

But it was those rotten mosquitos that made me do it. I blame them. Just when a gal's getting ready to take off her shoes at the river's edge, the mosquitos will start landing on every exposed piece of flesh.

The proper way to cross any stream is to remove shoes, tie the laces together and sling them around your neck. Then cross in socks, or barefoot, it's your choice. Head slightly downstream at an angle. Don't try to buck a strong current. No matter how cold or numb your feet get, take it slow and feel the rocks under your foot before taking another step. Experts warn to unfasten your hip belt. If you get swept away, you'll want to lose the pack and save your life instead of floundering under a ton of wet gear. Hiking poles are life savers, in my books. They allow the wader to maintain several points of contact against a rushing current.

Hiking poles really help a person maintain balance while crossing a log, but often I'd rather wade across a stream than balance on a sketchy log which could roll once your weight is on it. Sometimes a person can rock hop but falling from that exercise can mean a nasty bruise.

Late one evening I crossed a large river before heading towards Echo Lake resort. Alone and tired, I figured to cook, maybe even camp right along the shore. Why not, I asked myself. I was in no hurry. I had plenty of time before my partner flew in to meet me for the last leg of the journey to Canada.

I sat down in the soft sand and pulled out my heavy sack of treats. As I started cooking ramen, I sighed, resigned to the thin pasty noodles. I was sure getting sick of that stuff but it was always cheap and available and plus, a person can eat it raw like pretzels, or solar cooked in a plastic jar.

I snacked as the noodles cooked. Once the pasta was tender, I began eating it with my spoon. My eyes grew wide while I watched a black bear casually walk into the brush not one hundred yards upstream. I blinked, disbelievingly, stood and stared as he crossed that stream. Right away I knew this wasn't going to work. I couldn't camp here, especially now that I had cooked. I threw my stuff into my pack and hiked onward, soon crossed another river and forgot to get water. That night I piled my food under rocks and slept soundly. In the morning I woke to a waterless Snickers bar breakfast.

Lesson: just because you see a bear is no reason to forget to get water.

These three thru hikers posed before heading down to Lone Pine for Deet! They gave us a pound of cheese. Cobweb, Becky and I cut it into thirds and scarfed it down standing on the spot. Left to right: Sassafras, Patch, Rambo John.

5. Colorado Trail

Trail Overview

Abandoned mines and rusty bed springs, herds of cattle and sheep guarded by monstrous white dogs, cowboys toting high powered rifles and riding sleek horses, country so high the lightening becomes your brother, water so scarce the beaver ponds are welcomed, these are a few of my most vivid memories from forty days and nights spent in central Colorado. The magnificent Colorado Trail holds the most adventure you could pack into a 468 mile trail. I admit when I researched it and saw it was less than 500 miles long, I sort of thought, piece of cake. Wrong!

Its northern terminus is just outside the mile high city of Denver. Then it heads west and swinging around to Copper Mountain where it joins the Continental Divide Trail for a spell taking you over 10,000 foot passes. The southern terminus is just 2.5 miles outside of Durango, an easy two and a half miles road walk to town from the trailhead.

Heading south is preferred. After all, it's much easier to acclimate from the mile high city to nearly 14,000 feet over the course of a couple weeks than abruptly mount the monster overnight. This trail is not for wimps.

People plan on 5-6 weeks to cover this trail, enjoying 12 mile days. We did the entire trail in 40 days and nights, with only 2 nights spent in town. Salida is about half way and has a lot of motels and amenities.

During our thru hike of the CT, Rainmaker and I spent serious time hunkered under tarps, waiting out the lightning storms, sometimes camping early while dark clouds sought our warms bodies. We witnessed white bolts hitting the ground right in front of us. Once we even ditched our packs and laid low in the small depression. It was only 10:30 in the morning. But being warned by the gods that we were still mere mortals, we bid our time, in no rush to test the powers that be. While we were out there, 4 people died from lighting strikes.

Anyone who wants to hike above tree line for extended periods with views extending to neighboring mountain ranges, this is for you. People say to hike it in September when the daily cycles of morning bliss interrupted by life threatening thunderstorms are over. You can get snowed in any month. We planned our trip during January in Georgia, waiting for the snow to melt on the high slopes, deciding to begin the trail mid-July. When the guide book arrived, I paged through the glossy pages, wondering how much weight we could shave off by removing the cover and introductions. Not that much. It was just going to be heavy. The companion data book didn't seem to give enough information to wing it without the big book. I designed another silnylon pack, added some pockets and figured, oh well.

I tend to get lost easily. I compensate by checking my backtrail often and stay pointed in the right direction until I stop. Not every northbounder hikes north. Sometimes a trail swings south, heads east then reroutes over a ridge before reclaiming its compass direction. The Colorado Trail is such. If you look at a map, you'll see a wide swing westward before it heads east and then finally south. I've heard a hiker refer to the fantastic switchbacks as "Yonder-fucks" as in "Why is the trail going way over yonder? Fuck!"

I think the worst one is just north of Copper Mountain. You can see your destination yet hike for miles away from it across the mountain, then drop down to cross a road then finally sneak up right behind it. Once right behind the resort, it's an easy stroll smack into town. Don't get distracted and take the road down to the gas station to resupply like we did. Stay on the trail and drop right into the backyard of the resort.

Near Death by Strangulation

Our Tacoma for Two Tent doesn't have zippers. The screen doors are like drapes and hang down gracefully, long enough to tuck under the floor to keep bugs out. It's very spacious. Backpackers sleep parallel to their own long vestibule, each with their own double doors to open and shut as needed for ventilation and exit.

My black down sleeping bag was thrown over me on the first night out on the trail. Because it was so hot I was using it quilt style. Once the night cooled off, I would climb in it proper and zip it up.

Somewhere after midnight I needed to pee. Rainmaker was finally sleeping peacefully after a stray coyote black dog had quit barking and left us alone. The dog had followed us, yapping annoyingly for half a mile, before we chose our campsite. The poor animal seemed abandoned and very irritated when we camped on his sandy strip all along the Platte River.

In the middle of the night, I noiselessly threw back my "quilt", lifted the screen and crawled out of the tent. This was the same tent we designed ourselves and which earned the Backpacker's Editor's Award in 2003. Because of its design, neither partner has to crawl over the other to get out of it. No one has to sleep by a back wall. No one has to worry if a knee will end up in their face while the partner makes the night trip.

As I left the tent, I checked the river bank, and sighed happily. The dog was nowhere to be seen. Apparently he had left. The moon provided enough light so I didn't need to use the tiny photo LED light. I stood, crossed the soft sand, peed, then walked silently back to the tent.

Just as I lifted the screen, Rainmaker, in all his fury, lunged across the tent at me.

I fell back and yelled, "Rain, it's me." His arms were outstretched, his fingers curved at the ends of strong hands like the talons of an eagle. I feared for my life. Rainmaker is a Viet Nam vet. He is schooled in hand to hand combat. I backed away, anxiously waiting outside the tent, repeating, "Rain, it's me. David, it's me!"

Angrily he glanced at the sleeping bag, felt it and visibly relaxed. I waited. Was he really awake now? Did he believe it was me?

"Ok, Carol," he finally said softly, "But, next time tell me when you go out. I thought it was that goddamn dog." I looked down at my clothing. I was wearing black: black shorts and a black top.

The full length doors of each vestibule have Velcro stitched the entire length. This configuration allows each hiker to vent as needed, store wet gear and block wild animals from just walking up for a sniff. When they are rolled up and out of the way, the Velcro "ripping" noise won't be heard either when a person exits the tent.

Fire and Ice

We had hiked miles through burned out forest. With an early morning start our first hours were cool and refreshing. The trail guide had warned that Section 2 could be very hot and waterless. Rainmaker and I congratulated ourselves for the 16 miles we did yesterday, first day on the trail, thereby allowing us to jump on this burnout around 7:30 a.m.

The heat began building as the morning wore on. The land became an oven. Rainmaker's tiny thermometer registered 100 degrees. He has always been able to walk through it. He maintains the same pace knowing by 5 there will be a camp and coffee. His mind is focused on that reprieve, no matter what.

Meanwhile, I get hot. I quicken my pace, find a scrap of shade and breathe slowly, take a sip of water, and relax until he catches up. Somehow those little rests keep me going. This goes on all day. At last we come to the highway. "There's supposed to be water down the road at the fire station," I told my partner. He agreed to watch everything under the shade tree while I run down with some empty soda bottles to see. We did this on the PCT a lot. If you can drop your pack before heading to water, carrying 5 quarts back is much easier, but the rule of thumb is to never leave the pack unattended. If I don't have a partner to do this with, I take my pack.

A PCT guy once told me he had left his pack on the trail, heading down a slope for a photo shoot. He heard a ruckus behind him and turned to find a bear trashing out his pack. He ran back up the slope shouting. A couple friends heard him and ran to join in driving the bear away. A person learns from trail stories.

It took just a few minutes to get to the fire station. I walked around the parking lot, looked in the windows, but the station was completely deserted. Where in the world was the faucet, I wondered. I knew we couldn't last in this heat without water especially at these elevations. Staying hydrated keeps the altitude sickness at bay and holds off heat exhaustion. With the next on-trail water about 2 miles away, Rainmaker and I had agreed, if there was no water there, we might have to hitchhike into a nearby town.

I walked around the empty fire station, pounding on doors, looking through the tiny windows, daring any cop to please come by and find this suspicious person lurking by the fire station. A police man would probably have water. Water! Trails are gained and lost by water.

Finally, I stood back and surveyed the building asking myself, if I was going to put a faucet someplace on a fire station, where would I put it? By the door and kind of low, I figured, that's where I would install it. I walked over to the door, looked down and voila, there it was. Sometimes I'm just blind. Quickly I filled the bottles, returned to my waiting partner. We drank a bottle each and we headed out.

The very next day we were hailed on soundly. Lightning flashed against the tree. The cool air was refreshing. Patiently we waited it out, only half an hour, then hiked on marveling at the change of scenery. Eventually we found a flat spot but it was covered with ice. Everything was iced. We pitched the tent on ice and found if you sleep on an ice cube, you'll probably get cold.

My short ultralight pad was a too scanty. That's when I started sliding my shorty pad inside my sleeping bag. This served two purposes. It snugged up the fit and kept all the insulation around me, regardless of a slippery silnylon floor. This did expose the down bag to the tent floor. So far that was not a problem and my sleeping bag did not get wet.

The Colorado Trail is one of contrasts. One day I'm dying from heat exhaustion, the next day I'm freezing my butt off. The old saying is: It's all just part of the trail experience.

Note: an ultralight silnylon backpack doesn't make up for a short pad. It doesn't offer insulation and it's too wet to bring inside the sleeping bag for a footie vapor barrier bag.

Of Bikes and Bears

You will be run down by mountain bikers on the Colorado Trail, I swear. If you're not intently listening for the click- click- click of pending bikers and jump off the trail in time, they honest to god won't alert you. Occasionally, this will happen on the Pacific Crest Trail near Lake Tahoe even though it's illegal for the bikers to use the PCT. However on the Colorado Trail, human powered locomotion is encouraged and is the main mode of transportation, even more common than horses.

I was hiking along, minding my own business when suddenly I felt a weird sensation, like when someone is looking over my shoulder while I'm chatting online, sort of like a teacher walking around the room while you're struggling with the SAT. Yeah, like a security guard following you around in a store cause they think maybe you stole something.

I looked behind me. Just a few feet from where I am hiking, a mountain biker was coasting along, waiting for me to notice. I jumped back, startled at his nearness and stumbled aside. He stomped on the pedals and sped past. I peered back down the trail, and here came another. I called out, "Rainmaker!" He turned around to look at me and stepped aside, scowling. Do mountain bikers not have bells or horns? Back when I was growing up that was a normal accessory. I don't mind sharing the trail, I just wished they'd let a girl know!

131

Bears

One night as we were pitching the tent above 10,000 feet in a nice little campground, another camper sauntered over to visit. He pointed to a large dome tent a couple sites down and said, "I'm putting an electric fence around my campsite tonight. The bears are bad in these parts."

I will admit to having slept with my food while backpacking. I've read and learned this habit was acceptable in stealth situations where no humans had camped previously and hunting was allowed. Tonight seemed a good time to reconsider our location. Rainmaker and I brainstormed the situation. We did not want to impose on anyone by throwing our food into his ring and we didn't want to draw bears near our tent with the food bag at our feet. Finally, we decided to hang our food bags in the privy, just before dark.

The night was fairly uneventful. After we were in bed and well after dark, we heard some vehicles and voices. More people had come to camp. I wondered if anyone would be visiting the outhouse and what they would think of two silnylon food bags suspended from the ceiling. If all went well, our food would be untouched and still hanging there in the morning.

Immediately upon waking at day break, I went to retrieve our food bags from the privy. Along the way I noticed huge ice chests and grills strewn around the campground. Not one sign of a bear all night. I guess the privy was over-kill.

The Poncho Lesson- Take 2

I should have known better but sometimes the second time around is different. I knew plenty of hikers who had ponchos. I'd watched thru hikers pull their arms underneath the poncho, grab poles and head down trail in pouring rain. Their sleeves weren't getting wet. They looked like a big cardboard box covered in silnylon, fabric whipping in the wind, every inch of their pack covered while they were getting it done.

I had designed a poncho which used the diagonal of a large square of silnylon (65 x 65) for the shoulder line. This made the sleeves plenty long, amble enough to provide full coverage for even the longest arms. Also, this poncho could be used for a vestibule on an ultralight Tarp system. This poncho could be pitched high and provide shade or protection from rain while cooking in camp. I am very proud of my innovation. It's very multi-purpose and only weighted 7 ounces. Rainmaker dubbed it the PonchoVilla. I loved my brown prototype and wore it often on training hikes.

Rainmaker named it the PonchoVilla because the space it created was awesome.

The poncho also took the place of a pack-cover and jacket. This was definitely a gram weenies dream: a three-fold purpose piece of backpacking gear. The trouble is, sometimes you need all three purposes fulfilled at once.

Being the Ultralighter that I am, I just had to test it full bore. I knew that if I gave myself any easy outs, I would take them. I had to commit to the project completely. When things get tough, the tough come up with solutions.

So, in spite of my early poncho experiences (see the details in the River to River Adventure, Chapter 1.) my rain gear for the Colorado Trail was a poncho and silnylon rain pants. By the time I got to Salida, I was praying I had packed my silnylon rain jacket in the one drop box we'd shipped ourselves. Nope. I hadn't.

Several times during these 40 days of Rocky Mountain Hiking Rainmaker and I would have to hole up and wait for a thunderstorm to blow over before we could cross the high mountain pass. I would sit leaning against a tree wearing my poncho, ultralight pack on my back. If we figured it would be a while before the storms abated, I'd remove my pack, prop it between my feet, letting the front corner cover it for protection.

If I took off the poncho so I could walk around yet still keep my pack protected, I'd get wet. Or if I I wore it and walked around I'd have to carry the ultralight pack. Not what you want to do for a couple hours. I felt stuck in an imperfect world.

Then one night after the Lake City Resupply, we pitched our tent in half mile off the trail in an abandoned horse camp. I hated hiking half a mile off the trail just to camp, but there were no level spots on top nor water for cooking. But, it turned out to be a godsend. Someone had left a big black garbage bag lying in the mud. I claimed the torn bag, cleaned it up with my wet bandana and used it for my pack-cover. This was a bad omen, yet at the same time a gift from the gods. When a gear designer has to scrounge in the mud for plastic bags, things are at low ebb. I was humbled.

Still, there are people who swear by ponchos. Brian Robinson, Triple Crowner in One Calendar Year had an awesome poncho at the Pacific Trail Kick Off Party in 2001. His dad had made it. It was 65 inches wide by 118 inches long, give or take. He had special tabs for hiking poles to be inserted and Velcro for attaching bug screening. The guy was and is a genius, but it didn't work for me.

I read Brian's journals and I specifically remember him using an emergency bivy in conjunction with his poncho. I still have my PonchoVilla, the original prototype. It's in my day pack and serves as my survival Go-to shelter and raingear, but for serious long distance hiking, I take my silnylon rain suit.

Now, there is no way anyone can accuse me of not thinking these issues through before heading to the high peaks on the Colorado Trail. I wrote this webpage for Trailquest and it got thousands of hits.

So you think you want a Poncho-Tarp-Pack cover?

Maybe you are just getting into ultra-lighting and plan to swap a heavy pack cover, Gortex rain suit and 3 season double wall freestanding tent for this single piece of gear. Sure, you'll shave well over 7 pounds off your pack weight, but please consider the following points before buying one.

Remember if it's raining, you and your pack must stay together to both be protected. If you're above tree line, you may want a separate pack cover so that during a lightning storm you can leave your pack and all of its metal cook system and tent stakes up the trail while you take cover in a low spot.

If it's raining, and you're inside your shelter (tarp) and you need to dig a cat hole, you will have no rain protection while venturing outside. You'll either have to strip down naked, go take your dump, then come and dry off before reentering your shelter or you will have to dig a cat hole in your sleeping area. This brings new meaning to the phrase "sleeping with your shit". Please figure out your plan of action here because if you don't Murphy's Law of Backpacking will make sure you need to do it. Also, avoiding the consumption of anything that gives you diarrhea would be a smart move.

Do you already use hiking poles? If not, you will need some other type of support when this poncho is used as your shelter. You may need to bring along a shock-corded pole or rig a line so you can suspend this poncho-tarp from a branch.

Are you comfortable with a shelter, a rectangular tarp that is 5 feet wide by 9.5 feet long? Have you ever even slept under a tarp before? This size shelter is adequate for someone who is 6'2" when pitched in a configuration such as the "Tacoma Tarp".

If you plan to use this poncho-tarp- pack cover in conjunction with a bivy or as a door-vestibule structure with an existing tarp, and you are a reasonably intelligent person, you will find it's easy to configure the poncho-tarp-pack cover for this purpose because there are many staking points and guy out loops.

As a personal rain cover, the hood is ample and the shoulder and torso area is well covered. However, your arms must be bent to be covered. In cold wet weather, your arms might get wet if you're using hiking poles with arms extended upward. By using the finger loops on the poncho, or wearing vapor barrier mittens, you can protect your arms.   Also, by shortening your hiking poles so that your arms are angled downwards, in conjunction with using the finger loops and clipping the poncho together, you will achieve adequate cover in windy conditions. You can use extra elastic cord to expand the torso area if you're too chubby to do this otherwise.

 Have you visualized setting up your poncho-tarp-pack cover as a shelter in the pouring rain? One way to do this is to have 5 tent stakes available in your hand. Then, kneel down in a suitable spot. Stake out the front corner, then the back corner on one side of the poncho, say the left, spreading it out as far as you can. A taut, straight line is best. Take care not to fall on your face when attempting this task while in the kneeling position or you will dislodge one or both of the stakes.

Next, stake out the other front corner and other back corner, which would be the right edge, so that it is about 3 feet less than the back wall that you created with the left edge. You then insert one hiking pole in that slack side, straightening this pole until the slack is taken up. Now, remove yourself from the poncho, take off your pack and guy out that front pole. You can now adjust the poncho tarp while inside the shelter.

Please note that you will want to perfect this technique while at home, not on the trail. Or, simply take off the poncho and get wet while pitching your shelter quickly.

These next two paragraphs I wanted to add online, but didn't for obvious reasons:

On this item alone, should you decide to return the poncho-tarp-pack-cover, a 10% restocking fee will be assessed. You will be blacklisted and your e-mail address sold to our registry of current spam clients.

Above all, using a poncho-tarp-pack cover takes preparedness, a willingness to suffer some inconveniences in exchange for dropping some serious weight, and a certain level of experience and co-ordination. If you think you still are interested in spite of my best efforts to dissuade you, then go ahead and order one, you bone head.

But, all kidding aside, I know and have met long distance hikers who swear by their ponchos and I respect them, no matter what.

Trail Gods

I believe in trail gods. At one time the mere thought of plural gods would have sent me into a fanatical seizure. Heathens! Now I am sure they exist and mess with long distance hikers on a regular basis. They sit back and laugh at our misfortunes then bestow amazing gifts to lure us again into the world of which they are masters.

Consider the Sucker Hole: dark storm clouds parting for an instant, allowing perfect blue sky to peek through, making the backpacker think things are clearing up and yeah, why not try to get over the pass? Eagerly shouldering our packs, we stride forward, away from cover, smiling at the benevolent powers that be. Then, once you're committed to crossing that narrow notch in the mountains, that same blue hole closes and the deluge begins.

I am totally in favor of honoring the Trail Gods by accepting all gifts they give a person, and of humoring their wacky sense of adventure. Whether on the trail, in camp or even in trail towns, the deities will mess with you just because they can.

If this sounds weird or slightly off kilter, bear with me and allow me to give some examples, including both experiences and real objects. Over the years, the Trail Gods have supplied the most amazing things while displaying a sense of humor and amusement.

On the Colorado trail, Rainmaker kept finding loose change. It started adding up to the substantial amount of 73 cents. He was so lucky, I started wondering why he was favored while the gods ignored me.

Finally, I found a really super pair of sunglasses and a Mickey Mouse watch. If you are reading either of these items were yours, my condolences. It was pretty awesome. Another time we found a perfect sun baked, extra-large Fuji apple sitting on a rock, right in bear country. Of course, we shared the apple and it was delicious, very much like a baked apple pie.

About 2 days before arriving in Sailda we seemed to hit the jackpot. Coming around a narrow bend, I glimpsed a really neat long sleeved yellow t-shirt and Thermos. The stainless steel thermos was nearly brand new and had potential. I put it in my pack, but the shirt was 100% cotton, so I left it on the branch, deferring to others who might pass this way and need another layer.

Farther on, I caught sight of something black hanging from a tree branch. Amazingly, it was a small pair of fleece pants, just what I needed. Either they had been abandoned as too bulky, or had been summoned by the gods for me alone. Perhaps they were just following the traditional Lost and Found cycle.

"Wow," I exclaimed, delighted. "Now, I could really use these!" Rainmaker silently watched me retrieve them. I checked the label, said, "Yup, 100% polyester, size small." I nodded and smiled at my good luck, simultaneously stretching the waistband for size, allowing Rainmaker the opportunity to agree. "Do you think they'll fit? They look like they will, size small," I reminded him. He said nothing, just stood contemplating the garment. I looked up at him and asked, "What do you think? Are they worth carrying?" It's not like I could tuck them in the closet, along with the rest of the stuff I will eventually wear, one day when my girlish figure returns.

"Humm," he pondered, thoughtfully lifting them with his hand, gently hefting them up and down. "About 11 ounces. Well, you could carry them until you can try them on. Then if they don't fit, you can leave them on a branch like you found them."

I frowned. This was not the reassurance I expected. I tucked them into the top of my pack and we continued down the trail, eventually arriving at a trailhead, a privy and parking lot. I looked at Rainmaker, thought about having to remove my hiking boots and shorts, try them on, then replace shorts and boots. "Well, these ain't gonna fit me and you didn't want to say it," I challenged.

He smiled, his blue eyes showing a lifetime of male education, refusing to comment. "Next time don't let me carry this stuff, ok?" I said testily, then slid my pack to the ground, removed the pants and hung them on the trail sign. Angrily I left the thermos as well, thinking, why on god's green earth would I need a thermos on the trail? Fine! Now that the trail gods had their laugh, it was time to get in some miles.

When the Gods take a break from bestowing gifts, they will test you to see how bad you want the journey.

After generously resupplying in Twin Lakes, we headed back to the trail. Afternoon was approaching and with it another thunderstorm was building up steam. The landscape was wide open, not a shelter in sight, unless you counted a few brown buildings. Closer inspection showed they were public buildings surrounded by a tall wooden fence. I told Rainmaker I'd run over and see if we could wait inside.

He nodded and I hurried over, soon finding the locked gate. I didn't let that stop me. I climbed the fence, walked over to the front door and saw no one in sight. In fact, I soon discovered all the doors were locked. It was a power plant facility. I retraced my steps, climbed back over the fence and jumped to the ground. That's when I heard a sickening shredding sound. My silnylon pack had ripped ten inches along the web reinforcement.

I hurried towards my partner who had noticed several deserted buildings up ahead, alongside the trail. We hurried and arrived just before an incredibly fierce and lengthy thunderstorm broke out.

Under the eaves, I took off my pack and analyzed the damage. The silnylon pack I had sewn just two months ago was gapping open in one straight rip, along the black webbing, vertically aligned with my shoulder straps. That web strap had served as a ridge. When I landed on the ground from a five food jump, the weight of the pack carried the silnylon downward. It had been exactly like creasing a paper, then ripping along that fold in one confident tear.

Rainmaker saw my dismay. The pack would need careful mending now, before hiking further fully loaded. He dug out his murphy kit and lent me his needle and dental floss. While the storm raged and blew against the back side of the building, I sewed a tight overhand stitch, hunkered under the eaves of a bunk house. Two hours later the storm finally blew itself out and the dark clouds abated. Rainmaker and I packed up our gear and hiked around the dam. We saw a side trail down to a calm blue lake. The shore was sandy and soft so we made camp and cooked our lowly meals.

Twin Lakes had nothing for fuel. No rubbing alcohol or denatured alcohol, no petroleum jelly nor Heet or fuel line additive. I ended up with some Coglan's woodchip fuel sticks. I was thankful to have them, too, even though they burned sooty. At least I could enjoy my coffee hot. I just flipped the little soda can stove over and used the bottom to hold portions of fuel sticks, feeding them in slowly as needed.

The next morning we packed up as usual. Our packs were really heavy, loaded with food for six days. The tent was heavy with wet sand. I asked to carry the tent at least until we could get it dried out, knowing Rainmaker's back was giving him trouble. Reluctantly he agreed. Slowly we started up the trail, taking our time up the gradual ascent, climbing easily. Rainmaker was in the lead. Suddenly, he gasped and jerked his buckle open and flung off his pack. I hurried to his side. His face was a mirror of agony. "What? What's going on?" I asked, terrified. I'd never seen him in so much pain.

"My back!" he moaned, "My back!" It's all he would say. He started pacing the trail while I watched, horrified. This is what he had warned me of, so many times, warning me that one day his back would totally give out on the trail. He expected it to happen and said his main hope was that he would be able to hike out on his own and not have to be carried out.

Immediately I started thinking of plans and solutions, how or where to get help. Maybe we should hike back down to Twin Lakes? Or maybe I should go out to the road and hitch back to town or to our car parked in a storage unit in Denver? He told me he couldn't carry his pack 30 feet. Then I wondered aloud, Should I leave everything with him while he waits for me to return with the car? Maybe I should watch everything, including his pack, while he hitches out to get the car? I pulled out the guidebook and started looking at road access points and nearby towns. I knew we were heading into a section with very little road access. It would be 50 miles before another opportunity presented itself to get help.

I offered several suggestions but nothing was right. He continued pacing, angry at the change of circumstances. I fell silent. It seemed my words made it worse. It was one of the most helpless times of my life. Watching someone you love in such pain is a heart wrenching experience.

Finally, Rainmaker swore, picked up his pack and said, "Let's hike!" This experience intensified the daily concerns of thunderstorms, sufficient food and water and mileages. Somehow, our inner drives must overcome all these obstacles, and everything just hung in the balance. Everything seemed out of my control, out of my reach.

We took one day at a time, covering enough miles to get to water, knowing that to push too hard would push us right off the trail. We planned a zero day, at least one night in a motel in Salida. Once we make it to Salida, we could regroup.

Secretly I wondered if Rainmaker chose to leave the trail, would I go on, alone? Probably. I hoped I would. It took too much to get out here, and once we were in Salida, we would be over half way.

If Rainmaker decided to leave the trail, I hoped my Mileage Madness would kick in. In a couple weeks I could finish. I lay awake at night worrying about trail data, his body status and the nimbostratus. Becoming consumed with worry is not the way to hike a trail. Rainmaker's brother once told him "Short term planning is breakfast, long term is supper." At the end of the day, all that really matters is that somehow we had made progress.

And the trail gods were asking: How much do you really want this? Rainmaker and I were not speaking much either. He was certain I wanted to ditch him, which was never the case. It hurt me deeply that he never believed I was terrified of the possibility of leaving him alone in the wilderness while I raced to find help as quickly as possible.

A Sudden Stampede

Rainmaker was finishing the last of his coffee, leaning against his camp tree. I stood to take down the tent. It had been damp camping by the river but the water had been plentiful. I dropped the Tacoma in the early morning light and unstaked it. I grabbed two corners and gave the gray silnylon several hearty shakes to knock off some of the condensation before stuffing it into the bag.

Suddenly, right across the river and all along the bank, cows began to scatter, running up hill through the brush as though being chased by a wild animal. We looked across the water and watched the cattle tearing up trail, madly fleeing an unknown danger. This continued long after the tent had been shaken, proving that stampedes are easier to start than stop. Rainmaker and I packed up slowly. That was the trail we needed to be on after crossing the bridge from our campsite.

Cows and calves who'd not seen nor heard the gray flying tent still stampeded, heading up the slope as they drew abreast of the disturbance. I guess that's what they mean by following the herd. Finally the cattle passed. We crossed the bridge and got on the trail, heading south again.

We carried a gray Tacoma on the Colorado Trail. During lunch breaks, we would hang it from a branch to dry.

A Desperate Resupply

Rainmaker stood back and watched in awe, a slight smile on his gray-bearded face. When you look up Frugal at Wikipedia, you will see my photo. But in my defense, I'd had enough of this hitchhiking and standing on the side of the road for hours, like bums with our thumbs out, eyes beseeching travelers to stop and give us a lift. I knew Rainmaker and I looked too scary for most to take a chance on.

The Colorado guidebook had said there was a store here at this campground with basics. All the way here we'd planned what we would order for lunch. I was ready to sink my teeth into a double cheeseburger and fries, wash it down with a large milkshake then demolish an entire package of Oreos for dessert.

But, this year, all they stocked were snack foods and sodas. Rainmaker and I had circled the shelves in the store unbelievingly. It couldn't be. Lake Molas was supposed to have food, where was the food. After paying someone at Lake City to take us back to the trailhead, we were determined to resupply at this camp store, just a short walk down from the CT.

Fine, I thought, and briskly gathered up my choices and plopped them on the counter. I pulled out a couple twenties, slapped them down, certain that should cover the cost. After paying for my assortment of goods, I left the store and headed out to the picnic table to eat a lunch of chips and soda while stripping down the packaging for 5.5 days of food.

Here's what I bought for 5 days of trail:
--11 packages of Grandmas cookies, 2.5 ounces each, making my breakfasts and afternoon breaks loaded with fat and calories.
--3 bags each cashews, peanuts and beef jerky, to be eaten after dinner and pre breakfast, weighting a total of 8 ounces.
--1 Snickers and 5 Milky Way candy bars, for lunch desserts.
--6 packages of hot cocoa. I was running low on coffee and saw no instant coffee.
--4 small packages of assorted chips. These would be my lunches and soup enhancers, for about 16 ounces total.
--about 6 ounces of dehydrated refried beans and 10 tortillas, donated when I told the clerk I would buy any bread off her. We rationed this between us, providing 3 meals each for both Rainmaker and I.
--5 snack crackers and 2 snack cookie packages, intended for a.m. snacks.
--Leftovers from previous resupply were 2 ramen seasoning packages and 2 tablespoons mashed potatoes which would form the base of two soup suppers.

Lesson I learned from this menu: drink plenty of water. There's not enough fiber here to create one decent bowl movement.

Nearing the southern terminus we felt the border fever. Every day we rose by 6:15 and packed up, anticipating a quick clean finish in Durango. Rainmaker did his back warm up exercises and I'd take smaller steps to ease my feet and knees through their issues.

From the first day on the Colorado Trail, I used just one hiking pole. The other one had bit the dust in Waterman Canyon. I being the gear tester, thought, "Perfect, I'll see what one hiking pole feels like in the mountains." Never again. One hand is always hanging down, blood pooling uncomfortably. A person can stick their hand in a pocket or the strap of the pack and trade off, but two poles give a hiker much more stability over snow, shale, fighting off dogs and setting up tarps. I'm a two pole person.

Desperate Camp
Friday night we camped just 22 miles from the Durango Trail head near Taylor Lake. It was peaceful and the site lovely. Within a couple days

Rainmaker and I knew we'd be off the trail and headed back to Georgia in a little blue Geo Metro. While the evening sun warmed the tent, we cooked and washed our supper pots, then headed to bed. During the night the rains started.

By the next morning the clouds had thinned and we hiked this one last full day thoughtfully. By 2:30 the rains caught up to us once more, descending in sheets, completely drenching us, streaming off our packcovers as we looked for a camping spot. The rule seemed to be: If there was water there was no place to pitch a tent. If there was a tent spot the water was nowhere near.

By the time we crossed lower Junction Creek the two tiny creek-side camp spots were flooded and muddy. We kept hiking as evening drew near. It was 7 p.m. and still the rained poured down. I figured, whatever, we'll just walk straight through to Durango tonight. I followed Rainmaker, my head bowed to keep the water off my nose, watching his sodden feet when suddenly he stopped and asked, "How about here?" I raised my head to see from under my hood. It was a wide spot in on an old logging road, right beside the trail. The spot was packed down and level. "Sure!"

Rainmaker uncinched the tent bag from his external pack and held it out. I pulled the tent from the bag, found the black floor and handed him his side. Together we spread it, each grabbing 4 stakes for our sides. While his were pounded in magically, mine refused to go in. I bent several while attempting to set up my side. He was raising his hiking pole. Still I struggled, looking for a rock while the rain pounded our tent. At last I got two stakes in and inserted my hiking pole.

Rainmaker hurried over to help, crouching beside me just as my stakes flew out of the ground. My side collapsed on my head. He grabbed each stake and straightened them, swiftly pounding them both in. I inserted my hiking pole into it's position and raised the Tacoma.

With our shelter standing large and strong, Rainmaker returned to his side. Simultaneously we crawled into our own spaces and kept all the wet stuff under the vestibules. I was so glad we each had our own doors and vestibules because my muddy mess didn't interfere with his. He had plenty of his own to deal with.

Now inside the 5 x 8 floored tent, we each leaned into our vestibules, knowing we could eat whatever we wanted, as much coffee as we pleased. Tomorrow we could even eat breakfast in town. I ate a couple packages of Grandma Cookies and the last of my jerky, then heated some concoction I called "survival soup", a mixture of crumbs and ramen seasoning package. It's no wonder I couldn't look another Grandma Cookie in the face again.

Early the next morning, we packed up our wet gear, stuffed it roughly into wet packs and hiked the remaining two miles to the southern terminus, then 3.5 miles into Durango. A car passed us. The driver leaned out and asked, "Is this the way to Durango?" We nodded, replied, "Sure," both surprised the man didn't offer us a ride in his empty car.

An hour later we walked into town, The Colorado Trail was completed and we were headed home.

Rainmaker and I walked along the main drag, passing a construction site. We looked both ways, then snuck in behind the fence to use their porta-potty. Then we hurried on, arriving at McDonald's. I ordered coffee and a sausage biscuit, Rainmaker had several, and second cups of steaming coffee. Our rental car would be available by 1 p.m., just across the street.

Back view of PonchoVilla, with red rain pants.

6. Continental Divide Trail

Trail Overview

While growing up in Madison, Wisconsin, the very notion of backpacking through heavy griz country had always impressed me as foolhardy. I had read stories about folks backpacking through Yellowstone and wondered why anyone would harbor such death wishes. It borders on suicide. But the CDT's northern terminus is the Canadian Border. It goes straight through Glacier National Park and into the Bob Marshal Wilderness and then traverses the Scapegoat Wilderness, all in Montana. A person has to get comfortable with the notion or go home.

Heading south from the Canadian border, I was really glad Rainmaker was with me. He had spent serious time backpacking alone in Alaska. In fact, one evening while cooking supper, he said he watched two young grizzlies wrestling.

I'll mention right now that I was expecting my period on that first week. Rainmaker wasn't worried. I figured either the dude was nuts or had more guts than any guy I'd ever met. After all we've been through together, I'll go with the latter. Guts.

And it's not fair. It doesn't matter how long I've been on a trail or what I eat or how much weight I lose. It never fails. I always get my period, on schedule and in bear country. So I deal with it. I treat all feminine products like food. The smells are known to draw critters. Wrap well and store in Garcia canister. Sorry guys if you're grossed out. I couldn't help it. I do know they make hormone pills to take care of cycles, but I don't believe in messing like that with nature. Studies have shown that down the road, synthetic hormones can bite back.

Rainmaker and I left our home in Georgia, drove across the country to Helena, Montana. We parked the car in a self- storage unit, then took a bus up to Shelby, Montana where we caught the train bound for East Glacier. We arrived late in the day and got a room at the backpacker's hostel. We spent the evening scoping out the cute little town, eating at a local diner, burgers and fries.

The next day Rainmaker volunteered to fulfill the trip leader's obligation of watching a video and signing backcountry permits. I spent the day hiking around East Glacier, heading up to the massive lodge with three floors of wooden beam opulence. The atmosphere was at the same time relaxing and sophisticated. At last Rainmaker returned, told me about his day while we ate supper in a fine restaurant. Then we spent the night at the Backpacker's Hostel.

The next day we hired a young woman who waited tables at the local breakfast joint to drive us to Chief Mountain Trailhead. Both Rainmaker and I would just as soon pay someone than hitch hike like beggars with thumbs flung out to passer-bys. Been there, done that.

We don't mind at all helping with gas and compensating someone for their time. It's a long drive. After she dropped us off, we hiked one-tenth mile up to the Canadian Border and got our photos taken by Gingerbread Man while the border patrol watched us from their booth.

Yesterday Gingerbread Man had spread some water stained maps out along a wooden dresser back at the hostel, and shown us some of his ideas highlighted with a red pencil, outlining a possible route through the Galatian and Madison Ranges north of Yellowstone. By doing the "Ennis" Cut Off a person could bypass the wide circling Anaconda Route heading out to Idaho. This alternative route cuts off about 300 miles, sometimes a critical and viable solution for northbound thru hikers with heavy snow threatening a Donner Party Experience.

As we listened to our new friend's proposed route, I was struck by the fact he'd never been on it. The maps were sketchy and he wouldn't be around when it didn't work or we faced a dead end. Rainmaker smiled at his enthusiasm and I nodded encouragement. Once alone, I told Rainmaker, "I don't want to be pissing around on someone else's bushwhack." To this day we use that observation to get off someone else's agenda.

Many opinions vary about such alternative routes. Purist AT hikers cringe. PCT hikers have some issues. CDT hikers quickly learn the Continental Divide Trail, starting at the Mexican Border, trailing through New Mexico, Colorado,

Wyoming, Idaho and Montana, is only 60% completed route anyways. Even the published trail guides differ in official routes from Canada to Mexico.

The huge Delorme Atlas contains detailed Topographic Maps showing all the known trails and back roads, highlighting BLM and State Lands in GPS Grids. These can be taken apart by the ultralighter and used for alternate routing. We used them in Montana. They were a wonderful backup. Be sure to take all the pages that could pertain to the route you're looking at.

Other maps that could be helpful are The Gallatin National Forest, The Lee Metcalf Wilderness and West Yellowstone Vicinity. All three can be purchased at Ranger's Stations in the area and are useful if you're sure you're going through there on an alternate route.

Wyoming's Continental Dived Trail Guide, The Official Guide by Lora Davis, photos by Scott. T. Smith, by the Continental Divide Trail Alliance. This is a beautiful book. I found it at a bookstore in West Yellowstone. This particular edition is 2000. When heading out to a trail, try to get the most recent edition possible. The few bucks saved in old copies will cost you later in reroutes and frustration. I love this book, more for dreaming. It reminds me of the Colorado Trail Guide with all its glossy pages and weighs 1 pound 2 ounces. I would take it apart, stripping out the covers and overview if I was actually using it for the trail.

The Wolf guides are very popular and put out by the Continental Divide Trail Society. Between the Delorme for Montana and the James Wolf guides, Rainmaker and I felt we had sufficient info. Note the dates on the guides. I loved the fact the author suggested several alternates like: **As an option, therefore, one may choose a shortcut from Butte to Yellowstone via the Tobacco Root, Madison and Gallatin Ranges. (This alternate route, which is equally fine scenically, passes through towns where supplies can be replenished.)**

This guide was written in 1979. Excerpts like this caused considerable trepidation: *The trail in this section, mostly cross country, follows the crest of the Continental Divide closely. Although it is quite strenuous, with a great deal of climbing....Aside from snow patches, which may linger at higher elevations well into July, there is no known water supply in close proximity to the trail....pick up a faint trail that contours to the right of the next minor summit.*

With many trails under our belts, both Rainmaker and I knew faint trails often disappeared, and my definition of the "next minor summit" and the author's definition of a "minor summit" could differ remarkably. The bottom line is you really can't have too many maps for the CDT.

After photo sessions at the Canadian Border, Gingerbread Man confided he had 16 pounds of food in his pack and wondered if we would like something. Sure, we say, we'd take few power bars. We were carrying just 3 days of food because it was only 2.5 days to Many Glacier Campground, the place we must go because it was marked on our permit. It was a good plan, too.

There was a restaurant/store complex at the Campground, making it equivalent to a town day. Three days of food was plenty and much easier to deal with each night in bear country.

Our packs were very light because we have left the "guerillas", our term of endearment for our Garcia bear canisters, back at East Glacier in custody of the understanding hostel owners. We'll be hauling those canisters once we get through the park. My external frame had been stripped of its original nylon pack. I sewed a custom fitted silnylon pack to accept the canister. This way I won't have to lash it on the outside.

This silnylon, custom fit pack has been used for several thousand miles at the time of this writing and I conclude that it will last a while longer if given good care. Because it is strapped to an aluminum frame, the durability is enhanced over just the 9 ounce silnylon pack I used on the AT.

Garcia Cannister with fuel bottle.

The lid of a Garcia Canister is locked via silver rotating screws, making the entire thing flush. Studies show even griz can't break into one of these things. Bears will bat it around, get frustrated and abandon it. That's why we put it next to a log and not near a slope where it could roll down into a lake or river

The first day on the trail we sang, chatted and watched for bears as we hiked through the lush dense forest. But Rainmaker and I are not verbacious people. Soon we realized a noise maker was in order, something that will clang every time we move, making enough noise to alert bears to our presence. Hiking over the passes each day and descending to rivers takes a lot of energy. Neither of us wanted to keep up the chatter. We were tired of singing **Where Have All the Flowers Gone?** and **Bad Moon Rising**.

Our noise makers were developed like all good gear. There was plenty of serious trial and error, which is critical for backcountry gear to meet these specifications: it must be ultralight, multi-purpose and cheap, better still, free. I would love to include 'nearly indestructible' but everyone knows that's not how ultralight gear is. If it survives one long trail, the piece of gear has done well.

At first, I tried tying my pot lid to the metal frame of my backpack, fully expecting it to swing freely against the metal frame. It remained suspiciously silent. I thought maybe the cord was too short, so I tested that concept using a longer cord. Still no luck. I tried tying it to my shoulder strap, giving the device more play. I expected more bang. Still nothing.

Then I noticed my hiking pole, but they had padding all along the shaft, for what reason I do not know. At lunch break, I sliced through the padding and removed the soft black foam glued on by the manufactures, carefully putting all the foam pieces into my trash bag. Then, I tied the pot lid onto the handle strap of my hiking pole. This worked really well. Every step I took my pot sang with a Clank clank-clank. Success!

Rainmaker has a theory he states this way: **Inanimate Objects will do exactly the opposite of what we wish them to do, unless forced to do otherwise.** I concur. Given half a chance, these same objects will run away, hide in the leaves, fall into the biggest mud puddle. Example: we carefully prop our hiking poles against a stout pine tree. Immediately these poles fall, slide away, trying to run off and usually downhill. The Downhill is the worst because it's also knee deep in muck.

Areas with abundant horse traffic have huge mucky trenches. You never see this on the AT. Horses are able to conjure up enough moisture to turn a trail into pure sludge. I figured this moisture was probably piss. When the tread-way becomes deeply trenched, about three feet deep or more, the horses refuse to walk in the trench and choose the ground right next to it. Eventually that space becomes eroded and the original trench is widened. Before you know it, you have an interstate.

Meanwhile, hikers are taught to Leave No Trace. Obediently, we hike in the muck. Every once in a while I feel rebellious, so I climb up on the grassy bank and hike on, scraping my muddy boots along the grass, getting some weight off the thick treads of my boots.

After the first week on the CDT we settled into a nice routine. I couldn't see getting up early to change into my hiking clothes and cook breakfast outside camp near the bear box, but Rainmaker needed his morning coffee so he would get up an hour before we wanted to be on the trail. Patiently he would go to the bear box, retrieve his hiking clothes and change from his warm sleepwear into his dirty shorts and shirt. Then he would head back over to the bear box while carrying his nearly empty pack. After retrieving his food bag, he would arrange his cushions to support his ailing back and cook oatmeal and make instant coffee. I would snuggle down into my down bag and wait for his return.

When Rainmaker returned from breakfast, I would hustle, knowing I had about fifteen minutes to dress while he warmed up his back. I'd drop the tent, shake it out and pack it for him. He carried the tent on his external frame. Quickly, I would run over and claim my food bag from the bear box, grabbing out a frosted blueberry poptart to eat, often pausing to chug plain cold water from the water bottle.

Once we passed through Glacier National Park, we carried Garcia Bear Canisters. Whatever didn't fit in them, we hung high up in a tree 100 yards from camp. Eventually everything, including tooth paste, fit inside the canisters.

Bear Lure Area

We had been noticing various trees with barbed wire wound around them for miles. We pondered the spacing, the height of the wires and figured it was the method the Park service chose to keep trees from being trashed out by animals.

But at the same time, we didn't notice any trail markers on these special trees. They were unevenly spaced. Sometimes several trees were wrapped, close together and then there would be long sections with nothing.

After we crossed the highway, leaving Glacier National Park and the Blackfeet Indian Reservation behind, we entered the Bob Marshal Wilderness. There were beautiful crystal clear streams and a variety of wildflowers growing beneath a perfectly blue sky. We sat down for lunch using our canisters as tables, facing each other while gazing farther out, watching the woods, enabling a 360 view. We were determined that no bears

153

would sneak up on our camp like they did on the PCT. A griz might be harder to route than a "candy-ass" black bear.

After a leisurely lunch, we approached a large white poster tacked to a tall pine tree. On the poster was a sketch of an angry griz standing up on hind feet. It read: **Bear Lure Area. Turn back now or proceed quickly.**

Rainmaker and I looked at each other. "Turn back to where?" I asked. "Proceed how far, and how quickly? What kind of sign is that?"

Rainmaker glanced around the woods and shrugged, "Let's go." It took us 15 seconds to decide to proceed quickly, making more noise as we approached each stream crossing. I could feel the adrenalin as we eased back on shore. No bears, yet.

Finally, seven miles later, we saw a Park Service campsite. There were no warnings posted. The place was empty but not barricaded. "I suppose we are past the lure area?" I asked.

"I figure so," Rainmaker replied thoughtfully. "They wouldn't want the liability of hosting a campsite in a lure zone."

We decided to hike on a few more miles before camping. Two days later still no signs stating if we were done with the lure area. Eventually, we came to a sign which explained that all the barbed wire was wrapped around the trees in order to capture fur from bears scratching against it. Please do not remove the fur, it read. The samples were being collected for research. We hadn't seen any fur on any of the trees and I wondered if in reality, no bears were in that area. Then it occurred to me to clean out my comb and stick it on the wire just for fun. Then I decided, maybe not, it could be a federal offence to mess with bear lure areas.

The Mule with Issues

The Chinese Wall is a marvelous section beloved by horse packers threading their way through the Bob Marshal Wilderness. We'd meet groups heading in any direction on a daily basis. Hikers must yield right of way, stepping aside until all of the party passes. This gives the horse people with their mules opportunity to cast observations our way.

We waited as a group of four passed by. Three men and one woman with heavy saddle packs indicated a lengthy trip was underway. As the woman rode by, her pocket dog barked furiously from the safety of its tiny pouch at her side. His little curly head bobbed up and down, with his rapid fire yapping. She looked down at the creature and smiled benevolently. After they passed, I muttered "Come over here and say that, you stupid pup!"

Once we met a ranger whose horses went nuts, thinking we were bears or something. She hadn't noticed us in time to rein them in. Her dogs circled around us and we called out, "Hello there!" alerting the ranger we were humans. She saw our noise makers and snapped, "Well, if you're so scared of bears, maybe you shouldn't be out here." We didn't reply, just let her get on past. It was easy for her to be so confident. She was riding a big mare and had 4 other horses, radio support, a gun visible in a holster at her side and two huge dogs ranging wide.

I really enjoyed those days of perfect weather, eating sparingly, watching each other's backs, hiking in wild country.

One day I stepped off trail while a man on horseback led his mules past. The youngest mule was not tethered. He walked next to me and stopped by my left shoulder. I waited. He looked at me and stood patiently. It looked like he hoped to be adopted. The man glanced over his shoulder and called him, whistled, "Here boy." The mule stood still, oblivious to the master's command.

I pointed to his master and said sternly, "Go!" Still the mule didn't budge. I think he noticed we carried our own stuff and decided that was what he wanted for his future: masters who carried their own packs.

Finally the owner road back, took hold of the mule's rope and led him away.

Blow-downs From Hell

Not all alternate routes are created equal. We noticed a particular route on the map and decided to take it. It trailed all along the left bank of a long river. It cut off several miles and was clearly marked, according to the trailhead marker.

The beginning was sweet, luring us into the wilderness route with plenty of green trees, a flowing river, hawks and chipmunks. It was charming, totally alluring. Off in the distance, wolves howled. We smiled. That was a rare event. The gods must be rewarding us for our determination.

Then we entered the burn area. Out west burn areas and trails don't mix. We had hiked about five miles along the beautiful river before the burn-out and blow-down hell began. It was too far to retrace our steps and we weren't dismayed. We figured it would quit. These blow downs couldn't go on forever. Horse packers would have come by and cleared them. We were so wrong. They nearly did.

Sometimes it would take 15 minutes to climb over a stack of blowdowns as tall as me, avoiding broken branches and rough boulders before we could get back on the trail. We knew it was essential to stay positive. Don't complain, just keep on keeping on.

A burned out forest goes from bad to worse. One strong wind will come through and blow down every burned pine like so many matchsticks.

Around 5 p.m. on the first night along that trail, we came to the confluence of rivers. We looked across the river and spied a lovely campsite on a little island used by horse packers. It was surrounded by water and had been protected from the burn. Thankfully we had the good sense to stop for the night.

The next morning we woke early, forded a swift branch of the Sun River and continued hiking through the burn area. Just across from our camping island, we noticed large bear prints, fairly fresh. By the size of the print and distinguishable claws I learned that these were indeed grizzly tracks. We hiked on, glad for our noise makers. After 5 more miles of excruciating blow downs, we neared grassy Gates Park, seriously scratched and bruised.

Love Under the Bridge

It had been incredibly hot all day. We'd gone thirsty, dropped down to a stream, refilled water bottles and took an afternoon break under a small shade tree.

Rainmaker and I resumed the trail, hiking late into the evening, unable to stop because of the rough terrain and lack of water.

Finally, we found a good level spot at Fletcher Pass and claimed it, setting up camp, cooking a simple supper of ramen. The night was still warm.

Exhausted, we went to bed and lay on our pads, sleeping bags thrown over our weary bodies. As we silently lay inside the thin single walled gray tent, Rainmaker raised his face to the sky and called out to the Trail gods, "How about some rain? How about some clouds tomorrow??" Then he turned to me and said, "Naw, it'll probably rain tonight then be hot and steaming again tomorrow."

"Probably," I agreed. We rolled over, peered into the darkness and fell asleep.

The next morning was warm with perfectly blue skies. Rainmaker's prediction would come true. We packed up and headed out as usual, hiking eight miles before pausing for lunch beneath a few scrubby pine trees. A shadow passed over the land and then another. As we stood up to leave, we checked the skies. They had darkened with thick storm clouds. "Well, here's your rain, David, thanks a lot!" Rainmaker chuckled while I rightly guessed the trail gods were going to have fun with us today. We began hiking, listening intently for the first claps of thunder, knowing we couldn't just hike through the rain because we were the tallest things out there. Suddenly a lightning bolt split the sky and we got serious.

Up ahead, Rainmaker noticed some small bushes lining a culvert and quickened his pace. I was thinking it would be one of those Lay- In-The Ditch days but Rainmaker had other ideas. We reached the bushes and quickly scrambled down the slope. Finding that the culvert was covered by a decent bridge and that it made the perfect refuge, we sighed with relief. There was a stream flowing sweetly right through the middle of our temporary shelter with generous embankments on both sides.

Without delay, we waded across the stream and took off our packs right below the bridge. If a car passed over that bridge, both of us knew they could not see us hunkered down there.

Rainmaker got out his two sleeping pads, spread them out. He dug in his food bag and pulled out some crackers. We ate a snack and I noticed he had that male gleam in his eye. Having been in griz country, he had gone without for a quite a while. Sources had told him that making love in the back country was more of a bear lure than a woman on her period.

We made ourselves comfortable on the pad and one thing led to another. Trail love under the bridge is something to remember. It was quick and down to business, an emotional release for me. Later, I remembered he had purposely called that storm up the night before. I figured the trails gods heard, proving that at least one of those gods are male.

After the skies cleared, we hiked to the tiny settlement of Canyon Creek, bought some Moose Tracks ice cream cones and learned there was "camping" just around the corner. "You go down the dirt road then turn on another dirt road. There's streams and everything," the cashier had said. That little "round the corner" to her turned into a 5-mile jaunt making a 21-mile day for us. As we quickened our pace along a dusty gravel road, a rancher drove up to ask if we were ok.

Instantly we assured him, "Yes, we're backpacking." He nodded and we asked, "Is there actually a stream along this old road, anywheres?"

"Yup," he replied, "About 2 miles more."

"Thanks," we said, and watched him drive off. Finally we found the tiny stream, green with algae and a cow skeleton lying 50 feet away. But there was a suitable campsite amongst the sagebrush with real cactus sporting 2-inch needles just waiting for some unlikely customer to transport it to another part of the earth.

We had a pleasant evening right out in the open, visible to all who might wonder what that gray thing was in the field.

Early the next morning I went to went to refill my water bottle. I hesitated and changed my mind when I saw the carcass of a coyote not 40 feet from our tent near the stream. His entire head, legs and paws were still intact, but the whole torso had been eaten by scavengers.

Karaoke in Helena

Rainmaker and I were normally a 15- mile a day couple who enjoyed our evenings in camp drinking coffee, writing in our journals, reading the trail guide. However, when I'm alone, I'll do more miles and hike late into the evening because I don't like sitting in camp alone twiddling my thumbs. I'd rather be hiking.

Rainmaker and I elected to do an alternate route into Helena after deciding to bypass Roger's Pass. This meant stretching out food from our Benchmark resupply, rationing it carefully to last over a few extra days. At the time we packed our food bags in Benchmark, we had no idea this would happen. Had I known we would be bypassing Roger's Pass, I would have definitely hauled out a few extra poptarts from the hiker box.

The alternate route passed through Silver City and we expected to buy some food there, but it was a sketchy little burg with no amenities so we continued onward down Birdseye Rd. We hiked faster, anticipating an early camp. Suddenly, we jumped aside, startled when 3 Saint Bernards lunged at the fence of a huge property fronting the road. We had some mace, but didn't need to use it. The dogs could not get out.

Happily we hiked on, arriving at Ft. Harrison which is a military establishment outside Helena. Nothing was to be had there either. We were hot and thirsty, without water and sucking on peppermints when we finally reached a state park just on the outskirts of Helena. Wearily we climbed the wooden fence, found a picnic table under a shade tree and sat down. Across the grassy lawn we could see soda machines in a small brick shelter, so we went over and bought four, each of us downing two Mountain Dews, shamelessly enjoying all the sugar and caffeine while eating some peanuts. I pulled out the city map and figured we'd already hiked 15 miles. Good enough. All we needed now was a motel and then we'd crash.

After a long break we hiked to the main drag, HWY 12 and saw one motel for sale, another one closed up with a No Vacancy sign and then a bar and grill with a sign reading, "Karaoke every Tuesday and Thursday, 9 p.m. until closing." I began laughing and told Rainmaker. He thought I was kidding. I pointed to the sign. His eyes lit up. Rainmaker and I had started doing Karaoke a year ago and decided we really liked it. I'm not much of a singer but what I lack in talent, I make up for in enthusiasm.

"We'll get a motel and go tonight!" Rainmaker said.

"Is this Tuesday, right?" I asked. He looked at his watch. Sure enough, it was Tuesday! Now our pace quickened, the skies thickened, but we had a mission. We stopped at the next motel which was just a series of run down yellow cabins. They wanted $68 bucks Plus Bed Tax. "No way," Rainmaker said. "The Motel 6 is less than 50 bucks, right down the road and much nicer." We agreed, and left immediately.

"Ok, here's the plan:" Rainmaker explained as we trudged on, "We walk to the Motel 6, get a room and drop the packs. Then we walk to the car stashed at the storage unit in East Helena, get the car and all our traveling clothes. We come back to the motel, clean up, and Drive to Karaoke, all by 9 p.m."

"Sounds great!" I agreed, nearly running to keep pace with his long legs now picking up speed. We didn't really stop to calculate how many miles that would be, whether we could do it or not or whether we would be dead on our feet. We just did it. It was 2:30 when we began this "Stampede". Around 3:30 a bad storm blew up, complete with lightning, thunder and hail. We sat it out under an overhang of a defunct luxury motel along with a young couple, both just kids on motorcycles. A street person on a bike joined us and told us about a free supper we could eat that night at a shelter, called "God's Love". "We're not as destitute as we look, but thanks," Rainmaker replied.

The storm finally blew over and we bid farewell and good luck to the young couple. We found the Motel 6, rented a room and dropped off our packs, then hiked to the car and suddenly we were rich!

After cleaning up at the motel, changing into jeans and a clean shirt, we made it to Karaoke. I sang **She Works Hard for the Money**, David did **Margaritaville**. We busted some moves, gave it our all and were roundly applauded by the young feisty crowd. They had the best sound system I have ever experienced.

About 1:30 a.m. we left the bar, returned to Motel 6 and crashed about 3 a.m. We had done 25 miles and partied into the wee hours of the morning. After packing up at coyote junction amidst cactus and briars we had ended up in the lap of luxury. Again we marveled at the ways of the trail.

As I edit this second edition, I'll add these few notes. After Karaoke, we took a zero day, got back on our alternate route and camped two nights later Townsend, Montana. We had wanted a motel, had hiked all day to that end, but all the rooms were taken. We ended up in the town's campground. During the night, several trains roared by. A fat cat snuck into our tent as the wind shook it, blowing the mesh screen out from under the floor. It didn't take us long to decide that was it. We had been fed up with the trail for a while and this was the last straw.

Nearly eight years later I still can't get the thought out of my mind that I am just 1500 miles away from being a Triple Crowner. I plan to pick up in Townsend where we left off and continue section hiking the CDT, mostly alone, if that's what it takes to get this obsession under control and gain some closure. Both of my blogs listed at the end of Chapter 11 have more details on my journeys.

A third book is underway. I'll describe the Ennis Cutoff as the Journey Continues.

7. Bartram Trail

I'm pretty proud of this next piece of work. In 2002 I bought the two volume, two part trail guide for the 117 mile Bartram Trail which begins at Russell Bridge in Northeast Georgia and goes all the way to Cheoah Bald in North Carolina. Years later I learned the Bartram Trail also heads into South Carolina from Russell Bridge but that's a whole other story. We later hiked that section and it was gorgeous.

As I prepared to cross this Favorite Trail off my list, I reviewed the guide. Wait, something was missing. How do I get from Buckeye Trailhead to Wallace Creek Trailhead? The authors told me they did not include the 14 mile road walk because it didn't fall into their category of "trail." I e-mailed the authors and asked what's up? I'd already paid $12 for the cardstock 8 x 12 inch trail guide, an ultralighter's nightmare, and I wanted the missing 14 miles. They told me to map quest it or, as they had the nerve to suggest, that because a road walk was so dangerous I should just take a cab.

This pissed me off. Immediately I fired off another e-mail giving them a list of my completed trails, among them the PCT, AT, and JMT and signed it Brawny. They replied with a dear MR. Wellman. Now I was seriously pissed and made sure they knew it was an Ultralighter and a female no less who was now very unhappy. They relented, did their homework and emailed me the rest of the guide.

I got my revenge by hiking the trail, forwards and backwards and writing my own free online guide. Here it is, updated and all yours.

Note: A hiking buddy told me the new edition of the Bartram Trail Guide now includes the road walk. The authors had held a seminar on backpacking, credited me with being the only one to have hiked the road section, which isn't true. Others have done the road walk as well. They finally realized the need for the complete road description, relented and gave us the whole thing.

Georgia Bartram Trail - 36.5 miles
Southern Terminus - Russell Bridge, parking lot is on the left side of Hwy 28, just south of the South Carolina/Georgia state line. Cross the road and get on the trail directly across near the guard railing.

.3(36.2) Cross a 112 foot metal footbridge

2 (34.5) Pass a rusty baler on left, and ruins of an old home site on right.

2.5 (34.0) Cross Adline Branch on wooden bridge. This is best water for next 3 miles.

3.2 (33.3) Cross Bynum Branch on wooden bridge. Water was scanty here, but there's a campsite on left hand side of trail.

4.3 (32.2) Cross another wooden bridge over a stream, with campsite.

6.3(30.2) Cross 66 ft. metal bridge, and in .2 cross Earl's Ford Road. There are some established, flat campsites here.

As you walk along the Chattooga River for the next 2 miles, there are some exceptional campsites. These are the last good campsites with water, until you reach Martin Creek, about 11 miles away.

9.1 (27.4) Dick's Creek Falls. Be sure to pick up water at the stream near Dicks Creek Falls, ****next sure water is near Warwoman Dell (9 miles), but you might cross a couple water sources in 6 miles depending on the season.

9.4 (27.1) Intersection with the Chattooga River Trail

9.5(27.0) Cross Sandy Ford Road, a carved rock says Bartram Trail.

11.4 (25.1) Cross road with rock carved, Speed Gap.

12.9(23.6) Cross Pool Creek Road, at Bob Gap. There are a couple dry campsites in the next 2 miles.

15.2(21.3) A 90 degree turn to the right, off an old jeep road. It's well marked and skirts Rainy Mountain to the north. There should be water in this vicinity in small streams, just off trail, which can be heard, if not seen.

17 (19.5) Intersect Goat Trail marked with metal goat-shaped blazes attached to trees.

17.3 (19.2) Green Gap

18.1 (18.4) Cross stream on wooden bridge.

18.8 (17.7) arrive at Warwoman Dell, with Picnic tables and Warwoman Road access. This is strictly a picnic area, no overnight camping allowed. The town of Clayton is 3 miles west. For northbounders, this would be a left hand turn; for southbounders, a right turn. Clayton has a Super Wal-Mart, lots of restaurants, and motels.

18.9 (17.6) Cross Warwoman Road

19.8 (16.7) Trail climbs and moves away from Warwoman Road, along small stream, and then approaches the bank of Martin Creek with decent campsites. There is an unusual trail routing here. When you cross Martin Creek on a small wooden bridge, walk up the other side to view a fantastic waterfall, cross Martin Creek again on a very well done wooden bridge with viewing platform, and return to nearly the same place you crossed previously. Then, following the blazes you head up the hill to continue north.

21.4 (15.1) Cross various streams on rocks

22.5 (14.0) Pass through Courthouse Gap, which is marked with a sign nailed to a tree. The Bartram trail ascends from here.

A short (.6 miles) side trail, marked with white splashes of paint, leads down to a parking area, easily accessible with a small car. To access this parking area, take Warwoman road out of Clayton for .8 miles, and you'll see a sign for Pinnacle Camp. Take a left turn off Warwoman Road onto Pinnacle Dr. Follow that road all the way, 1.1 miles, passing the camp, to Courthouse Gap Road. Take a right, and go .2 miles until you see a gravel road, with parking areas beneath power lines. Park there, and walk up that road about a tenth of a mile, over one culvert, until you see the trail heading left, up some rock steps, just before a second culvert. This trail passes water, but no campsites, as it ascends to the Bartram trail.

26.0 (10.5) Windy Gap

26.8 (9.7) Cross small stream in Rhododendron. This is the last campsite with water for next 3 miles

27.3 (9.2) Wilson Gap, cross a dirt road with dry campsites. Just south one tenth mile there is intermittent water. They say this gap is accessible with a four wheel drive in dry weather.

29.5 (7.0) Small stream and tiny campsite trailside. Continue a bit further and on the left is a short unmarked side trail leading to better campsite beside a stream.

30.5 (6.0) Saltrock Gap, elevation 3700 feet. Dry campsite.

32.3 (4.2) Rabun Bald, with observation platform, great views, elevation 4,696 feet.

33.9 (2.6) Bee Gum Gap, house 50 feet on left. Cross the road.

36.4 (.1) Cross many footbridges and streams, arriving Hale Ridge Rd.

36.5 GA/NC border

Winter in **Georgia** on the Bartram Trail can be cold. On January 11th a few of us from the Georgia Appalachian Trail Club headed out on an overnighter. It sounded like fun. Temperatures were predicted for the low teens, so I packed some extra food, a fleece liner and an ultralight tent.

We met at the McDonalds in Clayton, drove down Warwoman Road and left all the cars at the Dell. Pilling into one car, five of us headed to the NC/GA border, on Hale Ridge Road. It was already cold and I wore nearly all my clothes, with my black silnylon rain suit on top. A guy on the AT once asked me what's up with the black garbage bag clothing and pack cover. It's silnylon I said, thinking, you've never seen silnylon?

With a pack weight of just under 12 pounds, including 24 ounces of water, and two days of food, I felt very light for winter. After checking out the trail guide, I knew we would be climbing over Rabun Bald, and I would be feeling fine. The black absorbed heat from the sun and my companions thought that was a good idea for winter gear.

After parking just off the gravel road, we rugged GATCers headed south. At 10 a.m. ice still covered the trail, but the new wooden footbridges were basically clear. There was plenty of water flowing in these parts and no need to carry or treat it. Research shows that giardia dies in subfreezing weather and the streams flowed clear. Town sludge was in the valley, 10 miles away. I felt good to go and drank straight from the stream, suffering no ill effects.

We ate lunch on top of Rabun Bald. It is the highest point on the Georgia section at 4,696 feet. A 360-degree vantage and windbreak from the viewing tower facing into the sun made this a fairly comfortable stop. An hour later, we packed up and headed down to Wilson Gap to camp.

The hike was pleasant and the winter views expansive. We arrived in camp well before dark. Water could be had by hiking just one-tenth of a mile south, and near the trail. Quickly we found level spaces and set up our tents, filling our water bottles, knowing they would probably freeze.

That night the temperature plummeted to 11 degrees. Before going to sleep, I dumped my water after leaving just 6 ounces in a water bottle for midnight drinks and filling my pot and cup. I learned this trick from Rainmaker. My first frozen water experience of 4 pounds of ice in two soda bottles had taught me there had to be a better way.

One guy slept with his camelback full of water to prevent it from freezing, but the drinking tube froze solid and he ended up with no water and five pounds of extra weight. The problem with this is you also have nothing to put water in.

Some people say that Nalgene bottles don't burst. This is NOT TRUE. I've met enough people who told horror stories of freezing bottles and wet sleeping bags. One lady said she was sleeping on a bunk beneath a girl whose bottle broke during the night and dripped down onto her. Not fun. She woke with a wet sleeping bag.

Lesson: Water will freeze, even in your sleeping bag. If your bottles freeze, they are useless weight.

During the night I woke and shook the ice crystals in my bottle, eventually drinking all 6 ounces. In the morning I fired up the tiny backpacking stove and thawed the water frozen in my pot. I felt bad for my comrades who trudged down to the stream to get running water.

We packed up quickly, shaking frost from the tent, pulling staked from frozen ground. Our buddy checked his thermometer. Wow, it was only 11 degrees. "I'll meet you on the trail," I said, and shook the frost from my gloves. Ultralighters know that once they get moving, they'll warm up. Everyone decided to hike at their own pace and meet in the Dell, at the cars.

The trail was beautiful and mostly downhill. It was also well marked with yellow blazes. It had been rerouted around the campground listed in the guidebooks. Again, there was plenty of water. Becky Branch Falls is just .1 before the Dell, a photo opportunity no matter what season you view it.

Trip Report: Beginning at Russell Bridge, the Bartram Trail in Georgia swings west and follows the river. I was on the trail by 7 a.m. on a cloudless, cool morning in March.

The trail was deserted, although I heard the river and two vehicles on Hwy 28. The trail crossed a metal bridge then several new wooden footbridges. A sign was posted for no horses, then another and written beneath it in black magic marker, "Please!" Horses can really tear up the land. Hikers Leaving no traces are mere bugs in comparison.

Suddenly a large bird takes off. A few small birds twittered in the brush. All the pine trees, ferns, Rhododendron and moss keep this region green throughout the year. The metal diamond shaped, yellow blazes were well spaced and the well-graded trail headed towards a mountain. I was mentally prepared to climb the mountain expecting AT-type Pointless Ups and Downs (PUDS), this being Georgia and all. But, just like the profile showed, it stayed reasonably level and wound around the mountains. I passed Sandy Ford Road and heard a chainsaw down in a gully and headed towards Bob Gap. There was plenty of water all along this section.

The trail took a sharp right about 2 miles past Bob Gap as it skirted northwest of Rainy Mountain. I was daydreaming and blew past the well-marked turn still staying on a jeep road. It soon became obvious the trail had petered out, so back trailing quickly, I found the turn off. The trail became more rugged. The two mountains on the profile were reached and then I descended to Warwoman Dell. My ride was due in an hour and I relaxed in the modern pavilion, then walked down to sit at the picnic table in front of an large log shelter with fireplace. I noticed a guy panning for gold. In 7.5 hours, I had covered 19 miles. Not too shabby for a day hike.

A couple years later, two dear friends from my AT thru hike joined Rainmaker and I for a three day, two night jaunt on the Georgia Trail. I was the guide of sorts because I had hiked it before. It was weird being the "expert" among these seasoned hiker dudes. My memory didn't fail me and we camped the first night by the Chattooga River, near Earl's Ford and the second night by Martin Creek.

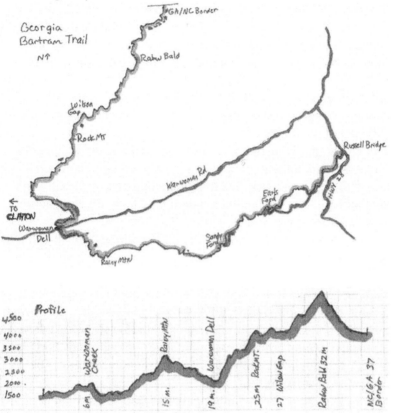

I drew this map and profile chart. A hiker e-mailed, thanking me for the Lewis and Clark rendition. I smiled. That's a compliment. It was a very rustic, workable, handmade interpretation of data.

North Carolina Bartram Trail : 74.4 miles

The northern terminus is atop Cheoah Bald. In October, the Forest Service Road 249, Nolton Ridge Road, is open and it's only a .9-mile hike to the top.

During the other eleven months, the hiker has two other alternatives. I decided to park at the Winding Stairs Trailhead and hike the 5.1-miles up to the Bald, then return via the same route. I carried just a daypack which made the 3,000-foot ascent from the Nantahala River to the Bald fairly easy. This 10.2 mile round trip is rugged but there's plenty of water because you cross

Ledbetter Creek about 7 times, often on slippery rock. Be sure to wear shoes with good tread. There are several decent campsites in this section as well.

From Cheoah Bald to the Wallace Branch Trail head there are 41.2 miles of well-marked trail. Then there is a 14.2-mile road walk through the town of Franklin, North Carolina. This is part of the blazed trail. The last segment of the N. C. Bartram Trail heads back into the forest at Buckeye Creek Trailhead. From there it is 19 miles to the North Carolina/ Georgia Border, just .1 of a mile past Hale Ridge Rd.

If one adds up all these mileages including the 5.1 to reach the summit to begin the hike, it is 79.5 miles.

Hunters use this trail during the various seasons. When you hear a gun go off, watch for deer and camouflaged dudes. Bright colors are a must unless it is turkey season. . During hunting season I tie orange or red streamers to my poles for visibility. It's good to check on these details before you go out.

I found hiking poles to be especially useful on this trail which is steep in places and sometimes narrow with uncompromising ridges. The trail can be very slippery with heavy leaf coverage and damp overgrowth.

The first number in the following data is miles from the GA/ North Carolina border, including the road walk, heading north. The number in parenthesis is from the northern terminus hiking south. These mileages were compiled using various data sources, and are approximate.

NC/GA Border, at Hale Ridge Rd, to HWY 106 (3.6 miles)

You can drive to Hale Ridge Trailhead by taking Hwy 106 west for 7.3 miles from Highlands, N.C until you come to the village of Scaly Mountain, NC. Then, turn left onto Hale Ridge Rd. and follow that 2 miles until it bears left, while Bald Mountain Rd. curves right. Continue on Hale Ridge Road. It becomes gravel and in three-tenths of a mile you'll see the Bartram Trail sign on the right hand side.   There's parking for about two vehicles.
This section is one of my favorite day hikes. As a round trip it's only 7.2 miles. It's marked with yellow rectangular blazes unlike the diamond ones found in Georgia. I park at Hwy 106, head south to Hale Ridge Rd. then return. It takes 3 hours. The data is given heading north into North Carolina.

.0 (74.4) From the crossing of Hale Ridge road, follow the sign, going to the left about .1 mile. There is a large sign directing you to the Bartram Trail. You will be crossing numerous plank bridges spanning creeks, waterfalls, and drainages.

.9 mile (73.5) Small campsite to right.

1.5 (72.9) Cross several intermittent streams on slippery rocks in the next half mile.

2.0 (71.2) Cross stream on plank bridge with rock steps heading down. There's a campsite up above trail on right.

2.6 (71.8) Intersect Hurrah Ridge Trail on the right. Watch for yellow blazes. The Hurrah Ridge Trail is blazed blue.

3.0 (71.4) Cross two plank bridges over fast flowing streams, then arrive at the West Fork Trail which bisects the Bartram Trail here. Great campsite to left of the intersection. Bartram Trail is straight ahead.

3.6 (71.8) Reach Osage Mtn. Overlook on Hwy 106. This is 5.8 miles west of Highlands, N. Carolina. There is parking here. Cross Highway to resume trail.

HWY 106 to Tessentee Creek Campsite (4.4 miles)

After crossing the very busy and potentially dangerous highway, begin climbing steeply, 1100 feet in just 1.5 miles. Once you reach the top of Scaly Mountain you'll enjoy fabulous vistas of the Appalachian Mountains.

3.9 (71.5) Cross stream on rocks and roots. This is the last sure water until you reach Tessentee Creek, 4 miles north. There were two other intermittent sources flowing this autumn, but in a dry season, not to be relied upon.

4.4 (70.0) A Big white house near trail. Take care, especially southbound, because a good trail splits off from the Bartram trail and leads directly to that house. Watch for the blazes.

5.0 (69.4) Trail intersection, and sign for Scaly Mountain, with a blue blaze trail for Hickory Knut Gap Road, elevation 4600 feet.

5.5 (68.9) arrive at Scaly Mtn. Summit, 4804 feet.

7.2 (67.2) Begin descending, at times steeply, passing a small dry campsite on right. Several well-made switchbacks take you from one ridge with a stream cascading out of sight, to another stream on the opposite end of the switchback. You can hear the water but cannot see it until you near the confluence at the bridge, a delightful surprise. As you hike down this mountain, two streams flow in valleys separated by the descending mountain and all of it meets at a marvelous campsite.

8.0 (66.4) Arrive at Tessentee Creek, with bridge and good, abundant water and large campsites. Note: *** No reliable on trail water for the next 9.7 miles.*

Rainmaker and I camped at this site and he called up several large owls. As they drew ever nearer on a full moon night, chills ran up my spine. I wondered if I had to leave the tent to pee, would they think me a mouse and swoop down on my head? It was a very surreal experience. Be aware though that this campsite seems to be on an old road bed. We did not see or hear any vehicles. Read the Foothills story about one scary incident for more on that subject.

Tessentee Creek to Fishhawk Mtn. (5.6 miles)

The trail merges with the road, then at:

8.2 (66.2) a sharp turn to right, up old log steps while the road continues straight ahead. Trail follows switchbacks, up, down and around marvelous views

9.7 (64.7) Switchback up to Hickory Gap. Cross old road with a sharp turn heading up another set of old log steps. Wooden sign reads Jones Gap and Osage Overlook.

10.8 (63.6) Jones Gap gravel parking area with information sign. (This parking area is accessible from HWY 106, via Turtle Pond road, then turn left onto Dendy Orchard Rd, then, after 1.7 miles, turn left onto gravel road just after house on right at the top of a hill). Cross parking area, and head up trail, north of the sign.

11.1 (63.3) Sharp turn to right, blue blaze trail goes left.

12.1 (62.3) Wooden sign for Whiterock Gap, elevation 4,150 feet. Steven Creek is 900 feet down steep side trail. Campsite.

12.5 (61.9) Short trail (50 feet) to right, intermittent water source.

12.6 (61.8) Trail to left for Whiterock Mtn. while Bartram Trail continues to the right.

Great views both east and west as you walk the ridges.

13.4 (61.0) Gap with small possible campsite, between Little Fishhawk and Fishhawk Mtn.

13.6 (60.8) Blue blaze trail up mountain.

Fishhawk Mtn. to Buckeye Creek Trailhead (5.4 miles)

13.8 (60.6) Water seepage across trail, too scanty to rely on, elevation 4,500 ft.

14.4 (60.0) Descend switchbacks, cross small gap, and continue on narrow ridge

15.0 (59.4) Expansive view, sign saying "Wolf Rock". Elevation 4,450 ft. Cross another narrow ridge, descend many more switchbacks, at times threading your way through rocks, to arrive at:

16.3 (58.1) Old school bus. There's also sheet metal and wood from a blown down shed.

16.7 (57.7) Switchbacks, arrive at sign "Buckeye Creek 3 miles". This sign is not accurate at this time. I am told a reroute is planned. But, according to my data and hiking time, it is 2.3 to Buckeye Creek from here. Elevation 3390 ft.
17.5 (56.9) Cross stream. This is the first reliable water since Tessentee Creek, 9.7 miles back. Southbounders take note.
17.7 (56.7) Turn right onto old log road. This intersection is well marked. Descend on this road for 1.3 miles.
17.8 (56.6) Good water, and some flat areas along this closed road. If heading north on the road walk, pick up water here. **** Next water will be at the bridge, at Prentis Bridge Road, about 8.4 miles. ****
19.0 (55.4) White forest service gate across the old road. Take a left and continue down Buckeye Branch Road about a tenth mile and arrive at the small parking lot on the left with informational sign. Elevation is approximately 2,300. (You can get to Buckeye Creek Trailhead by driving 13 miles on Hwy 441, heading north out of Clayton, GA. Then, take a right onto Tessentee Rd (SR1636) and stay on that for 3.3 miles. Take a left on the gravel Buckeye Branch RD. Stay on this road for about .6 mile. The trailhead will be on your right.)

As you leave this trailhead making your way north, you'll encounter many dogs. Most are leashed. For me, dogs represent one of the greatest dangers to backpackers, second only to thugs. Dogs are not generally afraid of humans. Often they feel protective of property and their owners and are unpredictable. Most of the dogs in this area are hunting dogs. I will cross the road to avoid walking near a yapper's property just to give us both some space.

The Road Walk

This portion of the trail is approximately 14 miles over paved, double yellow lined, backcountry road. The views are great and you walk by several branches of the Tessentee River with several possible water sources. There is no place to camp legally so this is a one day affair.

Take advantage of the mown grass shoulders along the road to alleviate pounding the pavement. The road had a few blazes but some are quite worn. Some blazes were spotted on telephone poles and trees. Mileages are heading north. State Route is abbreviated as SR. Road names are given when possible.

If you are resupplying in Franklin, an alternate section is described, so that you can walk right past a McDonald's, Super Kmart, and Burger King.

From the parking lot, on Buckeye Branch Rd, continue walking down the gravel road .6 miles

19.6 (54.8) Intersection of Tessentee Road (SR1636). Turn right, heading downhill. Stay on this road until you come to:

21.8 (52.6) "Y" intersection with Hickory Knoll Rd. (SR1643) a right hand turn. Take Hickory Knoll Rd. Continue until another:

24.4 (50.0) "Y" intersection with Clarks Chapel Rd, (SR1646). Hickory Knoll goes off to the right, you go basically straight. Stay on this road for two miles until you come to a:

26.4 (48.0) "T" intersection with Prentiss Bridge Rd. (SR1651). Take a left here, eventually crossing a bridge immediately over the Little Tennessee River. There is a parking area here, too, and "Public River Access".

26.7 (47.7) Cross another bridge and take a right at the T intersection going to Wide Horizon Drive (SR 1651, same as the Prentiss Bridge Rd). This road changes number when John Teague Rd. turns off to the left. Then, it will be called SR 1652, still Wide Horizon Drive and you continue down it until it runs into

29.7 (44.7) Old Georgia Rd. which is the same as HWY 441. Right now, you're at Macon County Fair Grounds, a group of long metal buildings. Cross the road (a very busy and potentially dangerous 4 lane affair). If you wish to resupply and hit some of the stores mentioned above, continue up 441, where you can see the Pizza Hut and the McDonalds. Cross in front of that smaller shopping center and then take a left and head up the frontage road where Lowe's, Kmart, and Burger King are situated near the Westgate Shopping Center. After eating and resupplying, stay on the frontage road (SR1170) until you come to Roller Mill Rd. (SR 1154) that's where you can resume the "official route" by taking right. To stay on the "official route", cross HWY 441 and walk up Beldon Rd. (SR1152), which is directly across from Wide Horizon Drive.

30.0 (44.4) Cross bridge and turn left onto Roller Mill Rd (SR1154). Continue on this road circling around behind the Westgate Shopping Center. Cross under HWY 64 by way of bridge.

30.8 (43.6) Take left onto Carolina Rd (SR1463)

31.0 (43.4) Take right onto Sloan Rd (1153). There is a gas station at this intersection with snacks available. Walk down this road .3 mile, passing the Wayah Ranger Station on your right. Come to the intersection with:

31.3 (43.1) Pressly Road (SR 1315). Head uphill. There's a trailer park on your right (this is a somewhat confusing intersection, so check the State Road numbers on the stop signs to be sure) and in 1.7 miles you will arrive at the:

33.0 (41.2) Wallace Branch Trailhead with informational sign. This has a good parking area, a campsite just inside the woods and plenty of water. There are some houses nearby but we did not note any signs that forbade camping.

Wallace Branch Trailhead to Sawmill Gap (14.7 miles)

This would be a great section to southbound because you go over Wayah Bald, at 5342 feet, and descend to 2260 ft. at the Wallace Branch Trailhead. This is not an easy section, however, whichever way it's hiked. Note there is no water between the last Wallace Branch crossing and just before the intersection with the AT, about 9.8 miles of undulating trail with about 5,000 feet elevation gain and loss over several peaks.

I hiked this section in the winter and then again in the summer with Rainmaker. In the summer there is a lot of poison ivy. If the trail crews have not cut it back, wash in the cold stream as soon as possible to avoid rash. If you're wearing gaiters, I'd treat them as contaminated and wash the toxic oils off them too.

33.1 (41.2) Cross stream over wooden bridge, with a waterfall to the right.

33.4 (41.0) Cross grassy jeep roads, possible campsites with nearby water. Note: ***last on trail water for 10 miles. Begin climbing, at times steeply.

34.6 (39.8) Forest Service Road 7190 visible down 100 feet to the right. Elevation 3,020 feet.

34.7 ((39.5) Sharp hairpin turn with a short trail to overlook, going off to the left. Lots of ascents and descents with great views for the next 8 miles, with narrow ridges, gaps and lots of down trees.

38.6 (35.8) Harrison Gap, with intersection of Forest Service Road 713, large gravel parking area. The next section has a few small grassy meadows with some old logging roads. Watch carefully as the trail winds through these.

42.5 (31.9) On a switchback, pass next to a wire fence. Also, there are diamond shaped North Carolina Bear Sanctuary signs tacked to the trees. Elevation approximately 4890 ft.

43.2 (31.2) Cross good stream, huge camping area just .1 miles down trail at the:

43.3 (31.1) Intersection of Appalachian Trail and Bartram Trail. They join for the next 2.9 miles, climbing up Wayah Bald.

43.9 (30.5) Summit of Wayah Bald with its stone observation tower, elevation 5342 ft. Walk down the sidewalk and there's even nice privies.

45.8 (28.6) Wine Spring (water) with campsites.

46.3 (28.1) Narrow ridge with "Danger Rifle Range" signs. The rifle range is below in a gap, so hikers are fairly safe up on the ridge.

47.8 (26.6) Sawmill Gap, paved Parking area along paved FS road 711. You can access this road via Wayah Road, SR 1310, just 1.7 miles north of the Wayah Bald sign. The turn is on the right hand side, if you are heading north. After turning off SR1310 onto FS 711, its 2.5 miles uphill to the parking lot.

I camped with a friend near the Bear Sanctuary sign in the very large, nearby comfortable campsite. We were heading south and she had no idea it was so close. When we passed it the next morning, she paused and looked wide eyed at me. "So?" I asked, "Nothing happened, did it?"

Sawmill Gap to Appletree Campground (9 miles)

I did this section December 1st as a day hike. There was snow and ice and all the streams were flowing well. Views were fantastic with lots of wildlife. Hunters use this trail too. Be sure to wear bright colors during the hunting season.

48.7 (25.7) West side of Jarrett Bald, at 4820 feet. Nantahala Lake visible way below.

48.1 (25.3)Steep descent begins on switchbacks. This continues all the way to the road, SR 1310.

51.2 (23.2) Cross small stream

51.4 (23.0) Arrive at SR 1310. Cross the road by the wooden sign saying Bartram Trail. This is the last blaze you'll see until you arrive at the Phillips 66 gas station.

Turn right so that you can see that last blaze behind you, heading north. You'll walk along this narrow, paved road for .7 miles. The following stuff is on the left side of the road, the same side you're on, facing oncoming traffic. First, within 100 yards, you'll pass a rugged, gravel parking area near the lake. Then, about a half mile down, a restaurant which was open in the winter from 7a.m-2 p.m. People were friendly and there's a pay phone in 2004, not sure about now.

Continue down the road, past the Phillips 66 station. There they sell some food and snack items. Just after the big 66 sign the trail turns left and goes down the gravel road. There is a blaze on the post there.

These next turns take you on the edge of a trailer campground.

52.0 (22.4) Cross Lee Branch on cement bridge. Turn right. Follow this gravel road as it turns left, ascending above SR 1310.

52.2 (22.2) The trail takes a sharp left turn onto an old, fairly obscure logging road and into the forest. This is easy to miss, especially if you're looking at the huge house straight ahead.

52.4 (22.0) Cross small stream. The trail uses old logging roads through here, crossing gravel roads. It's well marked.

53.9 (20.5) Cross a small stream. The trail is on old road paralleling the stream with some campsites.

54.7 (19.7)Cross cement bridge and turn right on High Water Trail Rd. Follow this gravel road for 2 miles. There are several streams which cross this road where you can get water easily without descending to the river which parallels this road.

56.7 (17.7) Right turn at T-Intersection with Cloudwalker Cove Rd. Walk down this road about a tenth of a mile until you come to SR 1401.

56.8 (17.6) Turn right and head up to the Appletree Campground informational sign. Just at the entrance, you'll see a wooden split rail fence. The blazes are abundant and direct you to climb over the fence to resume the trail.

Appletree Campground to Winding Stairs Parking Lot (12.4 miles)

This lovely section follows the river for several miles. There are several potential campsites, although few have been established and plenty of water. The trail is well graded and follows an old road-bed for much of the way.

57.1 (17.3) Trail emerges from path to gravel road FS 72908. Turn right, hiking along split rail fence at edge of campground. The trail does not actually enter the grassy camping area.

57.3 (17.1) Take a right turn heading away from campground, just past the metal road gate with a picnic shelter to the left. After one tenth mile, take sharp right turn off this road, heading into forest then descending to river.

57.9 (16.5) Flat areas in large trees for camping, although there are no established sites. This is the last spot that is fairly level for several miles. The next sites listed in the other trail guides are along the old road bed in 2.8 miles

58.9 (15.5) Descend and merge left on an old road. If south bounding, watch for this abrupt turn.

60.2 (14.2) Cross Poplar Cove Creek with water running down the trail for the next 175-200 feet, a very wet section.

60.7 (13.7) Cross small stream

61.4 (13.0) After a small stream, arrive at Y-road intersection and choose road to the right.

62.7 (11.7) Cross Piercy Creek, which is relatively wide and in wet seasons you may have to wade. No Bridge. Not an issue except during winter hiking. Shortly afterward, there's a blue blazed trail, the Piercy Creek Trail heading off to the right. Several good campsites in this area along the creek.

62.8 (11.6) Laurel Creek wooden trail sign. Laurel Creek Trail appears very overgrown while the well-marked Bartram trail goes straight here.

63.8 (10.6) London Bald trail intersection. Take a sharp right, ascending. This is well marked, but could be missed if you're hiking heads down.

64.2 (10.2) Cross another stream.

66.2(8.2) Walk around a huge pale green surge tank and small cement building on the right, elevation about 3500 ft. Join gravel road, which becomes the trail for the next 1.7 miles.

67.0 (7.4) Y intersection of gravel roads. Continue descending straight ahead. The wrong one goes down to a privy and private junk yard, visible only in winter.

67.8(6.6) Pass a pale green water tank. Roads and houses visible below. Within a tenth of a mile, take a sharp left turn off the gravel road, heading down a dirt trail through a weed patch, and under a power line. You'll arrive at the Bartram Trail informational sign, another gravel road and a gravel parking area. Head down the road to intersect SR 1310. Turn right and walk along the highway, over the bridge and to the end of a guard rail.

68.1 (6.3) Take a left at the end of the guard rail, crossing a large parking area, then joining the Mountain-to-the-Sea paved bike path. This level path follows the river for 1.2 miles.

69.3 (5.1) Take a left to cross the bridge over the Nantahala River, and arrive at Winding Stairs Parking Area.

Winding Stairs Parking Area to Cheoah Bald (5.1 miles)

I did Cheoah Bald as a day hike. It's easy to find Winding Stairs parking area. From the Hwy 441/ U S 64 intersection on the south side of Franklin, North Carolina, you head west on U.S 64. After 3.8 miles you see a sign for Wayah Bald and LBJ Job Corp. Take that right turn onto Old Murphy Rd and go about .3 mile. On the left you see a gas station, and Wayah Rd (State Route 1310) heading off to the left. Stay on that road for about 27 miles until you come to a T intersection with Hwy 19. Take a right and go about .8 miles, passing a Historical Marker turn off. The parking area can hold about 8 cars and has a huge sign just after the driveway for the Rocky Water Campground. The campground listed its phone number as 828-321-3660. It looked promising for people who wanted a nice place to camp along the river with amenities.

I got on the trail by 10 a.m. on June 28th. It was a pretty morning, but knowing what a difference 3,000 feet elevation change can make, I took a rain poncho, a water bottle and snacks. Within half a mile to the summit, a storm and cold rain began to fall. I tagged the tree with the sign saying **Cheoah Bald** and headed down. Back at the parking lot, all was sunny again, 4 hours later.

Cross Hwy 19, get on the trail directly across.

69.4 (5.0) Cross railroad tracks, continue through tall grassy area until you reach the forest.

69.8 (4.6) Cross Ledbetter Creek, with several good campsites, but they're near the rail road tracks. A much nicer, wilder site is ahead 1.7 miles. You will be able to see the train tracks for about a mile, while the sound of the creek diminishes.

70.4 (4.0) Trail turns north and climbs steeply, elevation 2,400. Soon you will hear the rushing waters of Ledbetter Creek again.

71.3 (3.1) Cross Ledbetter Creek on very slippery rocks, then follow feeder stream 100 feet on the trail.

71.5 (2.9) Campsite along Ledbetter Creek

72.0 (2.4) Several waterfalls in this area, along with crossings of Ledbetter Creek.

73.5 (.9) Merge with FS 259, Nolton Ridge Road, a gravel road accessible by 4 wheel drive, but only in October when the gate is open.

73.7 (.7) Climb steeply up Little Bald Mtn. elevation 4600 ft.

74.2 (.2) T-intersection with Appalachian Trail. Turn right.

74.4 (0.0) After a narrow ridge walk of .1 mile, you'll see a tree on the left with a wooden sign saying Cheoah Bald. This is the Northern Terminus, at 5062 feet elevation.

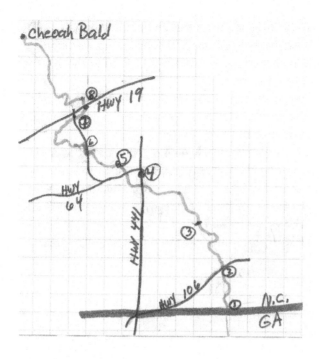

1. NC/GA border. Hale Ridge Road
2. HWY 106- Osage Mtn. Overlook
3. Buckeye Creek Trail Head
4. City of Franklin
5. Wallace Branch Trailhead
6. Phillips 66 Gas Station on SR 1310
7. Bike Path
8. Winding Stairs Parking Area, off HWY 19

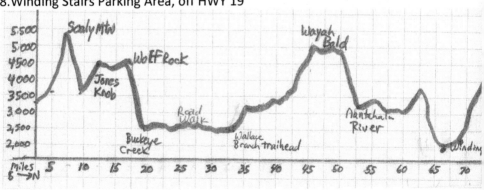

When Rainmaker and I hiked this trail, we used this guide and were also testing our Garcia bear canisters for the CDT hike. The last camp was made 1.7 miles from the summit. We cooked supper, put all our food in the canisters and hid them up stream for the night.

In the morning, I woke up and went out of the tent to collect our canisters before preparing breakfast. Right where we had stashed the canisters stood a large black bear. I called out and he fled.

I told Rainmaker about the bear. We decided I would just wait in the camp while he hit the summit, completing his trail and I would guard the stuff. The original plan was for both of us to day hike it, leaving our tent standing. We changed our plans because we knew the bear could ravish our gear while we were gone.

I read, wrote and waited patiently for Rainmaker to do his hike. The bear never returned.

8. Foothills Trail

Trail Overview

The Foothills Trail is nearly 76 miles long and routes through South Carolina, a pinch of Georgia and then North Carolina. It's located south of Rosman, North Carolina, east of Walhalla, South Carolina and west of Greenville, South Carolina. Some thru hiker friends used it for training camp in preparation for their CDT hike. This trail, while short, will definitely build calf muscles.

The southern terminus is in Oconee State Park in South Carolina off Hwy. 107. The northern terminus is in Table Rock State Park, South Carolina off Hwy. 11. Elevations range from about 1,000 ft. at Table Rock State Park to about 3,600 ft. at Sassafras Mtn.

We used the guidebook published by The Foothills Trail Conference, PO Box 3041, Greenville, SC 29602. Their website is located at www.foothillstrail.org . This guide book has excellent fold out maps, section mileages but no cumulative mileages. I created a cheat sheet, and stapled it into our book for references. I wanted to know, for instance, if you're doing sections A-C, how many miles would that be? I removed the pages as needed and didn't carry the entire guide, ever.

Never Camp Near A Gravel Road

Rainmaker and I have always shared a tent. On all of our long and short trails, we would choose something that fit the climate, the distance and expected pack weight. North of Crater Lake on the PCT, we had a double wall Coleman for Two. He carried the body of the tent. I had the fly, stakes and poles. I liked sharing the weight and gear. If we got separated, both of us would have a makeshift shelter. When together, we have a sweet little love nest.

On the Colorado Trail and CDT Montana section, we took a Tacoma for Two.

When we were on the AT-Vermont leg, we had The Coleman for Two. It was a little narrow, but warm.

For some reason, Rainmaker wanted separate tents for this trail. I wasn't happy about it. I was hurt and bewildered, but whatever. I'd learned from the moment I moved in with him, he always got his way. Disagreeing only meant lots of apologies later. I packed my new Eureka. He took the Arapaho that I'd made for him a couple years back.

I'd done this trail four years previous just after Katrina struck in 2005. Other than tons of trail steps used to construct the winding, vertically undulating trail, I loved it. I visualized the trail and remembered crossing many designated scenic rivers on a trail with plenty of water right from the start. It also has great mountain scenery and sees very little foot traffic.

Parking is easy to find, if not somewhat unsafe, in numerous pull outs. As the economy continued its downward spiral in 2009, more cars were being broken into near trailheads. We decided to utilize the few lots under surveillance for our adventure.

Early one morning we drove to Table Rock State Park. The rangers required us to fill out an anticipated end date and leave it in the car which we could leave in the big parking lot. If we didn't return in time, they'd come looking. I've never been threatened with a search and rescue before. Rainmaker and I both knew we would get out on time to avoid the rescue teams and subsequent charges.

After parking my car and making sure it was locked, we drove to Bad Creek Access. You have to go through a gate to get to that parking lot, a steel gate which is locked at 6 p.m. each evening. The parking lot is enormous. Many people like to park there and day hike to the tallest waterfall in South Carolina, the magnificent Whitewater Falls. Those who don't want to hike, choose to see these falls by driving right into an overlooking parking lot straight from the highway.

From the Bad Creek Access parking lot we hiked 2.6 miles, crossing a wide river with people already camping nearby. They invited us to join them but it was too early so we pushed on through pleasant trails with thick foliage.

Back in 2005 I had noticed a lot of hog damage in this area. I had been nervous about setting up in an open area, figuring more hogs could come scavenging while I slept, alone and unarmed. Eventually I had arrived at a flat area which appeared relatively clean and undisturbed. With me were some moth balls I had carried to use as bear deterrents. I set those out at both ends of the trail and pitched my tent back in the bushes. It was an uneventful night and I filed that away for future reference.

This was the campsite I had in mind for Rainmaker and me. There was plenty of room for two tents pitched far enough apart to give each other personal space. We'd known each other 9 years, and hiked thousands of miles together. Couples go through this, I told myself over and over. I cooked silently far enough from his special tree so we didn't have to interact and wondered why I was even there. I should have just helped him with his shuttle and returned home.

My online excuse: I was gear testing. What I really felt was that our relationship was at an all-time low. There are usually at least three versions of every couple's story: his, hers, and reality.

From Rainmakers Online Journal: After the scary incident with the people in the Ford 4WD in the middle of the night, I was glad to see the sun come up. Carol and I were out of our tents at first light, and talked about what had happened the previous night. She had made the correct decision to stay in her tent during the ordeal, thereby not letting the folks in the truck know that there was a woman in the other tent. For all they knew, our group consisted of several men. I'm not convinced that they had been looking for a dog. They may have been there to harass and rob us (or worse), then changed their minds. I suppose we'll never know for sure.

From My Online Journal: We hiked a leisurely 6 miles, camping at Bear Creek Camp. No signs of hog damage that I noted in 2005. Another group was camped up a ways, and we spent a pleasant evening relaxing in camp, and then went to sleep in our separate tents.

Suddenly I was awakened in the middle of the night by a roaring engine, bright lights and voices. I wondered how a vehicle could access the area and was glad I was surrounded by trees. I sat up, alone in my tent, to await events. I heard Rainmaker's low voice, some more exchanges, but could not distinguish words. Hoping it was a ranger, I looked at my watch. One a.m. Finally, after what seemed an eternity of racing heart and pulse, the vehicle turned around and left. All was quiet. I cautiously unzipped my tent, walked over to Rainmaker's tent, and called to him, "What was that all about?" He replied, "They said please don't shoot, cause they were unarmed. They were looking for their dog and asked if I wanted a beer."

Behind the Scenes What Really Happened

I set my tent up across the campground from Rainmaker. He wanted his own tent for this trail. Fine, I thought, and I'll give him plenty of space besides. We cooked separately, always have. From the first time he met me he wanted this rule of cooking separately. He'd seen too many couples fighting on the AT over food. Whatever, I didn't care. It was easier to cook for myself than worry about cooking for both of us.

Not only was I gear testing my new Eureka solo winter tent (double wall, 1.9 silnylon) I was testing the viability of the hobo backpacking stove. This stove was made from a large juice can and allows one to maintain a small campfire inside it, utilizing twigs, pinecones and bits of wood. It was messier but sustainable. At 4 ounces, it replaced the windscreen, pot support and stove of other backpacking systems.

I made two videos: How to make the Hobo Backpacker's Stove, and Gear Testing the Backpackers Hobo Stove. You can watch them on my channel at YouTube: Brawny03.

We finished our suppers, washed our dishes and maintained a friendly atmosphere. After dark we crawled in our tents and went to bed.

Suddenly I was awakened by bright lights and a roaring engine. Totally bewildered, I peeked out the tent and saw a big truck pulling in and swinging around. I was terrified. I wondered if that truck would run me over or if big burly guys would jump out and come see who was in the little tent under the trees. They swung around, pulled up near Rainmaker's tent and left the truck idling. Maybe it was a ranger, but how did they get back here? I thought the campsite was inaccessible. Next morning I would discover that an old logging road came within a hundred yards of the place. No doubt hunters camped there in the fall. I didn't recall noticing that old road in 2005. If I did, I chalked it up to one of many defunct roads that had been blocked off when the trail was built.

Whatever the men were saying to each other, I knew Rainmaker was in his tent, alone, with a flare gun and probably wishing he had something a little heavier. I checked my watch, it's after 1 a.m.

I pulled out my razor knife, figuring if there was a fight, I'd need to run into the woods. I realized I could very well be the only female here and I didn't like it one bit. Of course, had we been in the same tent, I would have known they were asking about a stray dog and offering beer. I would be waiting next to my partner, waiting for a clue of what to do. I felt if we were in the tent together, Rainmaker would be coaching me on whether to sit tight or flee.

But, sitting up, alone in my tent, ready to slice it open and flee out the back if things turned ugly, I realized the truck people had no idea who was in this little tent. It could even be a couple with guns. I figured it was best for me not to say a thing and just stay put. It was best for me to still my beating heart, breathe slowly and be prepared for action.

Finally, the truck backs up, pulls up to my tent and swings around. They leave. I wait. I have no clue what just went down. Were they looking for someone?

I wait. Several minutes passed. Still nothing. I actually expected Rainmaker to walk over and tell me all was fine and see if I was ok. I continued waiting. Years ago, when we first met, he would have been worried about how terrified I was. Reluctantly, I unzip the tent and walk across the site in the dark, find his tent and ask. He gave it to me short and sweet. Nothing. They were looking for their dog.

Next morning he says it crossed his mind to leave his tent and head for safety, but he couldn't, not with me there. He realized he couldn't just leave me and I felt a silent accusation from him. He was at jeopardy because of me.

This was another step in a long turning point in our relationship. Like a great vortex, its hard to reverse the whirlpool. I began asking myself what I was doing there. We weren't married and never would be. Why was I struggling to make this work?

Sometimes I read long distance trail journals online. Suddenly couples no longer refer to each other. One has gone home. They've split up. These things happen, and it's heart wrenching.

Note: Rainmaker and I worked it out for a little while. Still I left for the summer and spent 5 months cooking in Yellowstone National Park. The next summer I cooked in Zion, the following in the Tetons. Subsequently we split for good, realizing the love was gone.

Who Took The Lake?

But, back to the Foothill Trail Stories.

Next, we approached the Toxaway River and Canebrake Boat Access. I glanced around, puzzled. Where was the Lake? Last time I was here boaters were enjoying Labor Day weekend, even going up beneath the legendary 225 foot bridge across the river! This time, four years later, all was a mass of tall grass. Until we neared the enormous bridge, the river's flow could not even be seen. The campground was deserted. It seemed like a completely different location.

We continued onward, alone with our own thoughts. After hiking over the ridge we camped at Rock Creek. That night it began to rain.

I ate a cold breakfast and packed up in the rain. My new tent served quite well. It's a little trickier packing up a double wall tent with separate shock corded poles, but it went well. I learned how to quickly drop the tent while leaving the fly on top. Then I'd place all the poles at one end of the fabric and roll it while standing up, letting as much rain drip off it as possible. This works well for any wet tent.

We hiked through the Laurels Falls area crossing more than 15 substantial bridges as it winds back and forth over the river. Several wooden steps were missing on the ascent to Virginia Falls which made that trail dangerous and slippery in the rain.

Test of the Hobo Stove

We camped on a knoll 2 miles south of Sassafras Mountain, the highest point in South Carolina. I managed to cook and set up my tent during a brief respite in the drizzle using dry branches from a standing pine tree. I was pleased with the hobo backpacking system. With a combination of cold foods and this stove system an AT hiker would not have to worry about buying fuel along the trail. I realized, though, the PCT was way too dry and susceptible to wild fires to adopt this system.

We woke once again to a steady rain. I opted for a cold breakfast because I didn't feel like dealing with an actual fire building scenario. This stove system doesn't lend itself to any sort of vestibule cooking. I actually had a dangerous flare up while attempting to use a hexamine tablet and raced to smother the flames before it set my vestibule on fire.

Silently we packed up in the rain and began the dreary climb up Sassafras Mountain. Then we checked out the old homestead site and continued onward. The rain finally quit and the sun peeked out. Descending the mountain, we joined the yellow blazed Foothills/Pinnacle Trail and noted the reroute. No longer does the Foothills Trail pass Mill Creek Falls. Instead, a side hill trail winds around for a couple extra miles.

If you have an old trail guide, be aware that this has changed as well. Finally, we intersected the Carrick Creek trail and once again got to hike the old, unfortunately eroded Foothills/Pinnacle Trail. This beautiful portion brings you past natural waterslides and waterfalls.

There was nothing so sweet as seeing my own car parked and waiting undamaged at the trailhead. However, we were too late to pick up Rainmaker's car that evening. We went home and in the morning, headed back to Bad Creek Trailhead to get his.

9. Vermont Trail

Rainmaker's Skills

Rainmaker and I hiked the first 100 miles together in 2002. I was on the AT heading to Katahdin. He had thru hiked the AT in 1992. We joined up for this section, using a double wall tent, mailing our separate, solo tents to Killington, about 1.5 miles down from the Inn at the Long Trail.

Hiking this section as a northbound AT thru hiker, it seemed pretty easy. I didn't remember it as strenuous. I remembered it as growing wilder than the previous 1500 miles and really enjoyed the thick canopy and narrow rugged trail. It almost seemed like Oregon.

Rainmaker and I had enjoyed a night at the Inn. We resupplied at the store in Killington and carried cell phones for the first time ever on a trail. Once we headed to our own trails, I would call him from my town stops, leave him a voice mail, listen to mine and plan for our reunion. When he finished at the Canadian Border he would make his way back to my car parked at Cobweb's house, (my friend from the PCT hike) and find me somewhere along the AT. Then, he'd hole up until I finished at Katahdin and we'd head home together. That was the plan, anyways.

Rainmaker is an expert at finding his way from one remote location to another. Once he was backpacking solo in the Alps, got snowed in for three days and read Steven King novels by candle light. Periodically he told me he would leave the tent to brush the snowfall off his shelter, then go back in again. During those long nights, he'd hear avalanches.

When the weather cleared, he hiked down out of those mountains, found his way to an obscure village and then back to a train depot. He made it back to the United States, five years before we ever met.

Inn at the Long Trail. Rainmaker and I took different routes north from here. He finished the Vermont Trail and I finished the Appalachian Trail in 2002.

So when I took a notion in 2007 to go do the entire Vermont Trail, I sort of took it lightly. That's when perception totally messed up my reality.

Early in July I found myself in New York City all alone and waiting for my connecting ride to Williamsburg, Massachusetts. From there I'd hitch a ride to the southern access trail for the Vermont Trail. The border is actually up a few miles. One begins the Vermont trail by hiking up the AT, which shares the same tread-way for the next 100 miles.

I looked like a total disaster and felt like one too, after having spent the last 18 hours on the greyhound bus. What a confusion. I looked for the line to wait for the Bonanza bus. The service people were rude. No one knew anything. No one wanted to help. Why ask any one standing around in a uniform? Tired and frustrated, walking around with my backpack, I figured I would just show up at 10 a.m. and somehow get on the right bus. I was looking forward to being in the woods again and off on a manageable adventure. Just take one step at a time, I kept telling myself. Anything more is way too overwhelming. It was 6 a.m. and I had four hours to kill. I was a white woman alone being approached by various black males asking for spare change. I was rude as well. I'd shoot them a dirty look and ask, "You're asking me for money?"

At last I caught the 10:00 bus and met a nice older gentleman. We chatted and when he found out my destination, he offered me a ride to the trail head from his mom who would be meeting him in Williamsburg. I gladly accepted.

We're facebook friends now. He still lives on a houseboat on the Hudson River, in Manhattan. He fed me cheese and bread and handed me a non-alcoholic beer.

When Reality Sucks

Every morning, as is my custom, I rose with the sun, packed quickly and headed out. Two southbounders were leaving the camping area as well, waving as they passed silently. The guy in the shelter and his dog were awake. Two college kids and their dog had tarped behind the shelter and were still asleep. I noted the flat roofed configuration using a blue Wal-Mart poly tarp. Not ultralight, but these guys are strong and can carry anything.

When I hiked past the Congdon Shelter, I saw that 4 people were just getting ready to head out. It was nearly 10 a.m. It seemed late to me, but I know we all have our rhythms. Then I crossed a road and met a guy in pickup truck. He had food and sodas and was enticing hikers to stay and chat. I enjoyed some brownies and a soda, chatted awhile and continued on to Goddard Shelter, doing a 21.2 mile day.

It continued to storm daily, so I planned to sleep in one of many new, clean wonderful shelters built by the Green Mountain Club. After 19.4 miles, I arrived at the Stratton Pond Shelter. The caretaker collected $5 from each of us. One guy claimed to have "run" here from Route 2 this morning doing 48 miles. Yeah, right. He's not even muddy, in spite of the last hours of drenching rain. No one believed him but no one wanted to argue, either.

As always, I was testing something. This time I had fancy prepackaged trail food to evaluate, a cook- in- the-bag product a gear company sent me. It reminded me of the survival food dehydrated disaster I began my AT thru hike with. I feared it would be way too spicy for me, inadequate and time consuming. Each night I tried something different, but I found I missed my simple oatmeal and ramen. Several nights later, I traded a package of this gourmet trail stuff for a package of simple ramen noodles.

My pack had enough food to get me all the way to Killington at Route 4, nearly 100 miles away so I can avoid a hitching into Manchester. I know some hikers don't mind hitchhiking and look forward to town days. Hitching alone has never been my first plan. I will make sacrifices to avoid it, having been in close proximity to drivers who make suggestive remarks and talk about murdered females all along the way.

I waved goodbye to my friends hitching into town, then crossed the Highway, hiking on to Bromley Shelter. A while later I arrived and discovered it was another new beautiful structure. There I met five teenagers and two

189

counselors from Maine who were doing the Long Trail in five weeks. Others pull in, get water and push on, while some plan to stay the night. They filled us in with news from town. We enjoyed a night of laugher with the youth out on their first great adventure.

It stormed again that night and nothing dries out. The trail was muddy and slick. My feet are blistering from the metatarsal pads the doctor said would ease my debilitating foot pain. I later learned stretching would do much more good after self-diagnosing the plantar fasciitis and tight heel tendons afflicting me.

The Big Branch Shelter was really scenic. While sleeping in the shelter, we could look out at the magnificent river. We arrived early enough to swim, rinse out trail clothes and play along the shore.

A large plastic box filled with cookies and candy was here inside the shelter. Trail magic once again. I look inside, chose some oreos and lean against the shelter wall, removing my socks and shoes to let my feel dry out. I was dealing with deep blisters on the bottom of both feet and in between my toes. This was so unusual for me. I never got blisters.

After putting on my flip flops, I hobbled to the river and washed out my smart wool socks while considering all the mud and continual wetness. It was a little depressing not having any ready solutions in mind. I'd also been dealing with sharp recurring pains in my feet, reminders of past trail injuries I thought were under control. I stretched frequently that evening and removed the offending metatarsal pads. My knees were complaining but that was manageable by using Rainmaker's proven techniques of leaning upon the hiking poles on the downhill and taking shorter steps on the uphill.

But, bottom line I just was not feeling it, not feeling the magic of the trail, nor feeling the lure of the northern terminus. I asked myself repeatedly, "What is missing this year on this trail?"

It wasn't the people. I was camping with cool people. That night there were 4 AT thru hikers in the shelter and a young woman who broke her leg last year on the Long Trail. She was back at it this year, trying again to backpack the entire trail. She knew lots of important details, and updated us on the fact that the store we were counting on in Jonesville was closed. This meant a hitch into Watesfield. Or, a person could stock a drop box and mail it from Killington to the new post office in Jonesville.

I decided to figure it out while hiking tomorrow and took several ibuprofen, climbed into my sleeping bag and closed my eyes. I shut out the worries, or I thought I did, but still I couldn't sleep. Outside the storms rage. I remembered the young man tarping behind us. His structure seemed vulnerable. It's two a.m. and I asked the man next to me to scoot over just in case the young man and his dog decide to jump in to the shelter to join us.

We drifted back to sleep. Half an hour later, the woman a few bodies down starts yelling. A large animal had entered the shelter and it was licking her face. Someone grabbed a flashlight and aimed it at her. Thank god it was the dog and not a bear. The dog finally settled down when his master joined us. We wondered how the guy who pitched his tent on a large rock in the middle of the river was faring.

Bailing

In the morning, two men hiked out ahead of me. The young man with his dog had a buddy bail last week because of bad knee injuries. Rumors said he was seriously considering calling it good enough and going home. I hurried, packed up and caught the guy who was hiking Vermont in 20 mile segments. He told me about his aching feet and possibly leaving the trail, too. I realized the three of us were thinking the same things. He stopped to swim in a pond but I pressed on.

My foot pain increased and I had a splitting headache. I could have suffered through it, but it occurred to me I just didn't want the Long Trail enough to work through the pain and loneliness and I know that where ever I get off this trail, a major route finding and dreadful hitchhiking awaits me to reconnect with the bus lines to get back home. These damaging thoughts plagued me for miles as I anticipated more rain and more sleepless nights. Somehow I couldn't stop the fateful negative thoughts. My mantra "my pack will get lighter and I will get stronger" had deserted me.

I caught up to the young man and his dog. He told me he'd gotten a signal on his cell phone and called his friends who were coming to get him within the hour. Eagerly I jumped at the chance and spontaneously asked, "Can I get a ride from you to a bus connection?"

"Sure, no problem, I totally understand," he replied. The die was cast. I was on my way home. That's how fast a bail can happen. I have some regrets now, here, in the comfort of home, at my desk. My partner supported my decision and said I made the right choice. But the decision plagued me. I was a failure. I had to let it go.

I spent a night in Rutland, caught a bus that took me to White River Junction and the connection to NYC. I got to the terminal plenty early, started to sketch and write while sitting on the curb, waiting outside like other passengers. I pondered how I ended up here and why I quit so soon. I wrote my conclusions:

We forget the pain, that's why we keep going back for more. We remember the joy, the power, and in our finite world we think it actually matters to someone besides ourselves. But, in the end you find no one wins and the race was only with yourself.

I know what it's like to finish, to slack off, to be broke and be successful. And now I know what it feels like to bail. Ouch. Bailing hurts.

We all must fail, if not just for the humility it brings, then to know you have pressed the limits.

Thirty- two hours of southbound travel via Greyhound Bus lines and I am met by Rainmaker in Anderson, SC. While it was good to be home, I knew I would deal with the deep sense of failure for a long time.

Object Lesson: Never quit in the rain.

Moral of the Story: You talk your feet into hurting. They really did, but quitting a trail really sucks big time.

And a last thought, leaving a trail before you are truly ready can haunt you for years to come.

10. My Ultralight Gear List Evolution
Ultralight Philosophy
"Out of clutter, find simplicity, from discord, find harmony. In the middle of difficulty lies Opportunity"--**Albert Einstein's Three Rules of Work**

I love this quote. It summarizes my philosophy for life and ultralight backpacking. I take what I want to enjoy the journey yet strive for the lightest, most basic gear with all components fitting into a harmonious system. Over the years and thousands of trail miles, my needs and wants have been redefined or eliminated, making an incredibly low pack weight possible. In this ever learning, ongoing process, any difficulty in the journey brings opportunity and an amazing confidence born of hardship without luxury.

An ultralight attitude can be developed over a period of time. Henry David Thoreau said "How many a poor immortal soul have I met well-nigh crushed and smothered under its load, creeping down the road of life, pushing before it a barn seventy-five feet by forty, its Augean stables never cleansed, and one hundred acres of land, tillage, mowing, pasture, and wood-lot! The portion-less, who struggle with no such unnecessary inherited encumbrances, find it labor enough to subdue and cultivate a few cubic feet of flesh."

My takeaway from this quote is to not carry anything too big. It just drags us down. We want enough, but just enough. Less material goods does not indicate poverty but the power of personal restraint, a very satisfying concept and lifestyle. Embracing this philosophy may require an adjustment of attitude for most Americans, brought up to believe that two chickens are needed in every pot, two cars belong in every garage and a home with one full bathroom is substandard.

This ultralight concept does not refer to financial resources or money in the bank. A wise man once said, "Most emergencies can be solved with the proper application of a Master or Visa Card." Instead of pushing stuff through life, I prefer to live lightly with back up funds kept safe and accessible.

A self-sufficient ultralighter shows personal power. They do not borrow gear, food, water, fuel or guide pages from others. I will not advocate that anyone go to a trail ill equipped or unprepared because they want to eliminate extra pack weight, figuring they will come across some good Samaritan or trail magic to bail them out. An ultralighter's goal is to have all the essentials or learn how to improvise until they get it.

In some areas, a person may not meet another hiker for days or even weeks. Also, it is not fair to put others at risk, obligation or inconvenience because of our lack of planning. At times, ultralighters have been disparaged as "moochers". I feel duty bound to help shake that image by never borrowing or accepting anything, except for rare trail magic.

In real terms it means that as a petite woman, I carry clothes that fit me. Nothing is baggy, too large or too long. All can be layered harmoniously for maximum warmth. It means keeping body weight down, which has a double impact. By staying lean, not only do I feel better and can climb hills easily, but the volume and weight of my pack is reduced because of smaller clothes and sleep systems. My shelter is a minimalist. It is a single wall silnylon structure, just large enough to sit up in, and sleep.

I analyze each gear item, both for weight and volume, replacing them with newfound substitutes. For instance, my only knife, a 5 gram cutting tool found at office supply stores, has worked well for over 5, 000 miles. The food is adequate and simple, requiring minimal cooking time with less fuel on an alcohol stove. I utilize town stops by eating a lot of extra calories and carry about a pound of food per day on the trail. I take advantage of natural daylight, to cook, clean, write or read. I avoid doing anything that requires batteries. The two exceptions are a waterproof watch, and photon LED light. Both still have the same battery after 5, 500 miles. I use well-made gear that can be repaired with superglue, electrical tape or needle and dental floss.

Ultralight living and backpacking are natural for me. I have never been a collector of material goods. Instead, curiosity and love of personal challenges cause me to try all sorts of new ideas, and I collect experiences.

Sometimes there's a lot of discomfort in these adventures. I concede the failures and recognize each success, however marginal. This firsthand knowledge is applied to future escapades. Some of the techniques I learned hiking the Pacific Crest Trail did not apply to the Appalachian Trail nor the Colorado Trail.

Researching trail conditions always helps in making appropriate gear choices and resupply plans. I believe in carrying trail data and developing a strong understanding of the trail you're on, especially if it's a long hike. The most important piece of gear a backpacker has is his or her brain. The knowledge you carry in your head can save you many pounds of pack weight, prevent miles of missed trail and wrong turns, give you options and back up plans, and the confidence to press preconceived, and often erroneous, limits.

True Cost and Sleeping Bag Issues
Rainmaker told me that a long distance backpacker would spend $100 to save an ounce. I thought that was preposterous. Later I found out if you could get

by that cheap, you were doing good. On the AT I dropped $269 dollars in Damascus at the outfitters to buy an 800 Powerfill goose down bag. I have it still. It saved me 16 ounces over my cat's meow. But it wasn't that simple. I couldn't just buy a new bag and send the old one home.

My friend had a brand new 20 degree Cat's Meow that she wanted to trade me for a 10 x 12 ultralight tarp. Sure, I said, I'll trade you, good deal. Sleeping bags were running over 100 bucks and I had 8 yards of gray silnylon to spare. So, I made the tarp, got the sleeping bag and modified it. I thought it was way too wide and too long for me. A bag that is over sized is hard to warm up. There were too many extra ounces to haul around. And as I soon found out, it was way too bulky for a serious ultralight backpack.

So this Cat's Meow was narrowed and shortened and test driven one cold February when temps wished they could sneak up to 17 degrees. It had snowed all night while I was camping at Plum Orchard Gap Shelter in my single wall tent. I was gear testing my systems before heading out for my AT thru hike, scheduled to begin mid-March.

I slept warm and decided this was a fine bag to start the trail, even though it was a bit bulky. Once I got farther north and things warmed up a bit, I planned to swap out for a fleece bag and liner. What in the world was I thinking? Just 2 days shy of Damascus I froze my butt off twice, curling up in a ball, wearing everything I had and waking first light so I could pack up, get moving and thaw out.

I had already sent the Cat's Meow home and this was not sustainable. The mountains were still cold and fronts came in often, delivering ice and snow into May. Hikers argued about down and synthetic. Down is so light but very expensive. It packs down to the size of a baseball. But get it wet? Shit, you might as well have cotton.

On the other hand, synthetic is bulky and it's really hard to buy something my size. I used a youth bag on the PCT, but out grew that, not in size but mentally. A woman's got to have a decent sleeping bag. We sleep cold and we need our rest.

Then it finally dawned on me that in all my wilderness experiences, having gone through record rains on the PCT, I had never gotten my bag wet. Why couldn't I get a serious down bag? I could manage to keep it dry, I was sure of it. Hence, I spent the 269 bucks. It was the best money dropped on gear in my whole career. When I arrived in Damascus, I pulled out the Credit card and selected the 30 Degree Marmot bag. I've been a believer ever since.

My sleeping bag originally was a man's bag and 6 foot long. To solve the frozen foot dilemma, I shortened it. This is an easy procedure. Simply lay the bag flat, right side out. At the very bottom, punch in the foot bed so it goes up inside the bag, sort of like starting to turn it inside out, until it is the correct length.

Then, pull the bag smooth and stitch across the new bottom with dental floss. This holds the extra fabric and insulation up on the inside, giving you a toasty little foot nest.

After lots of bag nights, any sleeping bag looses its loft. The insulation will absorb body oils and dust and might have a beverage or supper spilled on it. One guy peed on his, by accident. He figured a zip lock baggie would be a very cool pee bottle. It collected fine, it just didn't stay sealed. Not fun. Guys, go out and pee like we do, or use a gatoraide bottle . Sheesh. Where was I?

Two years ago I washed my down bag in light dishwashing detergent and dried it in a dryer set on delicate. It took a long time but bottom line my Marmot is completely restored to its full loft and beauty. Best piece of gear I ever bought.

Using an actual trail trowel is a total luxury. I normally just use my hiking poles, find lose ground and excavate 6 inches. The best place is next to a pine tree. Lots of pine needles drop near the trunk, plus a person can use the trunk for privacy and steady hands. I've never seen a vine creeping up a pine tree. Such vines, found in deciduous forests are probably poison ivy. Never lean against that. Even your clothes can become contaminated, causing outbreaks later. I know these things from experience.

If you have a shelter which requires using your hiking poles, digging a cat hole after dark is more interesting. I had my trowel cut down to a more packable size, thereby eliminating volume as well as weight. The hole is drilled to facilitate hanging from the pack. I like mine tucked into a pocket. Actually, I don't carry one anymore.

Evolution of the Gear List

I created this gear list for the online community. I'm always messing with it, although some things are tried and true. For instance, I always carry a small Cook Set, and that Cook Set is always in an outside pocket or near the top of the pack and easily accessible.

Keep the Cook Set at Hand

After killing my knees on the first 30 miles of the Appalachian Trail, I limped into Neel's Gap and called home. I was embarrassed. How could I have failed so soon? Rainmaker knew I was dealing with a lot of pain. It took him about 20 seconds to have the answer. Hiking in sandals was not working for me. Go back to what works, he advised then added, I'll be there in an hour or two to get you.

I pulled out the Cook Set and sat near the steps at Neel' Gap. I had instant coffee in a little baggie, my fuel bottle and water bottle. Nothing else mattered right then as I waited for a ride home. I wasn't quitting the trail. Just regrouping.

Another thru hiker crossed the road, heading towards me. He watched me fire up the little soda can stove, pour water into the pint aluminum pot and set it on the flame. "How's it going?" he asks.

"Not so good," I said, "I've got to take a little time to recoup and get some trail runners."

"My knees are trashed," he confided. "I'm calling my girlfriend, and taking two weeks off. Then I'll be back." He was a young man and strong. I felt a little better. You have to really want it. If you can stand the pain you can keep going. If you can't, something's got to change.

I had watched friends on the Pacific Crest Trail come to water and pull out their cook stoves. They never bothered to cook unless they were at water. Made sense to me. I like to watch people. Sometimes they'll come up with genius solutions I would never have thought of.
Cooking at a water source, especially in the evening, allows a person to totally rehydrate over the course of an hour, wash the dish, wash the feet, brush teeth and wash the face. Then, the person can hike a little farther and all those animal attractants are left behind at the water source.

Leave no trace principles always apply. Don't dump crap into the water. Broadcast any quantifiable food scraps or dig a hole and bury it. As an ultralighter, I put clean water into the pot, scrub with my index finger and drink it.

One day, Rainmaker and I had hiked all morning in the cold rain. We were doing different trails. He was on the Vermont Trail. I was doing my AT thru hike. We took advantage of the fact they share the same path for 100 miles and spent a week together. We crossed the road, hiked another mile and saw the sign for the shelter. "Let's take a break, make some coffee and eat lunch," he suggested. This is really easy with the cook set in the side pocket and lunch separated from the main food bag each morning. All these little methods make a long trail enjoyable.

Electronics and Batteries

We live in a power filled life, everything from entertainment to lighting to food preparations. Cameras and headlamps, GPS units, cell phones and watches are all things a backpacker might want at some level.

For the ultralighter, the question is how am I going to keep it running? When the batteries die, it's just dead weight.

Just north of Damascus I pulled into the shelter. Five thru hikers were already there. Damascus is 468 miles up the trail and a great place to reprovision or hang at the House, a three story free "hostel" maintained by a local church. It's got a post office so hikers can send stuff home or get stuff shipped. By this time, most have been on the trail a month and they have definite ideas of what they wished they had or could definitely do without. Many will drop serious money at the Outfitter's store.

This dude got his full sized CD player and full headphones sent. It looked weird seeing huge headphones like that but whatever. Each must hike their own hike. He said he did a lot of solo hiking and couldn't take the introspection anymore.

I understand that. I've sung songs, played mind games and practiced math formulas. A hiker can zone out, going mindless with the proper self-discipline. I finally called home and asked for ideas. Rainmaker said he'd send my ultralight radio to Delaware Water Gap. "It only weighs 5 ounces," Rainmaker explained, "And you'll enjoy it. One AA battery will last you between resupplies." I'll try anything once.

Heading into New Jersey, a black-bears-gone-wild territory, I wore just one half of the ear buds, figuring I've got to hear the rattle of snakes and the brush breaking with bears wandering close by.

Of course it would start raining. I tucked my radio under my rain jacket, inside a zip lock bag and hiked on. Some local stations came in, others faded. I landed on a Chocolate Milk Challenge. This sounded very interesting. While following white blazes, I listened intently as the DJ outlined the concept, saying "No one can drink a whole gallon of chocolate milk." This was an interesting thought. Could a stomach hold that much fluid?

Well, it's not just the fluid. 128 ounces of fat and sugar can make a normal stomach rebel. That was the guy's point. I decided to stay tuned in to find out.

"Keep going," one animated DJ encouraged the contestant. A female voice chimed in, cheerleading with enthusiasm, "You're half way, keep going."

"He's turning green," another guy said excitedly. "Get the garbage can!"

"Don't think about it man, you're almost there," the first DJ warned. White blazes streamed by. I was mesmerized as the Milk Battle raged.

"Look out!" the woman cried out, obviously alarmed. "Hold it, hold it for him."

Suddenly violent retching erupted and then a soft chuckling sounded over the air waves. "Man, you almost had it, you almost did." Back slapping followed and I switched to some music before I lost my cookies.

I love the head lamp. You really feel visible and comfortable in the neighborhood but it's much heavier than a solar powered LED. I take mine locally. This ultralighter uses daylight to read, write in the journal, do supper and wash the dish.

Interestingly, four guys with head lamps will attempt night hikes. If you wait for a full moon, a night hike is pretty easy unless the trail is sketchy. If there's any danger of missing your turn off, forget it. Guys are strong and a little extra weight to them is worth the luxury. I maintain my minimalist approach and observe.

Creative ultralighter Fanny Pack taped two White LED lights to the brim of his baseball cap. When he wanted light, he flipped them on. That works. I got a couple lights with no permanent **on** switches. I can't get them to stay on no matter how much tape I put on them.   LED lights last forever. A person never has to get stingy with the lighting situation. I've since discovered solar powered LED lights. They are fantastic if you don't step on them. I own two.

Make the 9 Ounce Pack- Specs

The pack measures 22 x 8 x 13 inches, and has a capacity of 2,288 cubic inches with 5 pockets: one on the top cover flap, and 4 external that are 9 x 10 inches each. Overlapping flaps and Velcro closures keep the gear from sliding out.

There is a draw cord closure. A closed cell pad rolled up lengthwise and placed inside like a cylinder and then allowed to expand, gives the pack its shape. This pack is shown on page 78 of this book. As you can see, it will stand unaided if packed in this manner.

A 3 inch wide hip belt is sewn in with webbing reinforcement. It is ½ inch thick. Even for the serious ultralighter, hip belts have been proven both useful and necessary during long sections between resupply. My external frame carries heavy loads extremely well because of its hip belt and suspension. When I designed the 9 ounce pack, I created suspension via hip belt and structure.

I found if the food bag was placed in first, the silnylon hip belt didn't ride up.
A hiker buddy did 38-mile days and carried out nearly 20 pounds of food from town. With 9 pounds of gear and additional water weight, an ultralight pack can top 32 pounds in real life situations. His solution to the no-hip-belt

dilemma was to buy a fanny pack, stuff it completely full and use it as a ledge to rest the weight from his loaded pack.

Shoulder straps were made also from silnylon with closed cell padding inserted. They might appear to be overkill in this photo, measuring 3 inches wide and ½ inch thick. Thin straps cut into shoulders over the long haul. You'll find yourself stuffing clothing under skimpy straps. If you're making a pack, spread the impact over a larger area.

20 ounce capacity water bottles can be carried on the front straps utilizing a shock cord band, a trick I learned from Just Eric on the PCT. This easy access and counterbalance for pack weight makes picking up water at stream crossings simple. I carry a tiny bottle of chlorine for water purification in a side pocket.

Friends would watch me stoop and grab water while they sat and pumped through a filter. Next town stop, they would ditch their filters, locate a hiker box and pillage for empty plastic bottles. They would take that little bottle with them when they went out to eat and ask the waitress to fill it with chlorine. All food establishments use chlorine in the back of house. Ask and they'll help you out. Many motels have chlorine. I'd watch that just in case the person got confused and filled the bottle with something toxic.

A Few technical aspects of the pack's construction follows:

This pack was made totally out of silnylon and my design is based on the principle of one bag set within another. The bottoms of those concentric bags were then sewn together along the bottom seam and then up the sides forming the pockets.

The beauty of this construction is that the pack has a double thickness of fabric at the bottom. A cover flap for each pocket was incorporated by using length of the inner bag. My Colorado Pack was made with a single layer of silnylon and mesh pockets sewn on for gear. This let the gear dry as I hiked. The bottom will last for at least 500 miles of trail. The Appalachian Trail is 2,172 miles so I figured this pack needed a double thickness.

Start by making two large stuff sacks, one shorter than the other, for the main body of the pack. To determine cubic inches, multiply the height by the width times the depth. 2,500 to 3,000 cubic inches is large enough for most ultralighters.

Sew in various loops as you go, especially at the bottom seam of the outer bag. Sometimes a person might need to cinch on an extra sack or clip on sandals. All of my AT gear fit inside this pack, even for cold weather. The extension collar / cover flap allows extra clothing to be placed on top.

This pack was durable enough to last the entire AT thru hike in 2002. Weighing only 9 ounces, a custom silnylon pack is remarkably strong and easily repaired trailside.

To repair silnylon, use free flowing super glue, sealing the threads so they won't pull loose. Then thread a needle with dental floss and use the over hand stitch.

The Gear List

The following list is intended to be very complete. Its main purpose is to help you not forget anything. My gear list for the Appalachian Trail is discussed in detail on my homepage hosted at Trailquest: http://www.trailquest.net/BRindex.html. I list my weights here for your convenience. If no weight is listed, it's because I didn't carry it on the trail. Some of the smaller kits were grouped together and weighed as a unit. At times various components where mailed ahead and my webpage also details the management of gear for the AT.

The Big Three, and their components-From the AT list
-Sleeping Bag with stuff sack (24 ounces)-30 Degree Marmot Down 800 Power Fill
-Sleeping Pad (8 ounces closed cell pad, trimmed) from Wal-Mart
-Shelter with stakes, and guy lines, in stuff sack (18 ounces) I made this myself. It was a Tacoma Solo Prototype
-Ground cloth, if desired
-Pack, pack liner (garbage bag liner) - 9 ounces
-Packcover (1.5 ounces)
Clothing
-Silnylon Rain jacket and rain pants (6 ounces-Gram Weenie)
-Warm layer (fleece top-12 ounces, pants-7 ounces, hat, gloves, socks)
-Mid weight layer (tights 3 ounces, silk top- 4 ounces, socks-1 ounce)
-Hiking layer (shorts- 4 ounces, top-3ounces, socks-1 ounces, hat-none)
-Sandals (1 ounce) Gram weenie
-Stuff sack for clothing (half an ounce)
-Sleep wear (silk shorts-2 ounces, and silk top-three ounces)
-Town wear (optional) (none taken here)

Hygiene/ Medical/Murphy (about 8 ounces)
-Tooth brush, tooth paste, dental floss
-Comb

-Ultralight mirror
-Tweezers for tick removal
-Disposable Razor, cause I still shave my pits
-Rubbing alcohol, cotton balls
-Toilet paper
-Trowel
-Hand sanitizer, I just use rubbing alcohol
-Body lotion or Vaseline, travelers size
-Camp towel/ bandana (one ounce)
-Pain reliever
-Imodium
-Multi-Vitamins- they absorb moisture, I dropped these
-Sunblock
-Insect Repellent
-Electrical or duct tape –wind around the water bottles
-Needle and thread
-Safety pins
-Free flowing super glue
-Any prescriptions you are taking
-Eye glasses, sun glasses
-Two or three ditty bags for all this

Cook System(7 ounces, but no pot lifter, or pot scrubber)
-Stove
-Fuel
-Matches, lighter
-Windscreen, pot support, pot lifter
-Cooking pot
-Cup, spoon
-Pot scrubber, if desired
-Plastic bags for repackaging food
-Zip lock bag for trash
-Stuff sack for pot and stove
-Stuff sack for food-make sure you have enough capacity for 100 miles of trail

Water Treatment and Capacity
-Chemical treatment (always bring) I use chlorine, simple household bleach
-Filter, if desired
-Water bottles (2 ounces) Soda Bottles work great

-Water bag/platypus (one ounce)
-Water bottle carriers, or pockets (included with my pack)

Other Items and Tools
-Paper and Pencil/Pen
-Hiking Pole(s), or hiking staff(2 Komperdels-18 ounces, not included as Pack weight)
-Driver's license, and /or photo ID
-Non-debit credit card , just in case you need to rent a car
-Emergency telephone numbers, insurance card
-Flash light/ LED /photon light (two photons,6 grams each)
-Knife (5 grams)
-GI can opener (4 grams, for town stops)
-Watch (16 grams-watchband cut off)
-Trail guide, maps, data sheet (data sheets only, with paper and pencil, 4 ounces)
-Compass, if needed or desired
-Cash
-Ditty bag as wallet (with cards and cash-1 ounce)
-Quality zip lock bags for all paper products
- Light cordage or rope for hanging shelters, guy lines, or food bags

Luxury Items (none taken except the camera)
-Cell Phone
-Radio, batteries
-Pocket E-mail
-Camera (digital, disposable, or regular) (disposable-4 ounces), now I would bring my digital
-CD player, disks
-Quality zip lock bag and ditty bag for any luxury item
-Knee braces, if needed or desired
-Reading Material, books, never take any myself
-Mace/ bear spray
-Bear Canister @ 2 pounds 11 ounces, serious weight

11. Other Stuff

The second half of *My Journey to Freedom and Ultralight Backpacking* is all about ultralight tips and making your own gear. I share suggestions for making good gear choices and how to do an ultralight resupply in town, buying as you go. It is available in digital format at Amazon.com or Barnes and Noble. You can get it printed on demand at Create Space.com.

Bear Canister Food List for 7 Days

How to fully utilize your bear canister

Many people have never actually used a bear canister. A Garcia bear canister weighs 2 pounds 11 ounces when empty and this accounts for the problem. Some National Parks require you use one and have them for rental. These canisters have a lid which is flush with the top and opened with a dime or similar object inserted into a slot then turned to open.

I tested mine for the first time on a short four day backpacking trip on the Bartram Trail in 2004. This preparation was for our upcoming hike in Glacier, the Bob Marshall Wilderness, the Scapegoat Wilderness and on downward to Helena; prime grizzly territory.

Glacier has bear boxes at designated campsites and there are several camp stores-restaurants when hiking along the CDT route. So, you actually can get by without a canister here. Always follow proper cooking/food storage procedures as outlined by the Park.

However, The Bob Marshall Wilderness has no resupply points. There were 110 miles of wilderness before we would see town food again. Given the difficulty of navigating the trail we decided to haul 7 days of food.

I don't ship food to post offices but eat what I can find in local grocery stores. My list reflects my preferences.
All of this food can be bought in a regular store. Most of it can be found or substituted in a small convenience store.

The main purpose of the list is to give you an idea of calories, protein and serving sizes, plus packing methods.

There are some unusual items, like corn meal. I think of grains as the beginning of a meal. Then I look for the form that cooks and tastes the best. Corn meal is much easier to find and cook on the trail than Corn Pasta.

As you may notice, there is no meat in this list. Bring jerky or cheese if you like. Being in grizzly country, I aim towards food with little or no odors and that cooks fast. Long simmering times would just add more smells to the area.

Food List: 7 days in Garcia Bear Canister

Item-	Amount/ weight Meal	Grams of Protein	Calories	Notes
Instant coffee	2 ounces	0	0	One cup at breakfast One cup at supper
Pop tarts	14 ounces 4 double packages, 4 breakfasts	16	1,600	Be sure to buy the frosted ones.
Oatmeal	20 ounces 3 breakfasts/ 4 suppers	44	1,600	French Toast flavor, instant
M&Ms plain	34 ounces, for lunch GORP, use as filler in canister	48	5,040	This is a lot of chocolate, can substitute nuts. Take hiking style and digestion into account.
Raisons	15 ounce box, use for lunch GORP, can add to oatmeal	11	1,430	Too sticky to use as filler.
Peanuts	13 ounces, use for lunch GORP, or add to ramen supper for interest	78	1,950	Can use as filler, may leave salty residue
Pretzels	13 ounces, use for lunch GORP	39	1,560	Can add bits to soup as appetizer
Ramen	12 ounces (4 packages) 2 suppers	32	1,600	chicken flavors Can be eaten raw, or solar cooked
Self-Rising Corn meal &parmesan	6.75 ounces 2 suppers	8	400	Make into a mush, bring bacon bits
Bouillon cubes	2.5 ounces, 6 cubes For suppers (or soup-flavoring)	12	180	Tomato flavor Knorr brand

Hard candy	9.5 ounces 49 pieces	0	882	Great for dry areas, sore throats 7 per day
Animal crackers	7 ounces - use for lunch GORP	14	840	Had the room, so I threw them in
Instant mashed potatoes	5.25 ounces	12	480	These can be added to thicken soup.
Totals	154 ounces 9.625 pounds food	314 grams of protein (44.85 per day) WHO recommends 40/adult	17,562 calories (2,508.85 per day)	This is 7 full days of food. It can be stretched to 9 by diluting and rationing, and fits into canister. Bring plastic bag for packing lunch each day. All packaging has been removed, and no garbage will accrue.

Nutritional Stats

-154 ounces, or 9.625 pounds, total weight
-314 protein, or 44.85 per day (World Health Organization recommends 40 per day for Adults)
-17,562 calories (2,508.85 per day)

I can stretch this amount of food to provide 9 days of meals by diluting and rationing. All of it fits into a standard Garcia bear canister.

The Method
First, remove all excess packaging and cardboard.
Using high quality Ziploc bags, repackage the oatmeal, raisins, ramen noodles.
 I bring a couple empty quart Ziplocs so that every morning I can pack my "lunch" out of this mass of goodies. I carry my lunch in a silnylon belt loop

pouch during the day. If it is not gone by supper, I use it for dessert.

The bear canister came with a heavy plastic bag liner. This is a great way to keep all the filler clean and hold down food smells. Keep this bag. Some hikers use rice as "filler". I use high calorie foods like nuts and M&Ms.

Place the poptarts, still in their wrappers but without the box, Ziploc bags of oatmeal, grains, and raisons into canister which is lined with a thick plastic bag. Bust up the ramen noodles to make a more condensed package, placing them in a Ziploc as well.

Place each bag of food inside the canister, forming tight layers.
Once you have all the packaged food items in the canister, pour the peanuts and M&Ms into it and shake so they fill in all the holes.

The grains make good trail items because they don't leave many gaps in the packing process. However, you'll find you can put a lot of calories in the canister by using nuts and candies as filler, and following this method.

Unpacking for meals:

Have a clean plastic bag ready so that as you look for the breakfast fixings, you can carefully scoop aside the GORP mix, peanuts and M&Ms. Lay food on the plastic bag or in your clean, dry, cooking pot.
Using a spare Ziploc bag, use this time to ration out lunch. You'll carry lunch outside the canister while you hike during the day.

As you repack the canister, plan what you'll need for supper and be sure that it is near the top. Replace "filler". Lock securely.

Keep meals simple. As the days go by, you will find this gets easier.
Be sure to lock the canister so the lid doesn't pop off while hiking after each use.

Now that you have finished my book, won't you please consider writing a review at http://www.Amazon.com? *Reviews are the best way readers discover great new books. I would truly appreciate it.*

My Resume:

River to River Trail-Southern Illinois	Section
Sawtooth Mountains- Idaho	Section
Grand Canyon Kaibab Trail, Bright Angel Trail	
Pacific Crest Trail 2000-2001	Completed
John Muir Trail 2001	Completed
Appalachian Trail 2002	Completed

Colorado Trail 2003	Completed
Bartram Trail 2003	Completed
Continental Divide Trail 2004-present	Section Hiking in Progress
Foot Hills Trail 2005	Completed
Vermont Trail 2007	Section
Foothills Trail-2nd time 2009	
Yellowstone-Zion-Grand Tetons	Various Trails
Monte Bells Four Loop Pass, Aspen 2013	Completed
Alaska	Present

Website: http://www.trailquest.net/BRindex.html

Blogs:

http://www.brawnyview.blogspot.com

http://www.thefemalesurvivalist.blogspot.com

Other Books by Carol Wellman

Non-Fiction

My Journey To Freedom and Ultralight Backpacking

An Ultralighter's True Trail Stories-Beyond the Journey

Everything Except Corn Pasta

Wild Neighbors-a Children's Book

The Cookbook Project-Sharing Our Best

Fiction- C.J. Wellman

The River Survival Series

An End of Days- Book One

All Hell Won't Wait-Book Two

When Hell Comes Knocking-Book Three

No Storm Like This-Book Four

Expected Release 2014:

Darkened Trails-interlude with gods -Book Four Supplement

Delivered--Book Five

Primal Cut- --when a young cook goes to work the winter in remote Yellowstone National Park, she takes on the demons of the local ghost. What happens when men start disappearing, furniture goes flying, and Detectives find her diary pinning it all on the chef?

Fatal Loves-Sequel to Primal Cut
--pursued by a ghost and two cops, Madison changes her identity and lands a job cooking in Zion National Park. When bodies start showing up in strange places and men go missing, the Rangers step in to find a connection.

CPSIA information can be obtained at www.ICGtesting.com
Printed in the USA
LVOW04s1943220515

439574LV00030B/1217/P